D0944825

ERNESTO CARDENAL

COSMIC CANTICLE

translated by John Lyons

CURBSTONE PRESS

First U.S. Edition, 1993
Translation copyright © 1993, John Lyons
Cántico cósmico copyright © 1989, Ernesto Cardenal,
first published 1989 by Editorial Nueva Nicaragua, Managua.
ALL RIGHTS RESERVED

Front cover painting:
"Hombre" 1953
by Rufino Tamayo
Mural, vinyl with pigment on vinyl white lead ground
Cover design by Stone Graphics
Printed in the U.S. on acid-free paper by BookCrafters

Curbstone Press is a 501(c)(3) nonprofit literary arts organization whose operations are supported in part by private donations and by grants from the ADCO Foundation, the J. Walton Bissell Foundation, the Connecticut Commission on the Arts, the LEF Foundation, the Lila Wallace-Reader's Digest Literary Publishers Marketing Development Program, funded through a grant to the Council of Literary Magazines and Presses, the Andrew W. Mellon Foundation, the National Endowment for the Arts, and the Plumsock Fund.

Library of Congress Cataloging-in-Publication Data

Cardenal, Ernesto.
[Cántico cósmico. English]
Cosmic canticle / Ernesto Cardenal : translated by John Lyons.
p. cm.
ISBN 1-880684-07-1 : $24.95
I. Title.
PQ7519.C34C2913 1993
861—dc20 93-24154

distributed in the U.S. by
InBook
Box 120261
East Haven, CT 06512

CURBSTONE PRESS
321 Jackson Street
Willimantic, CT 06226

Contents

Ernesto Cardenal

Cosmic Canticle

CANTIGA 1

Big Bang

In the beginning there was nothing
neither space
nor time.
The entire universe concentrated
in the space of the nucleus of an atom,
and before that even less, much less than a proton,
and even less still, an infinitely dense mathematical point.
And that was Big Bang.
The Great Explosion.
The universe subjected to relations of uncertainty,
its radius of curvature undefined,
its geometry imprecise
with the uncertainty principle of Quantum Mechanics,
spherical geometry overall but not in its detail,
like any common or garden potato undecidedly round,
imprecise and constantly changing besides in imprecision
all in a wild agitation,
it was the quantic era of the universe,
period in which nothing was certain:
even the "constants" of nature fluctuating at random,
that is
real conjectures in the realm of the possible.
Protons, neutrons and electrons were
completely banal.
It was justified to say that in the beginning
matter was completely disintegrated.
Everything dark in the cosmos.
Searching,
(according to the mysterious Polynesian song)
anxiously searching in the deep darkness,

searching
there on the shore that divides day from night,
searching in the night,
the night conceived the seed of night,
the heart of the night had always been there
even in the deep darkness,
the palpitating pulpa of life
grows in the deep darkness,
out of the shadows even the most tenuous ray of light emerges,
the procreative power,
life's first known ecstasy,
with the joy of passing from silence to sound,
and thus the progeny of the Great Expander
filled the expansion of the skies,
the chorus of life arose and erupted in ecstasy
and then reposed in a delight of calm.
(Poem brought to New Zealand from Polynesia.)
Everything was dark in the cosmos.
Space full of electrons
which let no light through.
Until electrons united with protons
and space became transparent
and light flowed.
And the universe began
as in a Haydn oratorio.

Before the big explosion
there wasn't even empty space,
for space and time, and matter and energy, emerged from the explosion,
neither was there any "outside" into which the universe could explode
for the universe embraced it all, even the whole of empty space.
Before the beginning only Awonawilona existed,
no one else with him in the vast space of time
but the black darkness on all sides
in the space of time.
And he brought forth his thought into space...
Nothing existed, neither did nothingness exist.

Between day and night there was no frontier.
Everything at the beginning was hidden...
Or as they tell it in the Gilbert Islands:
Na Arean seated in space
like a cloud floating over the nothingness...
The expansion of the universe is
the velocities resulting from the great explosion.
And a diffuse background radio static
has remained floating,
a vague radio murmur dispersed in the universe
like a distant echo of Big Bang,
despite the "dielectric effect"
of pigeon droppings on the aerial
(a pair of pigeons)
that static
is the oldest signal picked up by astronomers
(earlier than the light of the farthest galaxies).
Vague radiation like an echo of when the universe was opaque,
1,000 times smaller and 1,000 times cooler than now,
that is, any pair of particles 1,000 times closer together.
...Before the sky and the earth took shape
everything was vague and amorphous.
When the sky and the earth were united in emptiness and pure simplicity,
then, without having been created, things existed.
This was the Great Oneness.
All things emerged from this Oneness
yet all being different...
...First was the great cosmic egg. Within the egg
there was chaos. And P'an Ku floated above the chaos.
Sky and earth without form.
Everything was vague and amorphous...
...In the beginning there were only mists.
White, blue, yellow mists.
The clouds he made from white mist.
The night he made from black mist.
The earth he made with all the mists.
He sang as he created the earth.

He made the earth singing...
...From the abyss the earth was born, when there were no skies nor earth.
There where once there had been no sky.
First, second, third, three times four-hundred epochs,
thousands of epochs.
Through his efforts alone, in the Deep Night,
the First Word sounded,
there where there was no sky nor earth...
The transition from the era of radiation
to the present era of matter.
Before, so great was the energy of the photons
that the greater part of the universe was radiation
and not mass.
Or we can say that everything was pure radiation
essentially without matter.
But the era of pure radiation
began only after the first minutes.
Before matter truly *was* important,
albeit a matter different from that of the present universe.
...In the beginning all dense darkness,
without forms, empty...
...Then the Tao had no name.
A name came and it was creation...
...All motionless, all still, all silent, all empty,
in the sky.
There was nothing united, nothing together,
there existed nothing that existed, only immobility,
silence, in the deep darkness, in the night...
Chaos in which it was impossible to distinguish what is, *asha*,
from what is not, *drug* (from the book burned by Alexander the Great
but which was reconstructed from memory)
...there was nothing but twilight...
is what the Cuna tell in their coral islands.
When the universe was 10,000 times smaller than now
its heat was 10,000 times greater.
There was a time when the temperature was so great
that the collision of protons with protons

produced material particles of pure energy.
...In the beginning only the One was without others;
that Being thought: I wish to be many...
...He was seated in the midst of space
and became aware of himself and that only he existed.
He began to consider what he could do. And he cried.
His tears are the Great Lakes.
He wished for the light, and the light was made...
...He came forth in the midst of the original deep darkness
with his crown of feathers which are drops of dew.
The mistress of the deep dark is the owl...
The positron is the electron's antiparticle.
When a positron collides with an electron
the energy of the two makes pure radiation.
(The relation between particle and particle is reciprocal,
The positron is the electron's antiparticle.
and the electron is the positron's antiparticle.)
Years were not earth revolving around the sun,
there was no earth nor was there sun,
time was that of the orbit of an electron
around a hydrogen atom nucleus.
...In that time there was darkness and there was no river...
First there was a zero time with infinite temperature.
One hundredth of a second after the beginning
(theoretical scientists believe it to have been
immediately after the beginning)
the universe was simpler than it will ever be again,
an undifferentiated mass of matter and radiation,
each particle colliding at great speed with other particles.
Which is why despite the rapid expansion
the universe was in a state of thermic equilibrium
and the temperature was 10^{11}° K.
The abundant particles were the electron with
its antiparticle the positron.
The heat was too great for these electrons and positrons
so they and the photons were nothing but radiation.
...Two twins put the finishing touches to creation.

They taught how to make fire, hunt seals.
They also taught man to make love.
They revealed the names of things to them...
...In the beginning he created two sexes and brought them together...
To the enormous density of the beginning
corresponds an enormous velocity of expansion.
The "characteristic expansion time," so they say,
is 100 times the length of time
in which the size of the universe would increase 1 per cent,
gravitation continually slowing down the expansion.
There is an electron for each proton
but too much heat for an atom to unite.
Then there's nothing more of interest for 700,000 years.
Then electrons and nuclei formed atoms.
The universe became transparent to radiation.
Recently formed atoms glowed with great light.
Then
the first stars began to shine in the first galaxies.
Once matter and radiation uncoupled
matter began to form in galaxies and stars,
gravity gravid with stars,
later gravid with planets around the stars,
and 10,000 million years later
Weinberg is telling this story.
But before protons and electrons
1 million million millionths of a second after the beginning
the world that existed
"could scarcely be called material."
(In California): The world was invisible
Transparent like the sky...
He existed, Ta'aroa was his name in the immensity,
there was no earth, there was no sky,
there was no sea, nor Tahiti.
Existing alone, he transformed himself into universe...
The very idea of 'particle' must have been meaningless,
each particle would have been the size of the observable universe
and the universe with a temperature of more than

100 million million million million million degrees
one tenth of a millionth of a millionth of a millionth
of a millionth of a millionth of a millionth of a millionth
of a second after the beginning.
 ...He made the earth of Hawaii like a sea conch
 and the earth began to dance...
It's at least logically possible that there was a beginning
prior to which, time can have had no meaning.
A zero temperature
since less heat than absolute no heat there cannot be.
A zero time,
a moment in the past
when it is impossible in principle for there to have been a before
no chain of cause and effect
no before.

 In the beginning was an explosion,
but not an explosion from a center outwards
but a simultaneous explosion on all sides, filling
the whole of space from the beginning, every particle
of matter drawing away from every other particle.
A hundredth of a second after
the temperature was 100,000 million degrees centigrade
still so high that there could not be molecules nor atoms nor
atomic nuclei, only elemental particles:
electrons, positrons
and ghostly neutrinos without electrical charge and without mass
 "the closest thing to nothing that physicists have conceived of"
 And the universe filled with light.
...Night oppressed the earth like dense jungle...
 ...It's said that when it was still night,
 when there was still no light,
 when dawn had yet to break,
 they say that they gathered together. They said: Who will bring the dawn?...
...When it was night.
The light was hidden away in a Big Thing.

Day began to break and to show the light it held within,
and it started to create in that first light...
At the end of the first three minutes
protons and electrons began to form nuclei,
first the hydrogen nuclei
with 1 proton and 1 neutron.
There were still no galaxies nor stars
but only an ionized and undifferentiated soup of matter and radiation.
There must have been a time
when the energy of radiation was greater
than the energy contained in the matter of the universe.
And it was the transition from the era of radiation, when
most of the universe's energy took the form of radiation,
to the present era of matter, when most
of the energy is in the masses of particles.
To start with he dwelt amongst dense and dark mists
there where the sky and sea meet.
In the sea he created a very large island
which he filled with mortal life...
...When the sky up above had still not been mentioned
and the name of the earth not even thought of.
No swamp formed yet. And there was no Mesopotamia...
...When the whole earth did not yet exist,
and all around there was water,
an immense mist...
Matter continued to disperse, to disperse,
ever colder and less dense,
and shortly after—a few hundred thousand years—
it had cooled sufficiently for electrons
united to nuclei to engender atoms of hydrogen and helium,
and this gas through gravitation began to gather, and to gather,
and then, to compress further in the form of galaxies and stars
of the present universe.
...The stars are women
who at night light frozen fires...
...Above there is a village of women
who at night weave their *molas* next to brilliant lamps...

...Shooting stars are star excrement...
From then on the pressure of matter, of mere matter,
was too weak to frustrate
the passionate union of matter in the galaxies
which we see in the sky.
The ingredients of the first stars
derive from those three minutes.
But the galaxies must have been so close together in that past
that neither galaxies nor stars nor atoms, nor atomic nuclei,
had a separate existence.
...Formerly our earth was in the place of the sky...
...In the beginning forms were created from cloud matter
but without life.
The creation of the first couple came later...
...The First World was black like black wool
that we know from our ancestors... (said the Navajo
to Aileen O'Bryan, and he said that the Navajos
had always known about evolution).
But if expansion continues on and on
the distance between particles will increase
until the entire universe will seem like
an empty space.
Thermonuclear reactions slowly petering out
in every star, just cinders left behind
from black dwarf stars, neutron stars and black holes,
the planets orbiting ever more slowly,
without ever coming to rest in any finite time.
Death by entropy.
The sky finally utterly black.
The distinction between shining stars and black space will evaporate.
Or matter will transform once again into radiation
and everything will be light again.
The universe will slowly begin to contract again.
The contraction will be an expansion in reverse.
As though the film were being rewound again
while the spectators are still seated in the theater.
the cow-boy on his white horse galloping backwards,

into the pistol the fired bullet,
the parted mouths returning to the slow kiss.
Within ten thousand million years astronomers
will observe the distant galaxies
begin to shift from red to blue.
The gravitational collapse of the universe.
When the universe is a hundredth of its present size
the noise of radiation background will dominate the sky.
The night sky as warm as our present sky at day.
Seventy million years later it will be brighter than the sun.
The molecules in planets and stars and interstellar space
will start to break down into atoms
and the atoms into electrons and atomic nuclei.
After another 700,000 years
the temperature will reach ten million degrees,
stars and planets liquefied in a cosmic cocktail
of electrons and nuclei and radiation.
The temperature will rise to ten thousand million degrees
in the following 22 days.
Nuclei will break down into protons and neutrons.
Soon after, electrons and positrons will emerge in great numbers
from the collisions between photons and photons,
and the ghostly neutrinos with their antineutrinos
will render the entire cosmos a thermic communion.
Until the last three minutes.
Is that when time will stop, in the last three minutes?
And beyond is there only infinite temperature and infinite density?
Beyond the last hundredth of a second we know nothing more
just as we know nothing prior to the first hundredth of a second
the author of the book about the first three minutes tells us.
Once again the universe would then reach
100 million million million million million degrees
but maybe the cosmic ball always bounces back
and it will begin to expand again,
and its expansion will proceed once more to strike the wall
and return again and so
bounce back again

and so again and again
and so on forever.
And what of us?
Endless cycle of expansion and contraction
over and over again in infinite past
that had no beginning.
An infinite bouncing between infinite infinities.

And what do we matter?
No monument—stone or metal—from the present universe.
You human being gazing from your window at the stars.
They shed tears in them too!
Death in plane crash, or election to president.
What do we matter?
Someone who says: tomorrow's Monday, have to go to work.
The hope in he who went to the place from which there's no return
and returned.
Who called himself an electromagnetic process.
After all, life's a process.
Everything's a process,
after all.
And why has it been given to us to know it,
and to set it out in blinding coherence on a blackboard
with chalk numbers, and a clutch of calculations?
And what if the tendency of the entire universe
is to become a single universal being?
And the final stage of evolution
the universal super-organism?
This universe repeating itself after each Big Bang
to be better each time
until it becomes the perfect cosmos,
present in it all times past,
recapitulated all beings.
Einstein, for all his efforts,
failed, his equations always gave him a non-static model
of the universe.

CANTIGA 2

The Word

In the beginning
—before spacetime—
was the Word
All that is then is true.
Poem.
Things exist in the form of word.
All was night, etc.
There was no sun, nor moon, nor people, nor animals, nor plants.
The word was. (Amorous word.)
Mystery and at the same time expression of that mystery.
What is and at the same time expresses what it is.
"When in the beginning there was not yet anyone
he created the words (*naikino*)
and gave them to us, just like the yucca"
in that anonymous yellowing translation from the German
of a part of that massive book by Presuss
which I came across in Bogotá's Museum of Ethnography
Spanish translation of Presuss translating from Witoto into German:
The word in their songs, which he gave them, they say,
is the same with which he made the rain
(he made it rain with his word and a drum),
the dead go to a region where "they speak words well"
downriver: the river is very big,
(what they've heard of the Amazon according to Presuss)
there they haven't died again
and they are well downriver without dying.
The day will come when we will head downriver ourselves.
In the beginning then was the word.
The one that is and communicates what it is.

That is:
the one that totally expresses itself.
Secret that surrenders itself. A yes.
He in himself is a yes.
Reality revealed.
Eternal reality which eternally reveals itself.
At the beginning...
Before spacetime,
before there was before,
at the beginning, when there wasn't even beginning,
at the beginning,
was the reality of the word.
When all was night, when
all beings were still obscure, before being beings,
a voice existed, a clear word,
a song in the night.

In the beginning was the Song.
Singing he created the cosmos.
And for that reason all things sing.
They don't dance except through words (through which the world was created)
say the Witotos. "We do not dance without a reason."
And the huge trees of the forest were born,
the canaguche palm, with its fruit for us to drink,
likewise the choruco-monkey to eat the trees,
the tapir that eats the fruit on the ground,
the small parrot, the borugo to eat the jungle,
he created all the animals like the otter, that eats fish,
and the small otter,
he made all the animals like the stag and the chonta-stag,
in the air the royal eagle that eats the chorucos,
he created the sidyi, the picon, the kuyudo parakeet,
the eifoke and forebeke turkey, the chilanga, the hokomaike,
the patilico, the sarok parakeet,
the kuikudyo, the fuikango, the siva and the tudyagi,
the stinking duck, the mariana that has learned now to eat fish,

the dyivuise, the siada, the hirina and the himegisinyos
and the Witoto poem goes on
in the anonymous Spanish translation
from Presuss's German translation of the Witoto
filed away in the Museum.
"Even if they say: they dance for no reason. We
in our festivities tell the tales."
Which Presuss patiently gathered on a gramophone years ago
and translated into German.
The dead: they have returned to the creative word
whence they sprang with the rain, the fruit and the songs.
"If our traditions were merely absurd,
we would be sad in our feasts."
And the rain a word from his mouth.
He created the world by means of a dream.
And he himself is something like a dream. A dream that dreams.
They call him *Nainuema*, according to Presuss:
"The one who is (or has) something non-existent."
Or like a dream that became real without losing its dream mystery.
Nainuema: "The one who is SOMETHING very real non-existent."
And the earth is *Nicarani*, "that dreamed," or "the vision dreamed":
that born from nothing like a dream of the Father.
Genesis according to the Witoto or Huitoto or Uitoto.
In the beginning
before Big Bang
was the Word.
There was no light
light was within the darkness
and he brought the light out of the darkness
drew the two apart
and that was Big Bang
or the first Revolution.
Word that never passes
("heaven and earth will pass away...")
A distant murmur from that explosion
lingers on in the universe
like radio static.

And the celestial dialectical dance began.
"The *yang* calls;
the *yin* responds."
He is in that which each thing is.
And in that which each thing enjoys.
Each thing coitus.
The entire cosmos copulation.
All things love, and he is the love with which they love.
"The *yang* calls;
the *yin* responds."
They are the two choruses.
They are the two choruses which take turns to sing.
And Pythagoras discovered the harmony of the universe
hearing a blacksmith hammer.
That is: the isotropic movement—uniform and harmonious—of the
universe.
Creation is a poem.
Poem, which is "creation" in Greek and thus
St. Paul calls God's Creation, POIEMA,
like a poem by Homer, Padre Ángel used to say.
Each thing is like a "like."
Like a "like" in a Huidobro poem.
The entire cosmos copulation.
And each thing is word,
word of love.
Only love reveals
but it veils what it reveals,
alone it reveals,
alone lover and beloved
in the illuminated solitude,
the nights of the lovers,
word that never passes
while the water flows beneath the bridge
and the slow moon above the houses passes.
The cosmos
secret word in the nuptial chamber.
Each thing that is is verbal.

Lie is what is not.
And each thing is secret.
Listen to the murmur of things...
They say it, but say it in secret.
Only alone is it revealed.
Only at night in a secret place does it lay itself bare.
The cosmic blushing.
Nature: timid, bashful.
All things lower their eyes in your presence.
—My secret is for my beloved alone.
And space is not speechless.
Who has ears to hear let him hear.
We are surrounded by sound.
Everything existing united by rhythm.
Cosmic jazz not chaotic or cacophonous.
In harmony. He made all things singing and the cosmos sings.
Cosmos like a dark record that spins and sings
in the dead of night
or romantic radio borne to us on the wind.
Each thing sings.
Things, not created by calculus
but by poetry.
By the Poet ("Creator"=POIÊTÊS)
Creator of the POIEMA.
With finite words an infinite meaning.
Things are words to whoever understands them.
As though everything were telephone or radio or t.v.
Words in an ear.
Do you hear those frogs?
and do you know what they wish to tell us?
Do you hear those stars? They have something to tell us.
The chorus of things.
Secret melody of the night.
Aeolian harp that sounds alone at the mere brush of the air.
The cosmos sings.
The two choruses.
"The *yang* calls;

the *yin* responds."
Dialectically.
Do you hear those stars? It is love that sings.
The silent music.
The sonorous solitude.
"The music in silence of the moon," mad Cortés.
Matter is waves.
And waves? Questions.
An I towards a you.
That is searching for a you.
And this because each being is word.
Because the word made the world
we can communicate in the world.
—His word and a drum...
We are word
in a world born of the word
and which exists only as something spoken.
A secret of two lovers in the night.
The firmament announces it as with neon letters.
Each night swapping secrets with another night.
People are words.
And thus one is not if one is not dialogue.
And so then each one is two
or is not.
Each person is for another person.
I am not I rather you are I!
One is the I of a you
or one is nothing.
I am nothing more than you otherwise if not I am not!
I am yes. I am Yes to a you, to a you for me,
to a you for me.
People are dialogue, I say,
if not their words would touch nothing
like waves in the cosmos picked up by no radio,
like messages to uninhabited planets,
or a bellowing in the lunar void
or a telephone call to an empty house.

(A person alone does not exist.)
I tell you again, my love:
I am you and you are me.
I am: love.

CANTIGA 3

Autumn Fugue

In the beginning
—Everything was dark.
There was no sun, nor moon, nor people, nor animals, nor plants.
Only the sea was everywhere:
        —A disorganized mass of poorly connected things.
        Nothing breathed in it.
        —Plants, animals did not exist,
    only the darkness,
    nothing was seen, neither the rivers nor the animals.
—An entity without a name sighed deeply
and there was nothing else in the world.
It was a darkness concealed by a darkness.

    The lamp in order to shine needs dark.
Planets, stars, clusters of stars,
galaxies, clusters of galaxies.
And 90% of the universe's matter is invisible
or perhaps 99%.
Stars are formed in dark and cold gases,
not in matter hot, luminous matter, *that* is expanding.
Matter is a form of energy,
which can be created from other forms of energy
    and vice-versa.

The second law of thermodynamics!:
energy is indestructible in quantity
but continually changes in form.
        And it always runs down like water.
    In the same direction as rivers to the sea.
The step is from a few high-energy quanta to

many low-energy quanta.
The fragmentation of big quanta into small quanta
(shortwave ones full of energy
and longwave ones with little)
and so it is impossible ever to rebuild the big quanta.
That is:
the inevitable decadence of the universe.
A day will come when the last erg of the universe's energy
will stop in its tracks,
and at that moment all movement in the universe
will be halted.
The millerwomen will be few and their labors cease.
The clatter of the mill will die down.
Birds will chirrup no more. Songs will be hushed.
The shattered jug by the fountain...
The second law of thermodynamics,
which no one can deny:
A final exhaustion.
A cold caloric death of the cosmos.
Order tends towards disorder.
The Acropolis corroding away through pollution.
Venice, its balconies crumbling like Gorgonzola cheese.

Like rivers to the sea.
But the energy which drives the rivers to the sea
is the sun's.
With radiation cut off,
the river ceases to run.
The energy of the whole universe is the same as that of the river:
emanating from the interior of stars
in the form of quanta
with very short waves
the waves have gradually lengthened as they lost heat.
From a few high-energy quanta
to many low-energy quanta.
Drawing away in space the waves gradually grow longer and longer.
The quanta increasing immensely in number

but each quantum now of less force.
Until the increasingly longer and longer waves come to die
on the most distant shores of the universe.
Like rivers to the sea,
        heat always in the direction of cold.
Towards the grave of entropy.
Will the day arrive when energy will regenerate itself
in new protons and electrons?
Will the universe which now consumes itself in radiation
rise again from its thermo-nuclear ashes?
                Will there be a new perturbation?
Waves of radiation arisen from a union,
                        from that union of protons and electrons
in the interior of a star
                sink into the shadows.
A thermodynamic equilibrium.
                        That will be the end,
when all matter convertible into radiation
will have been already converted.
Then time will extend to infinity
                                but time will not flow.
The universal tendency to decay.
To fall and fall as much as possible
in constant loss of energy and organization.

The starry sky is like a city by night
seen from an airplane: the stars like streets,
like brightly-lit supermarkets, neon signs,
like motels nightclubs cinemas and the lights
—white and red—of cars—which come and go—
along dark roads. And do they burn for nothing:
a gushing forth of energy in the perpetual night
like the energy here below lost in the emptiness
in avenues shops cafes nightclubs motels
cinemas with a Clark Gable super-production?

Only life creates order and maintains order.

Death is the loss of organization, molecules
return to the most simple, to increasingly
lower levels of organization.
Only life is the creation of order
against destruction,
and the heroic maintenance of order
against destruction.
But each microorganism that is born
is one less.
And is it not towards life that the whole universe is moving
and for its benefit the matter of the uninhabited stars
and of the barren nebulae
pouring out their radiation into empty spaces
for millions and millions of years
has been transforming itself?
Yet the second law of thermodynamics:
ay, the big quanta convert into small quanta
and then it is impossible ever to rebuild with them
the quanta which once were!

The second law of thermodynamics, the one which
determines that time has a single direction.
The film run backwards makes no sense.
And who after the explosion
could gather up the shards of shrapnel
and reassemble the bomb?
The stars' fuel finished.
I see them being extinguished one by one
as one puts out a cigarette butt.
Neutron stars have not been seen in telescopes
yet, but merely in the astronomers' imagination.
But a star a little heavier than a neutron star
is a black hole.
The fauces of a black hole.
Like a cosmic vacuum cleaner.
Where gravitation is so great, the curvature so great,
that light is swallowed up.

The entropy which in the end awaits us all.
The inevitable descent into final equilibrium
which is the grave.
The second law, which is that we are condemned to die.
Of the temple of this body protein upon protein shall not remain.
Why does our skull boast such a buffoonish grin,
and furthermore, macabre, sinister? My answer
would be this: None of all that matters.
About the grave. They're not us.

Energy falls like autumn leaves.
"Yellow leaves fall in the poplar grove,
where so many courting couples stroll."
Quanta fall...
A shift towards red in the spectrum...
The cold grave of entropy.

CANTIGA 4

Expansion

The galaxies are receding further and further away from us
and from each other
and we ourselves are receding
as our universe disperses.
And we will be ever more isolated.
Space ever emptier.
And ever colder.
When each galaxy is on its own
with no neighbor in sight,
the stars within them will go out one by one,
ever less stars to replace them.
Plunging one by one into black holes.
And the entire universe will plunge into black holes.
Or will the galaxies come together again
with ever more force as when they separated,
until their gases mix,
until all the atoms compress
and the cosmos regains the heat and chaos
from which it emerged?
And then? There are astronomers who maintain
that it would not re-emerge from that state.
Others speculate
that a new creation would explode again,
a new universe without a trace of the old one.
And thus the cosmos never ends,
with infinite creation after creation,
eternal cycle of birth and death and birth.
No discovery has been greater
than that of the expanding universe.
Distant nebulae shifting towards red.

Huge concave radio-telescope dishes listening in to them.
The 'immutable heavens'...
Continually changing.
And what there is where there are no stars
there where the sky is dark.
And the stars that already consumed their energy
and drift through space dark and dead.
And the quantity of matter that is perhaps invisible.
And whether other universes exist
in other spacetimes.

The elements found in meteorites
(South Kensington Geological Museum)
hailing from distant stars
are those of our planet.
All heavenly bodies solid or gaseous
are composed of carbon, oxygen, nitrogen and metals
in the same proportion as earth.
Are the stars just to be looked at?
So much extra-terrestrial matter has fallen upon the earth
that perhaps the soil we tread is extra-terrestrial.
From the depths of the cosmos.
Citizens of the universe through our earth
which is a heavenly body set among the others.
And consciousness in countless points of the universe.
1,000,000,000,000,000,000,000 stars
in the explorable universe.
Feast of fireworks
perhaps a million planetary systems.
New stars being born from the tenuous cloud of hydrogen.
Suns with their earth.
A shared universe.
One, without company, at a point on the surface
of a small planet
of a modest star on the outskirts of one of the galaxies.
Telescopes scan the remote universe,
and gigantic antennae try to listen in to it.

A space devoid of meaning? A
            shared universe!
The certainty of not being alone in the cosmos.

The color of light shifts towards red
as distant galaxies draw away faster and faster
and the radio waves grow longer and longer
whistle of melancholy train pulling off into the distance
                        grows deeper.
And the further away a galaxy the greater
its shift towards red and thus
the faster it is receding.
This receding of the galaxies
more and more towards red in the spectrum,
greater and greater wave length
                                    (train receding)
suggests a primordial explosion,
indicates
a primordial union, and a
common explosion.
            Explosion 20,000 million years ago.
There still remains a vague murmur of that explosion,
radio waves come from the depths of space,
something that can be detected on television screens, they say,
when turned to full volume with no channel tuned.
Telescopes have detected around a thousand million galaxies
in an area of a thousand million light years.
            Trains in the night pulling out of a station.
The whistle is sharper as they approach
and deeper as they recede into the distance.
First an infinite condensation of matter.
And from the marriage of protons with neutrons
life was produced.
What's in a star? Ourselves.
All the elements of our body and of the planet
were in the entrails of a star.
        We are stardust.

15,000,000,000 years ago we were a mass
of hydrogen floating in space, slowly rotating, dancing.
And the gas condensed more and more
gaining ever more mass
and mass became star and began to shine.
As they condensed they grew hot and bright.
Gravitation generated thermal energy: light and heat.
Like saying love.
They were born, grew and died, the stars.
And the galaxy gradually took on the form of a flower
as we now see it on starry nights.
Our flesh and our bones come from other stars
and perhaps even from other galaxies,
we are universal,
and after death we will contribute to form other stars
and other galaxies.
We come from the stars and to them we shall return.

Approaching train sharper.
And heavenly bodies bluer as they approach
and redder if they are receding.
Why is the night black...
It is black because of the expanding universe.
Otherwise, the whole sky would shine like the sun.
And there'd be no one to see that night.
And the galaxies where are they going?
Expanding like smoke dispersed by the wind.
The second law of thermodynamics:
This constant flow from light to the dark depths.
From love to oblivion.
He was 20, she 15 or just turned 16.
Illumination in the streets and in the sky. The sky
that of Granada.
It was the final farewell,
and it was when he read Neruda to her:
"...the saddest verses this night."
"The night is filled with stars

and blue, stars, in the distance, shiver."
Two people drew apart forever.
There were no witnesses to that farewell.
The two directions ever more divergent
like stars shifting towards red.
I have thought of you again because the night is filled with stars
and I see the stars flicker in the distance with their bluish light.

CANTIGA 5

Stars and Fireflies

The energy from their union
transformed into heat and light
that's what they are.
The universe lit up
by thousands of galaxies of thousands of millions of stars!
I gaze at the universe
and I am the universe gazing at itself.
The universe's most subtle retina gazing upon itself,
that's what we are.
That first time the heavens were seen
from the earth through pieces of glass,
when with sand transformed into lens
Galileo beheld the moon's craters and Venus in the first quarter,
the world gazing at itself.
Glow-worm on the ground.
Pointless light of the female on the ground
unless its fiery companion
plummets down from the sky.
Quite distinct the Milky Way
this summer night in Solentiname,
(300,000 million stars)
shoal of silver-plated fish.
Our local stars!
But the Earth indiscernible from them,
which makes it as good as non-existent.
One who is alone on this planet Earth
would love somehow to soar up towards those lights
and never again return.
He was twenty years old.
Glow-worm on the ground.
And can it have been after all a betrothal to an impersonal Being?

Alone, in a radius of 100,000 light years
            burning with love.
No companion body in the bed.
nor in the sand.
        Longing for the coming of the kingdom of heaven on earth.
            And at the end of spacetime
                the eternal coitus.

Essentially cosmic beings:
        We can't exclude the earth from eternity.
            Those lights there above, the Celestial Jerusalem.
If in mathematics numbers are infinite,
even and odd numbers
why not an infinite beauty and an infinite love?
It's a constant in nature,
beauty.
Whence poetry: song and delight in all that exists.
The earth could have been just as
functional, practical,
without beauty. Why then?
Every being is sumptuous. Did you really need to give
such luxurious jewels
            to such ephemeral fish
                leaping this twilight on the floor of the boat?
Love me, and if I am nothing,
I will be a nothing with your beauty refracted in it.
After all everything was born of nothing, empty nothing brimming
with the urgency of being.
Love certainly beyond this sublunar world.
With this vocation some have for a love without chromosomes...
            Your beauty permits you to be a tyrant.

Gazing in the night at those distant worlds,
distant also in the past.
Stars of the past. (And time
        is different for each of them.)
Alpha of Orion 5,000 times brighter than the sun.

Perhaps stars which no longer exist.
Alpha of the Lyre 300,000 light years away.
And 200 million away Boötes' nebulae.
Light's journey in the darkness.
Why does the light travel? And where is it going?
Gazing into the night.
The tremendous profusion of Earths up above.
The coincidence of man's being of intermediate size
between the planet and the atom.
And that in a planet the size of ours
an *agile* being bigger than man should be impossible.
Or the question why the universe is so big:
could human intelligence not exist
in a smaller, younger universe?
"A scientist is the atom's means of understanding the atom,"
and I who so hated physics with Father Muruzábal
and still more algebra with Father Stella.

Inhabitants of this heavenly body,
the gigantic cosmic spaces
act on our cells. As every molecule of the earth
attracts the moon, the sun and the stars.
Even in stones there are imperceptible
moontides.
Dust from very distant points of the cosmos falls on us.
Gases from the earth spread throughout the cosmos.
The brotherhood of all things.
Elements of our tears existed in other creatures.
The unity of all natures.
The galactic spiral copies the sea shell.
"A living creature not in constant interaction with its environment
is unthinkable."
As the sound of the sea has remained in the shell's aperture.
But isn't it the rhythm of the sea that has coiled the shell?
As coconut palms need the sound of the sea, so they say,
in order to grow.

We gaze at them in the night, and perhaps they no longer exist.
One day the sun will not exist,
and its light still reaching distant stars.
But
since each molecule attracts another molecule in the universe
the entire universe is a single star.
Since stars are no more than concentrations of interstellar matter,
everything is a star.

Matter is movement.
The universe, transformation.
The velocities within atoms
are like those in the heavens.
Matter in continuous dance.
Clouds of hydrogen in rotation
engendering rotating stars
which engender rotating planets,
and the galaxies in disks, spheres or spirals,
also rotating.
All of it (furthermore) harmoniously
expanding.
And what's it all about?
How came its creation?
And us, why are we here?
And who are we?
Could the universe have a soul
and are we that soul
with the entire cosmos for a body,
even the most distant gases, our body?
In this way the cosmos knows itself through us.
"Know thine own self."
Our own consciousness, also the consciousness of it all.
The secret of science transcends the scientific.
(The unity and interrelation of all things
in the *Avatamsaka Sutra*.)

"For an hour he tried to catch her eye

as she turned to her food without glancing at him.
Eventually she stopped eating and seemed to look at him.
Excited, he started dancing in front of her.
She took a few more mouthfuls,
and his dance became wilder; slowly he closed in.
She couldn't take her eyes off his blue back so it seemed.
Gently he caressed her leg with his leg
and she did the same.
For a moment they parted. Again he caressed her.
She seemed to have succumbed.
He withdrew a short distance. She chased after him.
And we never saw them again."

The fire which created the stars and us.
What we on earth call human nature
child of processes of nuclear reactions.
Stars are not believed to be born alone.
Although now the sun is seen alone, the sun alone
(we along with it)
we emerge as members of a huge group.
On those nights the Solentiname sky was clear
and I lay down with my head filled with stars
pondering my being a child of the creator of them all. But
a glow-worm in the long grass had more companionship
and compared with a physical love in the bay sands
the firmament is worthless, equivalent to a SEIKO watch
with luminous numbers
on the wrist of a lover with his sweetheart in the bay.
I solitary among the stars.
Just like Sappho and those Pleiades of hers.

Does the flow of time go from past to future
or from future to past?
Or does time not flow and is all present?
It's the other dimension we gaze at up there in the firmament.
Time doesn't pass.
Merely space, merely a permanent space

embracing the totality of time.
Time's not like a clock constantly ticking away
present-past present-past but
a clock that has ceased to beat.
Time doesn't pass,
but we pass.

Ah, St. Augustine my friend.
It's the passing of our lives
which appears to give movement to time
like the posts which from a train appear to pass
(the posts from that Naples train, at the age of 25, which flashed past
and never returned).
Airport runway lights which rush by
and then we gaze down motionless from above, the plane now in flight.
The cowboy at the gallop, the shot, the kiss,
all motionless wound tight in the canister.
A place in space is time.
Like railway timetables...
Distant hours in distant stations for the same train!
We journey in spacetime like a train in the night.
And with telescopes we gaze at the past in space:
2,000 million years back through the crystal,
galaxies as they existed those millions of years ago.

That old clock on La Merced, half-lit,
its hands on 8, the time for visiting her
—and time when old María Cabezas in her old armchair
at the rear of the house would begin her first rosary—
now as I write these lines, so many years later,
is it telling the present time, or is it out of order
stopped at any time, maybe 8 at night
of many years ago
pointlessly?

Gazing at this starry sky so utterly silent
and yet populated with millions of civilizations.

250,000 million suns in our galaxy alone
in a radius of a hundred thousand light years.
Millions of civilizations there, compañero planets.
The heavens.
Stars much older than the sun,
societies very much more advanced than us.
Or maybe like Hollywood's extra-terrestrial monsters?
Astronomers have gazed very far into space,
and very far into time,
15,000 million light years.
Now establishing our earth as a heavenly body.
An assembly of galaxies, the metagalaxy.
Perhaps the metagalaxy is disk-shaped
and rotates on its axis
and there may be clusters of metagalaxies...
Beyond the most distant world another even more distant,
even the most remote past has another past,
and every future another future.
The light of a visible star may be 1,000 light years
but that wait outside the brightly-lit house
was too long a time.
The round clock on La Merced filling the entire night
and never striking 8.

We, living beings still, with the ability to export
entropy.
A word which is not part of our everyday speech:
Entropy.
There is still that faint sound in the cosmos
which comes from the creation.
The Second Law: that cold does not become hot.
The Solentiname sunset bathed a head of hazel hair in light
and the breeze from the boat ruffled it. Hazel curls
which will be hazel but for a few years.
Mine was black.
Above us those black holes whence there's no return.
And where space and time end. Is the total gravitational collapse

of the universe into oblivion
really inevitable?
Whatever the case:
    the huge concave dish,
    the gigantic aerial, let's focus them
in the direction of Love.

CANTIGA 6

Beyond and Closer to Home

"One day is as a thousand years and a thousand years as one day"
(Epistle of St. Peter)

What days for instance? There are days and days.
Perhaps one day for someone a telephone
may assume cosmic importance.
It did once for me.
You see girls go by fresh as flowers: or rather
like fresh flowers: less ephemeral than flowers
but only a little less.
Notwithstanding Merejkovsky dared to say
and it's no irreverence to say
that sex is the human body's Trinity.
On the other hand
could space be matter and time consciousness?
And space and time be one like body and soul?
Time and space like one within the other?
He was twenty years old...
but one day is as a thousand years
to the relativist as to St. Peter.
Or like saying, after all,
time's a subjective phenomenon.
Or also, that perhaps time's composed of particles.
Or in accordance with the curvature of time...
"Now" means nothing more than "here."
Time is distance. Depending
on the distance an event
may be in the past of here and in the future of there.
(Space also subjective!)
"You who do not exist," Alfonso said to time.
They say

it should be possible to go back in time
                    if anti-gravity existed.
Where is spacetime flowing to?
            That hour which approaches from the tower.
And that mystery so simple:
in the seed of a tree
is enclosed all the space and time of the tree
including the seeds of that tree.
    All the dimensions of its age
    its foliage with fresh birds and its years,
including its seed, and the seed of its seed.
            A thousand years as a day
                    and one day as a thousand years.
Perhaps it's not that the universe is expanding in space
but space that is expanding.
Or are both things the same thing?
    According to Einstein's theory
    space is almost material.
And how can the science of the infinite
rank among the exact sciences?
Astronomy is no more exact than horse racing
says Murchie.
    As to whether creation was caused by anything...
Why does the golden oriole come in October
with its olive-green garb and red eye?
Or whither, for what purpose the V of ducks at dusk?
Humanity is like a child who has *whys* for everything.
    To leave time and being
                    —Eckhart sermon—
    and arrive at the Cause without cause.
What being is, we scarcely know. Much less
what is cause.
What does it mean to be without cause?
    and Cause without cause?
"*Motionless* is a word
for something that doesn't exist in the universe."
    And the opinion at present most widely-held

that there's a point in the universe beyond
which there are no heavenly bodies.
Still valid Aristotle's precept: in the face of the cosmos
adjust your toga with respect.

It appears that matter has the tendency
to produce life. In the interstellar spaces
organic compounds, rudiments of life
have been found.
We don't exist by chance in the universe,
or as an aberration.
As for death...
You die so that others may be born.
Were you not to die nobody would be born.
Reproduction battling it out against death.
On the other hand
only death makes immortality possible.
Oh eyes in which human immortality peeks through!
At that time he told them this parable: if the fertilized
and mature ovule does not fall into the earth,
the tegument covering it open
and the tiny root and gemma emerge with its cotyledons
while the tegument rots,
it remains alone. But...
If death's an absurdity, life is,
but if it makes sense, life does too.
Born into an increasingly dispersing universe.
But when death disperses your body into the universe,
you won't be dead,
your atoms, those of your life,
will remain alive,
they won't be dead atoms,
neither before your life
were they dead.
They go up as they don't die
though here they die,
said the Nicaraguas by the lakeside

to the conquistador.

In a cognizable universe
at least in part cognizable.
                The diversity of reality
                and its unity.
All us beings are of the same essence,
composed of the same elemental particles.
                    Physicists now speak like mystics.
"I am the son of the Earth and of the star-filled Heavens"
(engraved on an Orphic tablet which is in the museum
and which they took to the grave).
At least in part cognizable.
        They said that, like everything that moves, it has sound...
        And since those movements were ordered and harmonious
        those sounds also had to be a musical harmony,
        and if we couldn't hear the music of the great spheres
        it's because from birth we've been hearing it
        without the contrast of silence to pick it out.
The pentachord of the planets.
Like now in physics the music of atoms.
Although the interior of atoms is chaotic, note,
but with music.
                The hearth fire below
                is the same as the hearth above
                the Fan sing in their Fire Canticle.
Psychic interactions of electrons.
An exchange of virtual as if to say
spiritual impulses.
The confusion now between physics and spirit.
            Whether its future is finite or infinite
                    (the universe's).
Only fantastic theories stand a chance
of being true.
        "It's not sufficiently mad," thus Bohr
criticized a theory.
There may be infinities of universes.

The enigma is "where" and "when"
words of our universe alone.

I remember that Woolworth branch on Broadway, around 102nd,
and the cute salesgirl aged 17 or 18, at a cut-price counter
beset by greedy ladies,
        she snapped at another of them, she was beat
(it was close to closing time,
                she there on her feet all day)
and instantly the sharpness blossomed into a smile
when she saw me, 23 years old, in the entrance.
She gave me a smile. A warm smile as if to say, I'm beat.
        Slim, golden hair and pink skin.
Instead of that work she could have been in films.
Or I could have hung around outside for her until closing time.
I continued along Broadway. Down Broadway.
                Exactly 38 years ago now.
There by 102nd Street and Broadway
on the right as you come from Columbia
close to closing time,
that is, maybe something like a quarter to six.
                Now I'm 61.
Spacetime has shot by like an electric train
in a reality as illusory as film.

The stars, the colors come from them too.
        Colorless though the air is, the sky is blue.
And that green vastness, green how I want you green,
thanks to which we breathe and eat.
        The mutual attraction of matter. Gravity
attracts all matter to all matter.
Because of gravity, too, there's an atmosphere
and because of gravity we breathe.
All life lives off other life
in communion.
                        The corn seed has now been born
                                        (with the drum)

On cutting the umbilical cord.
Just as Dolmatoff witnessed it in the Sierra Nevada.
Also when the Spaniard asked:
And what do your gods eat?
The Nicaraguan *cacique*:
What we eat here, for it came to us from there [maize].
The root pulled down by the earth
the stem drawn up by the sky.

Diffuse gases become habitable worlds.
Energies from the cosmos produce interference
in our radiophonic broadcasts.
A grain of sand among the suns...
"Land of lakes and volcanoes"
Darío called this one.
But earthquakes and eruptions
are the delayed consequences of the explosion of the stars.
Which is why I maintain, I repeat,
the heavens are here on earth.
Aren't we the heavens for others?
The Pleiades still in their youth.
For argument's sake, say God laid out the stars
say for argument's sake that he laid them out,
but could it have been just for us to see them?
The sun is nothing but gas, the sun
that engendered life on the planet.
Do we know the universe's metabolism?
All living beings, relatives, to Pythagoras.
They say he was the first to call it *kosmos*
(order, harmony, beauty)
and man should be *kosmos* in miniature.
Anaxagoras questioned about his civic values:
to comply with the fatherland (pointing skywards).
Fatherland, in Plotinus. His "flight" to the fatherland.
Citizens of the universe.
Total Christ in Clement of Alexandria.
Polybius, long before the Roman Empire:

events were leading the world to a *unity*.
Not water, fire, etc for Anaximander
according to Theophrastus, but the essential element of beings
infinity.
And in Anaxagoras: that in all things there's something of each thing
since all things were together and in repose.
Even a pebble
part of the plan,
to the Maoris uprooted from Polynesia
who now rowing in New Zealand sing
"It was you that began this love affair with me."
From Brahmâ down to a blade of grass.
The order of this poem? It has no order
nor disorder.
Where the earth begins and where it ends.
Where a galaxy begins and a galaxy ends.
We among electrons and stars.
(As Socrates had seen: eyes are not chance.)
And *materially* made of stars.
According to what law of physics are molecules always
excited like children let out of school?
The hymns which the spheres sing in the skies
we attempt to reproduce with lutes,
with our throats.
And it's because we once heard that song,
we still retain the memory of that song.
So sang Chelalu-D-Din Rumí.
"Suffice it to say here
that nature would appear to be forcing mysticism
into science."

It was the Pleistocene era when a homonid became *Homo sapiens*.
To walk upright, speak with the mouth, build with the hands.
"Before all were in a huge village,
men and animals together.
The Creator frequently came down to the village.
No one is left in the village."

Or:

"God in the beginning lived in a cave
with animals and with men.
Animals are forever hankering for a delicious food
they once tasted."

Curiously, researchers
have found little trace of war
in the ice age. But
does biologically-based original sin exist in *Homo sapiens*?

Mr. Cummings' business
and the fascinating catalogue of his products
Finnish Lahti 20mm anti-tank cannons
bazookas: "the perfect weapon"...
International Armaments Corporation (INTERARMS)
or rather distributors of Death Ltd.
bought from Israel Soviet weapons captured from Egypt
to be sold to Latin Americans in the United States,
sold weapons to the Costa Rica of Figueres
likewise to Somoza enemy of Figueres,
it armed the RFG with Dutch MGs,
for a million bought all Franco's old weapons
and sold 500,000 FN rifles to an Argentine gorilla,
27 vampires to Trujillo bought from Sweden.
Mr. Cummings' business.
Weapons to invade Cuba, to prop up Somoza,
to kill blacks in Africa,
for the CIA, of untraceable origin.
Mr. Cummings' business
friend of Franco, of Somoza, the Shah.
Prosperous years these have been for his company.
97 wars for the United States since Pearl Harbor.
The sole business of Mr. Cummings, "Merchant of Death"
but a retail merchant of death:
More respectable firms have the Monopoly.
As for peace prospects
"deeply sceptical."

A Yankee soldier, on a camp bed, in shirt-sleeves,
smoking with eyes half-closed:
it's Humphrey Bogart, naturally.

Pythagoras inspired the poet Aratus
whom St. Paul quotes in the Areopagus
(men are of God's race according to Pythagoras).
The whole universe musical harmony.
Everything is number and harmony
in music and in heavenly bodies.
Or waves as we now understand,
melodic waves,
Hertzian waves, light waves, sea waves
and the waves of atoms.
A flower's color
is light waves which that flower fails to absorb.
And waves also the beauty of girls.
The flower's scent
is its song.
Vibration of its atoms.
The harmonious array of the atoms of the rose
is its scent.
From diffuse and shapeless gaseous states
to condensed and complex solidity.
From undefined clouds of random atoms
to structural symmetry and developed form.
The relationship between mass and light:
mass creates pressure which produces heat which generates light.
The sky spinning round.
And so then matter, all matter is nothing
but clouds, rotating shapes, or spheres
its steps uneven
and in harmonious proportion so equal.
The cosmos, like a circle to the Omaha.
Blue clay pot to the Jivaro.
The sky to the Maya a turtle shell.
And like a single tensed string Plotinus felt it

which when plucked at one end receives the movement at the other end too
and when another string's plucked there's a single harmony
and vibrations pass from one lyre to another, sympathetically,
in the universe, too, there's a single harmony.
Suddenly the first notes, and a pretty black girl
emerges, moving every mobile bit of her body
towards the multi-colored maypole
and a boy darts in close to her, close, with contortions
like those of a snake injected with alcohol
from behind to the front, the front and behind,
and she flirts
in surrender and rejection,
rejection and surrender
and now others are joining the circle
Mayo-Yaaaa! The rapid body movements
are the rapid movements of the music.
In the center of circles full of fire
and of other circles further off full of night,
urging on the union of female with male
and male with female: so God to Parmenides.
Which is why Shawn the dancer used to say,
he couldn't imagine God without rhythm.
"...his infinite Rhythmic Being"
Those that respond to the lengthening of the day in spring
or its shortening in autumn.
"Earth, sun, stars, such well-ordered seasons...
Is it not easy to prove that gods exist
dear guest?"
Being, for the Nuer tribes,
one and many at the same time.

As the bird emerges from its egg, say the Zuni.
The first men did not walk upright. They had tails.
When the world was still new and fresh.
The Sumerians spoke of an age without hyenas.
The Algonkin have scoured the lakes in their canoes for
the islands of the other world where hunger and war are unknown

(they claim to have seen them).
Pygmies remember the mighty tree which united heaven and earth.
"We have lost the heavens," the Ojibway sing.
The four seasons in their regular sequence, without confusion,
nothing harmed man and man harmed nothing,
but the order of the universe was disturbed say the Chinese.

For argument's sake let's say an immense wheat harvest.
Abundance is not more food for all
but hunger.
Over-production lowers production
and brings lay-offs
and due to unemployment
sales fall
and more factories fall idle
until scarcity increases production
once again
and over-production resumes
and crisis and once again the return...
unless the over-production is in weapons
and there's war
because this breaks the cycle
so there's really no over-production.
And thus they thrive on war.
Getty made his first million in the First War.
When the war ended
a Texan with more oil than the Axis: Hunt
(than Germany, Italy and Japan together).
D.K. Ludwing ship-welder when war broke out
already owned a fleet, fifth largest in the world
when the war ended.
The basic functions of war?
Young men died in the trenches so that
Republic Iron could grow from 3 million to 148 million
young men died in the trenches so that
Anaconda Copper could grow from 12 million to 58 million
young men died in the trenches so that

International Nickel could grow from 4 million to 74 million.
You'll hear talk of war and rumors of war
on the radios.
They'll end
when the monopolies end.
They ruin their opponents without hating them.
"Natural," like the heat or the rain.
...the rest like animals. Irrelevant
who said this
or where or when.
(In Mexico for example. they were sold for 40 pesos
in Guatemala for 2 pesos each.)
Which is why there'll soon be two human groups;
such a sharp division that within a short time
it will come to be
a true anthropological differentiation.
As for the spread of ideas
exactly equivalent to
a contraband in narcotics.
And Mills' point: a list
of the 100 most powerful people in the U.S.A.
and another of the 100 wisest
few would be on both
if any.
Mr. Daley chubby and bald, with loud ties
inscribed with THE WORLD'S A DELIGHT
surprised his banker colleagues
by entering the conference hall on a tricycle.
Flew from there to the Caribbean to set up the Jamaica Citizens Bank
the world's a delight.
In competition, unconsciously without hating them.
And ladies as hard as their diamonds.
(Its light elusive...all the colors everywhere
never twice in the same place
from red reflection to green scintillation to blue spark
an undying flame
in an infinity of prisms and mirrors without beginning nor end

created a million years ago this diamond
will continue to exist for another million years
it will cost madam merely $100,000 dollars
    at B.A. Ballow & Co. Inc.
the closest you can get to the eternal).
    And businesses whose abyss we barely glimpse.
Businesses which are like a bad check.
    "Allende's days are numbered":
the banker on Wall Street, one January morn, an icy
wind sweeping through the gloomy gorge of Wall Street.
    Deaths in Calcutta, not because of over-population
but because of capitalism.
Which explains: "Threat of rice over-production"
in India.
            "Threat of wheat over-production."
The horror of abundance and sufficiency.
General Electric invented the means
whereby a light-bulb instead of 1000 hours would last
750.
Corporation presidents: common criminals
                    bang! bang!
With planes that don't last too long.
And on purpose now the corporations
avoid inventing.
    "One of the greatest inventions of the 50s
was the tranquilizer."
    The 100,000 mile tire.
Can do it. But they don't want to.
Outboard motors increasingly perfected
to be less long-lasting.
        "Accelerate obsolescence"
            (President of Allied Stores Corporation)
    Our producers of scarcity.
As we know,
        bankers have no money.
So that
for naturalists it's enough to know a member of a species

or a few members
            but with the human species it seems
            unity does not exist.
In other words:
biological evolution is equal in species
but not social evolution in the human species.
Thus three quarters of the planet's wealth...etc.

The fierce Motilones
were gentle, B. Olson discovered in '63
(I was in Colombia then). They believed
that the white men ate human flesh.
    The Indian can hear the soul, say the Motilones.
Or Australian tribes for whom
the soul resides in the ear.
Pythagoras used to say according to Hippolytus that the universe sings.
There was geometry in the vibration of the strings
and music in the distance of the planets.
"They used to say the universe is musical [the Pythagoreans].
And that the soul is like a harmony, or like a music."
The protons in my body and the electrons in the moon.
Modern physics stepped back millennia
when it taught that the universe is a union
of complexity and simplicity, of variability and order.
Why are we attracted to music, rhythm, dance,
if not because it unites our atoms and molecules?
    The young Pleiades in the heavens
    and Sappho alone in her bed.
As for this poem's unity
it has none. The unity is outside.
The unity of everything.
The inanimate universe is not that separate from us.
Thus Sila who is also "universe"
(he's God to the Eskimos and simultaneously universe)
says to the children who are playing in the snow
Sila says to them:
                sila ersinarsinivdlugo

"have no fear of the universe"
in a soft voice like a woman's.
Soft voice of Sila with soft snow.
To the Arhuaco he speaks through waterfalls and rivers
and the murmur of leaves—in Arhuaco—.
He utters a Word in the Mahâbhârata without beginning or end.
Diverse manifestations and a single consciousness.
Beavers who communicate amongst themselves with tails
thrashing the water. Who makes the weasel
turn white in winter?
Butterflies amid flowers with colors of flowers,
of dry leaf amid dry leaves. The red-breast shapes
its mud nest with its feathers like a potter.
Like a potter
Ptah in turn shaped the egg of the world.
Or:
"God and man
...united in clay"
(the rest of the tablet is destroyed).
They said they were sad in Tierra del Fuego
for not knowing much about the Beyond.

CANTIGA 7

The Infinitesimal Calculation of the Apples

It was thought that atoms moved according to Newton's laws,
and could be predicted
like the falling of apples in the autumn afternoon.
Atoms are huge.
Vacuous atoms...
An Atom is as empty as the solar system.
Turned out to be an immense, desolate emptiness,
a space as vast and mysterious as that of the heavens.
An apple's a few elements:
hydrogen, oxygen, carbon...
like a woman too they're the same elements
with the same compounds:
water, sugar...
Apple and woman.
Even quasars are formed from our ordinary matter.
There's not an atom of hydrogen travelling in space and time
which cannot evolve, transmuting into helium.
With a great economy of resources you made the universe.
And this strange planet in the solar system
which spinning round and round, understood itself.
Acquired a mind and love.
This earth apple-shaped
(though to Columbus it was pear-like, or like a woman's breast
with paradise on the nipple)
thanks to gravity with its tendency
to concentrate matter in spheres.
Newton began to grasp it that autumn in Woolsthorpe's garden
with the falling apples,
upon which like English girls a blush had spread.
That the universe should be capable of the fragile biochemistry of life,

is it accident or design,
merely accident or quite the opposite...?
We're the products of trial and error
but with a destiny which can be neither error nor trial.

Proton and neutron equations
with their antiproton and antineutron
and the photon which is indistinguishable from the antiphoton,
or rather: the photon which is its own antiparticle.
If a boy falls in love with a girl of antimatter
(they say) their love couldn't but be platonic.
Like the music of the spheres
the sub-atomic music.
The sub-atomic chaos which produces a kind of order.
Background radiation allows us to deduce that the universe
is harmoniously curved
like a woman.
An atom's light spectrum
is similar to that emitted by a musical instrument.
The beautiful unity of the physical world in which we are,
whether we realize it or not.
The colors of hydrogen or carbon atoms
differ like the timbres of violin and drum.
Why the universe is as we perceive it
is the question.
Because were it different there'd be nobody to see it
is the answer.
In other words, it's so we might exist.
Which is the same as saying: literally a miracle.
Or what Wheeler says, that
a universe without life could not have existed.
A universe without an observer is no such thing.
Circles or ellipses... The stars' circumvallations
match those of our brain
or vice-versa, according to Galileo in Bertolt Brecht
(*Life of Galileo*)
or vice-versa.

Electrons gaze thanks to us at the galaxies.
In those cave times
bow and arrow were invented
(they're depicted in the caves)
and as the arrow was let fly and the twang of the cord heard
the lyre was invented.
And its harmony was attuned to the stars'.

Light displaces itself through a space which lengthens
in the same direction as the light.
Most ancient light.
Telescopes focused on the past.
Illume our nights' most ancient light.
It was only a grease stain in a gas station
and it shone with all the colors of the rainbow and the peacock.
That a thing may be both wave and particle.
So that there would be quantum mechanics
a hundred years earlier wave equations were discovered.
And earlier still the waves of bow and lyre strings.
Reality is not an invention of the mind
but it's not entirely out of the mind.
Minds are like television screens.
With a reality inside them but which is outside them.
There is a *real* reality which even in dreams we recognize.
(Everything I write is fragmentary
a collection of quanta.)
Particles appear to form part of an indivisible whole
and each one plays a part in what happens to the remainder:
reading up on Schrödinger's theoretical cat.
(Fragmentary and also incoherent.)
The cat in a box, which is neither alive nor dead,
can be alive or dead only if the box is opened.
Let's suppose we are traveling in a lift...
That a moving train...
Relativity is
that the observer is relative. Not reality relative.
Electrons, planets, or billiard balls,

what Nobel Laureate will explain to us
why we are in a universe which learned to think?
        And why this planet filled with metals?

Sub-atomic particles have no defined identity,
they say, and yet we are made up of them.
As also:
finally the mass of matter disappears and there is only immaterial energy.
We invent categories such as left and right
but there are mirrors where it's the reverse.
There having to be something greater than reality and the mirror.
I mean a reality that unifies reality and the mirror.
                Physicists talking now
of universes which are not solely physical.
"Mystical abstractions which appear to be the essence of matter,"
says Murchie.
                The more is known of it the less is understood.
There's speculation about illusive, illusory particles,
with very little mass, which never interact with anything,
or perhaps have too much mass...
"Scientific progress has not always advanced further
through having an open mind."
Or:
"It's not a question of not having theoretical prejudices
but of having the correct theoretical prejudices."

We are not merely atoms, or we're atoms
with an infinite thirst for dreams.
        Atoms whose lips touched under the poplars.
                        From poplars I come,
atoms, mother, that don't want to die.
The half-life of the atom which is today and gone tomorrow.
According to Prosser's theory:
                everything is in all places
although it may appear in just a particular spot.
        (Increasingly similar, physics and mysticism.)
Or according to Bohm: the entire universe is in each of its parts.

And death why fear it.
When you die, only what is not you dies.
Maybe matter's composed of a single particle
under various guises
        (didn't St. Benedict see the whole universe in a ray of sun?)
and all consciousness makes up a single consciousness,
the whole universe being conscious matter.
It's said that no theory on its own explains the entire real world
except one based on a hypothetical particle called...
But I tell you, girl, the hair on your head, your black eyes,
actively cooperate,
they follow a defined plan.
A "strange subjective element in the physical world," according to Davies.
Or that free will might obtrude into the microworld.
        A kind of mind domination over matter.
                ...and re-evaluate the traditional concept of reality.
Matter we are but not entirely matter.
Unless we were to talk along the lines of spiritual matter.

The Second Law is that the sun will fade away.
And that Myriam more beautiful than the sun will fade away.
It's not a figure from Góngora or Quevedo,
she was a Myriam once mine,
her black eyes came from the sun
                (whose black spots are so brilliant, they say)
but on the scale of evolution,
more beautiful and more complex than the sun.
The theory that the universe is a fluctuation of the void
with the explosion of an infinity of particles come out of nothing
and after a defined period of time reabsorbed into the void.
        Theory of the universe and everything in it.
That it's born from the ball of fire of Big Bang,
it expands, and it later contracts in a ball of fire
and vanishes.
And the theory that we exist only because of
a strange deflection in the equilibrium of the universe.
The possibility, they say, which emerged in 1971,

that the universe might have been born as fire,
expanded, and will finally collapse into nothing.
                    But as Aristotle observed
our life is programmed in computers.
Or Claude Bernard said:
It would appear an invisible guide is leading us.
Hyperactive matter, that's what life is.
For example Myriam on her 15th birthday
blowing out fifteen candles
(Avenida Bolívar, Managua, pre-earthquake)
a Myriam who (as this poem maintains)
will never be repeated.
            That characteristic of human beings:
                    unpredictability.
                              You had so much of that!
Molecules and atoms so alive in your cells... But
do molecules and atoms ever really die?
What marks the frontiers between what is alive and dead?
The atom from another galaxy in a girl.
What frontier between body and soul?
Who draws the line between life and non-life,
memory and matter?

First all was gas.
Then
from gas to atoms to cells to people and to the person you love.
The office worker who gets back exhausted to her 8th floor
and the cat that she pets on the pink sofa,
are they inevitable products of evolution?
            Our lives and our ephemeral and infinite destiny.
That we should be living in a universe that makes sense.
And that we're not merely chemical elements.
            My mathematical metaphors are in defence of life.
We're not alone in the cosmos, still less in the chaos.
We can conceive of a cosmos where chaos reigns,
as Paul Davies says,
where people and stars have no reason to exist.

Yet the evidence goes beyond unity...
The tendency is also toward complexity and order.
To the reductionist there's nothing fundamental in a cat
which isn't contained in that animal's atoms
never mind mysterious forces or laws or principles.
        But a cat is a cat and not another cat.
To what extent are electrons not individuals?

            And that we don't know what we don't know.
            Tears are H_20 and go down to the sea.
            But the sea and love where do they go?
                    Is it a particle or is it a wave?

CANTIGA 8

Condensations and Vision of San José de Costa Rica

Up above the stars call out
inviting us to awaken, to evolve
    to venture forth into the cosmos.
Engendered they by pressure and heat.
        Like merry boulevards lit up
        or towns seen by night from a plane.
    Love: which lit up the stars...
The universe is made of union.
        The universe is condensation.
Condensation is union, and it is heat. (Love.)
The universe is love.
        An electron never wants to be alone.
Condensation, union, that's what stars are.
The Law of Gravity
        che muove il sole e l'altre stelle
is an attraction between bodies, and the attraction
accelerates when bodies draw closer.
The force of attraction of chaotic matter.
            Each molecule
attracts every other molecule in the universe.
    The straightest line is curved.
            Only love is revolutionary.
            Hatred is always reactionary.
Heat is a movement (agitation) of molecules
as love is movement (and as love is heat).
        An electron strives to belong to a complete group or subgroup.
        All matter is attraction.
The electrons of an atom revolve in elliptical orbits
as the planets revolve in elliptical orbits
(and love orbits elliptically).

Every one of the earth's molecules attracts
the moon, the sun and the stars.
It has rained in the night and the toads are singing
under the moon, singing for their females, calling them
to copulation.
        And atoms, loving atoms join together
        until so many atoms have joined together
        that they begin to shine and it's a star.
(What happens in sexual union? And how does it produce
new life?) And dance came from the stars.
Amid stalactites and stalagmites (final gallery)
a bison shaped from clay from the cave itself
mounting a female shaped from the same clay
and on the floor prints, soles and heels in the clay
of ice age adolescents who danced
and danced before the two bison.
        The dance learned from the stars.

Sunday night, and on Wall Street a foul wind
blows newspapers along the empty sidewalk. Wall St. with stars
eerie and empty. The bank windows dark
though not all. A few rows lit up
in the black monstrosities. They can be identified:
the foreign departments of the big banks.
The iron doors barred and padlocked.
But by back doors some people have entered
the foreign departments. The lights—secret meetings,
decisions we're unaware of (and their cigar smoke
rising like shares) but they affect us all.
Devaluation sparks off a riot in Malaysia, buses burned
and blood flows in the streets like water from a hydrant.
At the hour that the stars shine over Wall Street
and the hour the banks open in London.

Matter attracts matter
and as condensation increases so its power
of attraction increases. Under equal conditions

a condensation two million miles in diameter
exerts eight times the attraction as one of a million. So
the greater the condensation the greater its capacity
to grow more, gathering in smaller condensations.
Let's suppose now that a huge mass of uniform vapor
spreads out in space for millions and millions of miles
in all directions: any slight alteration
in its uniformity can unleash condensation
after condensation, of every imaginable dimension.

Capitalism will pass away. You'll no longer see the Stock Exchange.
—Just as sure as spring follows winter...
My vision of San José de Costa Rica.
And if "the last enemy destroyed will be death"
selfishness will be destroyed before.
As different from present man as he is from Peking Man.
Competition impedes cooperation.
There is separation between man and man.
A broken humanity.
The first fish
died of suffocation. The first fish that leaped onto land
was like el Che.
But others followed after.

Anyone might think that a small disturbance
which only affects a small mass of gas
would produce a condensation of small proportions.
But the gravitation of the smallest body
is felt throughout the entire universe. The moon
creates tides on the earth and on the most distant stars.
When a baby throws his toy to the floor,
it disturbs the motion of every star in the universe.
While gravitation lasts, no
disturbance can remain confined
to an area less than the totality of space.

"An attempt to storm the heavens," said Lenin

Lenin no less (The Paris Commune).
        Communal and personal, without classes and without state.
A new man with new chromosomes.
Easy to produce and distribute what we need
            on this celestial body
(economics is not complicated).

The more violent the disturbance
the more intense will be the condensations
but even the most insignificant one develops
condensations, though they're of exceedingly weak intensity
and we've seen already that the destiny of a condensation
is not determined by its intensity but by its mass.
However weak their original intensity may have been
the large condensations continue to grow bigger
and bigger, and small condensations vanish, absorbed
by the larger ones, and nothing remains in the end but a clutch
of enormous condensations. Such are the phenomena that we call
socializations, and such is
                        the Revolution.

The universe is homogeneous. The star fragments
in the Geological Museum of South Kensington
demonstrate that they are of the same flesh as us.
            (We too are stars.)
"Celestial flesh," said Rubén.
        We too are children of the sun
(the heat of our blood is solar heat).
            Engendered by the stars!
"My black beauty, I am happy in the mountains
because I am at my people's battle front."
        And the battle's already twenty thousand million years old.
But: "the revolution doesn't end in this world"
if we don't defeat death
        the status quo triumphs once and for all
            death is the status quo.

And my Vision in San José de Costa Rica, I'll tell
of my Vision—in a taxi at night
having just arrived by plane for a Writers' Congress.
My Vision was: some neon signs, drugstores, cars
kids on motorbikes, gas stations, bars, people on the sidewalks
group of girls in uniform, workers in groups
            and I saw everything organized by love.
The color of a sweater spoke to me of love
love moved the cars, lit up those lights—all of them.
The girls' fashions, what were they but love
        the kids in the barrios, brought together by love
and red-flowering trees planted by love
        a long-haired youth—long-haired through love
an ad: IMPERIAL. Who knows what for but it has to be
something you share, you give.
A call box and somebody calling what person? which people?
Mother and daughter along the street and behold another love
        a couple goes by arm in arm, another love
            a pregnant woman virtually bellowing love.
My taxi moves on. Two on a sidewalk: one telling a story
(must be friends).
                Beautiful animal man is I tell myself.
Fried Chicken, Pâtisserie...love too.
Someone in a hurry—late arriving. Where? For a date
or a party, a house where he loves.
Another carrying bread. For him with others. Communion.
Brightly lit restaurants: they're also for a union
PILSEN beer: it too announces association, gathering together
        Coca-Cola
(real shit) but the sign tonight spells out:
                        C o m m u n i o n.
Beautiful species I said how I love it.
            All of us born of copulations
                born for love
(in a barrio, a house with a small party. And how moving.)
I saw that it was beautiful to die for others.
That was my vision that night in San José de Costa Rica

the whole of creation down to the hoardings groaned with pain
because of man's exploitation of man. The whole of creation
    was clamoring, clamoring in full cry for
the Revolution.

CANTIGA 9

Song of Spacetime

In the beginning.
The time before time?
Let's begin our speculation before the beginning.
When there was no matter nor motion, nor space nor time.
When in the words of the RIG-VEDA
neither non-being nor being existed.
What occurred before the Great Explosion?
Nothing, if there was no before.
Was Big Bang creation? Or merely the start
of creation, which is with us still?
Or is this a merely renewed universe,
without creation,
the authentic creation generations of universes back?

The sacred starry sky.
They and their inhabitants.
Our celestial community in the curvature of the void.
To a point beyond which no telescopes can reach.
So great the space of time of those lights
that we will be seeing the birth from the dark depths
of the first galaxies in constantly receding telescopes.
And Alfonso: does space expand or us in it?
(Space, where you and I are?
I who live in you and you that do not exist.)
Stars dying throughout the universe.
Order is born from chaos
and returns to chaos.
Unable to be order ever again.
The relationship, for example, between a refrigerator
and the final destiny of the universe.

When the sun's on the point of burning the last of its oxygen...

Newton thinking about that edge.
                Rejecting that edge.
Beyond which there would be a dark emptiness without limit or frontiers.
And Einstein:
        There is no center nor edge although the surface is finite.
A curved universe which meets on the opposite side.
In it galaxies rotating
rotating like gigantic girandoles of radiation.
                In an infinite universe
                there would be an infinity of inhabited planets
                an infinity of us's.

That it could be comprehensible was the great mystery to Einstein.
Gazing in the distance we gaze towards the universe's past.
At a distance greater than 5,000 Mpc
an age when quasars had yet to be born
            because God has so far
            failed to pinch the skin of the
            night!
(When it comes to such colossal distances there is
as Alfonso Cortés said
the distance to a star that has never existed.)
        Particles, atoms, molecules, dust,
        planets, stars, galaxies, clusters
        of galaxies and what else?

When it comes to such colossal distances
our problem, Lord,
is that one is never satisfied.

The galaxies are details in cosmic space.
And a million years like the blink of an eye.
Despite Copernicus, his five planets etc.
we continue to consider ourselves the center of the universe.

Atoms tend to unite in the direction of life,
it seems.
And life is an inevitable phenomenon.
That secret voice which tells you
that you are irreplaceable in the universe
and should live forever...
Biological death is not of the entire being,
it's another mode of being.
    A universal corporeity.
        Immersed in the totality of the universe.
In union with the radical unity of matter,
in communion
                in the heart of the earth (Matthew 12:40).
The death of a loved one
unites us with that world, Rilke noted, more or less.

Above the blue atmosphere
the sky is profoundly black.
    We see them neither in their proper place nor in the present.
    Radiation reaches us from the past.
    Even from times when there was no Milky Way.
And Bohm says: "naturally
there may be other universes expanding."
    Perhaps worlds in which our physical laws
are false.
So many worlds that not even the Buddha can count them
according to the Tibetan text.
Our middling star of average brilliance in the Milky Way.
Neither is our galaxy in the center
of our local group of galaxies.
No special place in the universe.
    And besides we see it as it was and not as it is.

Time is space.
    It's the advance of matter in space.
        There was nothing in space without time
        and there has only been time in space.

Matter moves and that is time-space.
Gazing into space we are gazing backwards in time,
backwards only.
Astronomers faced with present stars that no longer exist.
In today's telescopes the galaxies
    as they were millions of years
ago.
    And so in other heavenly bodies they'll see us in the future
present
as we once were.
        Time, a train itinerary...
    A space in time and a time in space.
And my recollection today of Mexico way back?
To give an example, her, and her house opposite the Parque España.
The getting off buses, puddles, and kisses in the rain
        —like stations and trains
    all space with a time and time in a space—
and we happily leapt those puddles, and splattered ourselves,
            coming back from the University.
But to astronomers: they're present, and they no longer exist.
I'm talking about a long time ago in Mexico.
        In the four-dimensional universe
        the past and the future always exist.
—Me forever helping her into that raincoat
as we left the Faculty—.
        In the three-dimensional one
        as though time *elapses.*
    But it's a mirage.
Time is an optical illusion of space.

Or:
    "Time is hunger and space is cold"
said Alfonso Cortés. What did he mean?
Hunger is felt with time. Like
if one does not eat the three times a day.
Space separates us. It is solitude and cold.
In spacetime we are

like those children sleeping on the street
wrapped up in newspapers in the great city
hungry and cold.

A light has travelled a thousand million light years
and is printed one night on a photographic plate.
Is it remote that galaxy?
It is remote but in time.
Just as remote from us the Maya observatories.
In space-time we are, we were, we will be forever.
Although here and now, with the cold of space and hunger of time.
Sacred time, sacred space...
(Eliade has studied them.)
Eternity and Paradise.
All myths and rituals are that nostalgia.
But time left the circle and became linear
thanks to St. Paul. With 2 aeons.
Linear and curved. Also the curvature of time
they speak of nowadays.
The fact that the curvatures of time are real
says Davies.
Gravity which is love we were saying, thanks to which kisses are given,
gravity is a consequence of the spacetime curve.
Gravity and all of us.
Also Paul Davies himself says:
Time and space, those approximate ideas...
(Perhaps a future theory
may not even use the notions of space and time.)
Past, present and future, it's linguistics.
But will the last thing to prevail be
the second law of thermodynamics?
Nothing but black hole after black hole after black hole
in which all has been submerged in oblivion. St. Paul says
the final enemy to be defeated will be death, will be
the second law of thermodynamics.
Perhaps matter again, as in the beginning,
reduced to an infinite density.

Apocalypse according to Davies.

The heavenly bodies
            and ours.
"Walking stars"—the Chaldeans. (About those not fixed.)
In Greek walking is *planetes*, so that
we inhabit a walking star.
Men who shaped Man
or rather will.
            Or the prospect before us is merely
a barren planet like Mars.
      A mushroom-shaped cloud slowly rising
on the horizon...
Star Wars which the *Wall Street Journal* called
"Dollars falling from the skies."
            Neanderthal *Wall Street Journal.*
But no. We have for example
evolution from the primitive shark until it transforms into dove.
Man's death instinct
                  is not inherited from animal ancestors.
Biology also teaches:
natural selection favours peace-loving animals.
Murderous groups within a same species do not prosper.
(Somozas, Pinochet, etc.)   Gorillas are meditative,
they like to spend their time in contemplation.
That the solution to all China's social problems
was love
was discovered five centuries before our era.
      One man helping another
      which to Pliny is God.
The incarnation of God in our biology.
In our still mammal condition.
      Jesus: with Adam's chromosomes...
Only a million years since *Pithecanthropus erectus.*
The government rooted in the sky which Confucius mentioned.
            Not dollars from the sky.
We've left excrement behind in plastic bags on the moon.

The Mayas had already discovered the lunar month
only out by 34 seconds.
34 seconds
in a time for them infinite, without beginning nor end.
The enemies of evolution (Somoza etc.).
Counter-evolutionaries.
How can there be unemployment on this planet?
But there is a tower we wish to build, Chuang-tse said,
that might reach to infinity.
Shit-eating counter-evolutionaries.
On that day even physical beauty will be egalitarian.

"Basically composed of bacteria."
Descendants of single-celled creatures still to be found in any drop of water.
Cephalopoda, vertebrates, vermiforms,
the one from Assisi called them brothers before the
Origin of the Species.
To believers in an author of evolution, that is
in a Creator, it's strange to us to see it making mistakes
creating creatures with a dead-end.
A premeditated evolutionary path? In reality, no.
But rectifying in hindsight.
Rectifying for example a defective air bladder.
Likewise *reversibilities* of evolution. Even
in human society. Even in the revolution.
Also living fossils in the depths of the sea,
the case of the crossopterygii, or in the White House.
Likewise Christian-Democrats, left or right wing,
and those whose paws and wings changed back to fins.
We are not only product of the process but the process
and responsible for the process being free from it.
There's a theory that the chimpanzee is ex-human. Out of fear
he regressed from man.
Evolution is not predictable but certainly controllable.
Will artificial intelligence be the next stage?
Silica beings superior to human beings of carbon?
We've already programmed computers to think.

Unlike us
        an error once committed they will never repeat.
    That's how they can beat us at chess.
Robots have freely ventured forth to explore the Solar System.
Those who at present answer, will they one day be able to ask?
Are we humans mere machines
to manufacture machines better than ourselves?
        Their information one day will be vaster than ours.
Will they then have consciousness or even emotions?
And reproduction even without love?
Will we be able, in the event of danger, to unplug them in time?

Energy
    matter
        galaxy
            sun
                planet
                    life
                        technology
and then what?

When the universe was the size of a grapefruit...
        And before, of an apple.
We're quite familiar with how the universe was born
but not how it will end.
                Will it end?
Either total entropy or the return to Big Bang.
Either death by ice or death by fire.
            Hence hope has to lie elsewhere.
Before there were distinctions between terrestrial and celestial.
When apples were falling in Woolsthorpe's garden
Newton saw that everything was attracted, apples like the moon.
Planets not yet seen were guessed at
because of the falling of apples. And the celestial
fell the same as the terrestrial.
Even the galactic system a living organism
(and beyond?)

The gas ever denser and hotter
until it is a star.
Why did the interior of the stars grow hot?
(The metabolism of the stars.)
Maybe love is particle and is wave.
The excitement of molecules which
is what the word heat signifies...
Waves of particles or particles of waves?
Whatever the case
the universe would seem to be overflowing with intelligence.
Permeated by consciousness.
They are not merely "jewels in the night."
Where chance and necessity go together
neither subordinated to the other.
There's a murmur of intelligence in every thing...
A subtle mental aspect to inanimate matter.
Is fire matter?
Fire's not matter but a process.
And life's not matter but a form of fire
and a process.
Biology is not excluded from the kingdom of heaven.
As for what came before
(For example ten seconds before the Great Explosion?)
Before time: what was there before?
The sun will change into a red sunflower.
I can only say that if time is simultaneous
(past, present and future simultaneous)
nothing is buried in oblivion.

CANTIGA 10

Canticle of the Sun

Slowly the sun rises from the sea,
rather, slowly the earth spinning...
seeming to us that the sun rises from the sea.
        Sun just gas.
And sun that we eat.
For plants eat solar energy,
and animals, plants or plant-devouring animals.
        Green chlorophyll and red hemoglobin.
        Thus the sun feeds us all.
Through solar radiation life was born,
organic compounds fusing together
in large molecular communities
under the influence of solar radiation.
Life: a few combinations of amino acids
with infinite forms.
        The pull of the earth draws down roots
        and the pull of the sun raises up stems.
And we also, like plants, between the earth and the light.
It had to remain stable through millions of years
of evolution, until consciousness came about beneath it.
            It did not burn out before us.
(We between the earth and the light.)
            And even the light of a torch
or of a pair of eyes,
                    comes from the sun.
The earth's colors have their origins there.
            (That mass of fibers
            which covers your entire head
            and hangs down your back in coils,
            from what mine did you plunder it or what jeweler's shop?)

Movement of the eye's molecules struck by light
that's the colors.
And we only see 30% of the light. Single-celled organisms
the entire solar light. They see the world as it is!
        As I will see it one day as it is.
Extra-planetarily perhaps. Or beyond the visible universe.

                And way out the dark frozen depths
the dark emptiness between star and star
where dead suns like extinguished coals,
                                    scoria, ash,
wander with their black and frozen planets.
Where matter plunges into the "never-again" of the black holes,
spacetime converted through gravity into black hole
into black hole from which not even light escapes.

But we, like the plants, between the sun and the earth,
earth from where Persephone emerges each year in spring.
Plants turned to humus turned to plants again.
And the blood of Adonis rises in red anemones.
Tissues unknit and knit again.
Organic matter, simple molecules, and once again organic matter.
And Persephone once again emerges from Hades
into the light.

Were there no eyes to see it
there'd be no light.
Can we imagine a light without eyes
        or eyes without light?
Would there be light everywhere in the universe
with no one to see it?
But, as we know, eyes were created by light
so that there'd be beings to behold it.
The Earth came from the sun (and its water).
From the sun comes this water, with its life and its colors
and its light.
                    This water in San Blas

full of light.
Where fish come and go
some like neon signs,
or traffic-light yellow.
Phosphorescent,
or as though painted with florescent paint,
iridescent,
scintillating,
others as though illuminated within
—strange light in their entrails–.
Tiny fish that nuzzle up curious like tourists.
Or where the angel-fish swims slantwise the better to display
its black and yellow stripes.
The light cuts through the transparency
and the white sand refracts it.
The atmosphere is turquoise
in the magic wood.
Creatures in the shape of trees
and others in the shape of grasses or mushrooms
and between them others dart and glint.
Motionless polyps or with tentacles in motion,
hungry whips.
Gentle corals swaying
and others turned to rock. Rock
carnations.
Colors upon colors
behind other colors
in quivering crystal.
The floor coral sand, calcareous algae, foraminifera.
A fish gaudily daubed like a clown
—red and black snout with a white patch–
and others pass by in masks
or with bulging eyes as though wearing glasses.
Bonsai groves
from which a tiny dragon peers out.
Medusas like an umbrella of water.
Molluscs soft as mucous membrane.

Petrified lettuces.
The light diffuse.
Fleshy escarpments
or of calcareous algae.
In a water like air.
Invisible like spectacles.
Black velvet fish
dragging the train of its ceremonial costume between corals.
Like tumbled-down terraces and abandoned gardens...
Filamentous shapes.
Curls, cacti, candelabra.
An air-like water.
Or like liquid light.
Purple fans fluttering in the water
like women fanning themselves.
Polished red pebbles that are plants.
Gelatinous carpets
trapping the light
for photosynthesis.
Transformation of the light
into food.
Bodies color of murky water
or color of whitish sand
or chine like clear water in sunlight.
Miró fish. Paul Klée fish.
Color-foods that come and go.
Living colors and lights
that come and go.
The sun drenching the water that stems from the sun.
Corals with circumvallations of brains.
Forked like deer antlers.
Like vanilla ice-creams melting away.
Like pine branches covered with snow.
There lilies sway. Huge bird feathers.
The green parrot-fish eats soft green corals
defecating a cloud of golden sand as it eats.
shoals of fish at dance

and the odd pensive one.
That harlequin.
Gold- and silver-plated fish.
Or even gold with black, and others black with silver.
Skyscrapers.
Cathedrals.
Millenary creatures these corals.
Light submerged.
The sun within the water come from the sun.
Liquid light, and the water seemingly solid.
The light is turned water and the water turned light.
Jungle beneath the water.
As in a dream.
Creatures the shape of dahlias or daisies.
Stone-strewn pastures.
And there the clefts teeming with fish.
Patches of opaque tangled algae.
Purple, cream, lilac: the sponges.
Fauces half-agape clustered with tentacles.
A voracious orange color coils and uncoils.
Silent undulating ferns.
Pliant chains of disks of flesh.
Luminous energy in food,
converted into food.
Branching stalks and on them
the baby off-spring of medusas.
The youthful barracuda
among terrified tiny silver fish.
Others on the curve, twisting, somersaulting,
looping-the-loop.
Up above the sun shimmers in the gold nose-pieces,
the gold rings in the noses
of the Cuna girls, who on the sea
shore, beneath the palm trees
sew their many-colored *molas,*
and from the sun come all the colors of their *molas*
on this island of San Blas which came from the sun

with its palms and everything
                —the sun is also San Blas
                        and the Indians are sun—.
Upon aquamarine water, in their canoes,
the men are fishing,
                        further out the long net deployed,
where it changes from aquamarine to deep blue
and you shield your eyes with your hand from light so fierce
        it burns your spectacles,
from so much light, in the eyes that the light created.
Light travels at 300,000 kilometers per second
why does light travel and where is it going?

CANTIGA 11

Gaia

In the beginning there was a turbulence.
(The Spirit of God was stirring...)

In the beginning was Chaos, father of Gaia, goddess of the earth.
Once there would have been only tenuous matter
spread uniformly throughout space.
The primeval Chaos.
Which produced the first perturbation.
First condensations of the most tenuous nebulae.
The condensations compressed into stars.
Those believed to be newest they called "nova" and "supernova."
Ironically, because they are the destruction of a star.
But a supernova created at least one new star:
the Sun.

As the earth maintains the moon revolving around it
the sun maintains the earth and the rest of the planets in circles
around it.
The planets were born as condensations of gas;
torn away from the sun they compressed, becoming liquid
and then solid.
The sun and its children the planets.
The planets and their off-spring the satellites.
Revolving around the sun.
Their unequal distances around the sun
produced as they moved together a harmony (to the Greeks)
like the uneven lengths of lyre strings
as they moved together.
Mercury first with its elliptical orbit and no atmosphere,
the most desolate of all the planets,

then Venus with its yellowish atmosphere of sulfuric acid,
the Earth with its moon
arid Mars, its pinkish atmosphere of carbon dioxide
and 2 moons,
the 60,000 asteroids, planetary debris,
giant Jupiter with its multi-colored stormy atmosphere
with 16 moons,
Saturn immense but vaporous with 3 rings and 21 moons,
Uranus of frozen methane with 15 moons and many rings,
Neptune pale green and little brightness, with 2 moons,
and much further out, the last one, Pluto, the planet with the longest year
(two and a half times our century) and the coldest, with one moon,
the 58 moons rotating on their axes
and around their planets
and the planets on their axes and around the Sun
and the Sun turning on its axis
and with all the planets and moons rotating in the galaxy
towards the constellations of Hercules and the Lyre
and the galaxy rotating around other galaxies
and all of it rotating around what or Whom?

The largest living creature on earth
is the Earth.
We've seen it in the photos:
sapphire sphere amid white fleeces
and gleaming white skull caps at its poles.
The new notion of *Gaia*—a living Earth.
The planet Earth, all of it a single living being.
It was so, long before there was "life" on its surface.
There is nowhere to live except in the sky,
therefore,
having emerged from the sun's equatorial region
it became round in order to spin.
Living being that needed neither legs nor arms nor mouth nor anus
but merely to be round and spin and spin around the sun.
It revolved quickly (5-hour days and 5-hour nights),
the moon already creating tides even then.

By itself it created conditions for supporting organisms
and later organisms with consciousness, people; and later
an organism which is both community and individuals.
Burning and arid, smouldering, gushing forth lava, molten glass,
it seemed that the Earth had no future.
Who'd have said that from that flaming magma
woods, and cities and songs and nostalgias would emerge.
But rains came. The rain evaporated and on and on it rained.
Torrential rain fell for one hundred thousand years.
A thousand million times it travelled around the Sun devoid of life.
At that stage the globe would not have been blue and white
with pinkish land.
The sun always the color of twilight.
The sky color of dried leaves and the sea copying that color.
Grey waves breaking on the grey and dead earth.
The eolic erosion of rocks was for life.
Continents very different from those today floated adrift.
        Everest was pushing up two inches a year.
The sky began to turn blue as it filled with oxygen.
The sky gradually turned blue because the sea was turning green
(with life) and later the earth green.
                        Chlorophyll and oxygen,
        all green and blue.
We had a wet planet, and already cooled down for life.
Still little chemical difference between cell and non-cell.
At first life was merely a purplish greenish tint.
Microcosmos that lives on within us.
Certain anomalous qualities of water
with exceptional properties of radiation
and temperature etc.
Until it became the dynamic system we call life.
        First in a foamy slime perhaps.
                Certainly microscopic.
But already with mouths, open microscopic mouths, avid
mouths still without song, and then later with fins,
fins foreshadowing the wing and the hand.
First life was very aqueous, delicate, slight,

and left no fossils not even microscopic ones.
Later there are *Limulus* fossils copulating in the Cambrian.
There were still no lobsters, oysters or fish.
The step onto land was like a trip to another planet.
The organisms were crushed by their own weight.
Whence bones. And skin, pelts, integuments
against the direct light of the sun which fell on the earth.
And the dryness, which is why water had to be carried internally.
Vertebrates on land, we continued to be aquatic.
Seals, dolphins, whales preferred to return to the water.
"The essential act of procreation is always in water."
And swimming in the waters of the womb the embryo grows.
And humans still sweat and weep sea water.
On its own the Globe learned to cover itself with plant-sustaining soil.
It is a living Earth, all of it, palpitating.
        Stone also vibrates although slowly.
In its core the planet palpates.
A living body which wanders through the sky among the stars.
An atmosphere protects us from harmful radiations.
The sun which gives us light allows us to sleep.
A cell is not just its molecules
and an organism is not just its cells,
so this living planet is not merely its living creatures.
        Extension of our body
is this spherical body floating in space.
Lakes and volcanoes are also our flesh.
Our flesh of carbon compounds
brought out of the depths of the earth by volcanoes.
With ultraviolet light it extracted ozone from oxygen,
ozone which was the defence against ultraviolet light.
In the Cambrian the sea was populated by invertebrates.
The earth was a sterile desert with volcanic eruptions.
In the Siluric the earth had plants as yet without leaves.
In the Carboniferous the first copulations took place on earth.
In the Eocene and Paleocene plants with flowers.
                        Then reptiles, birds,
                        and later, mammals.

The first tiny mammals, with warm blood
which enabled them to endure the night chill. They came out
at night by the moonlight, and the night dilated their eyes.
Then Gaia raised the temperature
and mankind abandoned the caves
to build cities.
Always superior forms after other inferior ones
in the structural organization.
Gaia:
Earth which is simply the largest living creature on the Earth.
All living beings being merely
part of the vast entity, of the total organism.
    A strange atmosphere, of incompatible gases.
And for the unstable atmosphere to remain the same
only a living creature can manage that: Gaia.
Its animals altered the atmosphere with their breath.
First it was poisonous
like the gas billowing from Union Carbide in Bhopal.
They invented how to breathe the lethal oxygen.
The red of our blood is on account of the iron.
And iron oxidizes quickly with oxygen.
    "To breathe is to burn."
Life evolved
not adapting to the environment as Darwin believed
but changing the environment.
Living beings transformed this chemically inert globe
into an immense organism.
Oxygen didn't appear until 2 thousand million years ago
when the first plants used photosynthesis,
and for hundreds of millions of years they have maintained
the ideal 21% oxygen.
The humble plankton submerged in the ocean
influences the density of the towering white clouds
which influence the earth's temperature.
    "That all the atoms should be swirling around,
    and that the planet should emerge by chance with life and all,
    the probability is zero."

Our anomalous Earth, says Lovelock.
Strange and beautiful anomaly.
Blue sky, sea and earth!
And the planet as a biological construction.
Against the flow of all chemistry.
This oxygen which makes it possible for us to light fires,
for birds to fly and for you to think.
With 21% oxygen we can light fires,
but with 4% more, the entire Amazon would set ablaze.
Neither very hot nor very cold, nor very acid nor very alkaline.
Sufficiently large for a thin, translucent atmosphere,
but not so large as to make it dense and opaque.
A little further from the sun it would be too cold,
a little closer too hot.
Control that only a living planet can exercise.
Its biological rhythm now altered by our technical rhythm.
A life created by chance, they say, is more difficult
than for a hurricane to assemble a Boeing 707.
And that life is fragile and delicate, is merely,
says Lovelock, the Victorian concept of woman.
The death of the individual is certain, certainly!
but there is a life in Gaia which will outlive us all.
Although only so long as the sun permits.

Living Earth that made itself in the sky life's habitat.
The celestial habitat of life.
And every living thing on Earth, from whales to viruses
a single living being.
Its depressions and mountains
like the curves of a living body,
and we inhabit a planet which is entirely alive.
A vast living thing,
which developed as something living from the beginning.
Gaia eats. It feeds on sunlight.
"Strange and beautiful anomaly of the solar system."
And we, as a species, its nervous system.
Five thousand million years ago

from dust and gas it took shape
and remained then as it is.
Rock and metal with a fine film of air and water.
The gas of farts and of the fetid bubbles of marshes
keep our oxygen level in check.
So that it's not so high as to set the woods ablaze.
Without foul-smelling marshlands neither you nor flowers would exist.
Water, they call:
one of the strangest substances to science.
So unusual and so abundant.
Both attributes which make the planet habitable.
    Organisms themselves invented blood:
    a piece of ocean within them.
The sailor thrown into the water one night by the Contras
    —he knowing it was 38 fathoms deep—
he remained hidden in the dark on his plank. Now
he goes under in his memories:
"At three I got my bearing from the star they call the Sloth.
When the sun rose, I was floating, lost, having swum and swum.
I saw huge waves in the sea the height of a coconut palm.
I spoke to the sea: Why are you treating me so unkindly? Let me sleep
which is what I want to do. And instantly it became calm.
When you live at sea you form a close relationship with the ocean.
I slept about half an hour. The swell and the huge waves returned
as though to awaken me, as though to receive the sea's message,
to tell me: the boats are there."

        Now Solentiname, hours from Bangkok.
Until all are conscious particles of a single organism.
    Bodies of a huge body.
A planet signals to another planet.
There's nowhere to live except in the sky.
The sight of the illuminated globe in dark space
inspired even the prosaic astronauts
    —"Gleaming blue and white jewel...
        ...in the immense sea of mysterious blackness."
Heiler quoted the African chief who said to the white man

"as though we'd had the same mother."
And Lovelock, the inventor of the Gaia theory wonders
whether another name for Gaia might not be Mary.

What song will the earth sing that day?

Lying in my bed in Managua
I'm dropping off to sleep
        and suddenly I ask myself:
        Where are we going? We are
on the dark side of the earth,
          the other side, lit up.
Tomorrow we will be in the light
and the others in darkness.
This night lying in my bed
I feel the journey. But where are we going?
I recall numbers learnt in other times:
Around the sun at 30 kilometers per second,
and together with the sun in the galaxy at 250 kilometers per second,
and the galaxy is travelling at what speed...?
Take it easy Felipe Peña, fallen we know not where,
and Donald and Elvis buried down by the Costa Rican border,
take it easy boys, we're doing fine.
        Spinning around in black space
wherever we're going, we're doing fine.
And also,
    the Revolution's doing fine.

CANTIGA 12

Birth of Venus

In the beginning was the Word
and the Word was light.
Or quarks without which there'd be no light.
Let there be light was let there be universe,
after all, the universe is really light, all light.
Since 1905 we've known that light is also mass
and conversely
mass can convert into radiation
just as a gram of matter was converted into radiation
above Hiroshima.

A disorganized mass of poorly connected things.
In the beginning God said: Let there be radiation.
The universe at that hour so hot and dense!
Although to Atkins we are merely children of a random chance.

Who'd have said that out of such confusion
there would one day emerge such a beautiful and fragile filigree,
life.
Fresh from the sea like Venus
life.
The sea was born from the wedding of hydrogen and oxygen
and life was born from the sea
In the salt transparency
molecules transforming into protoplasm.
Venus dripping, fresh from the sea.
The composition of our blood much akin,
according to Cousteau,
to that of sea water.

The salt of sweat and of our tears
is from the sea.
...dripping.
Even now our bodies gush sea water.
And the contents of each cell
a form of ocean water.
Hence our need for water. Thirst.
Venus gushing water—the first algae.
Then the first prints in the sand.
The first eyes opened
and already the earth was green.
Plants. (From gas and water and sunlight.)
The stench of mud and crushed leaves
created the sense of smell.
Toads and frogs were the first to hear.
Life came out of the sea, which explains
this oceanic to and fro in our veins.
And the moon's hold on us.
Life came out of the sea
like a bather on Corn Island beach.
Coconut palms in the foreground,
against the blue, the blues,
bluest of blues and
green swathes
like light-green rivers between the blue
dark blue
blue-black patches,
and the sky is scarcely blue at all against so many blues
and on the shore, on the stones: crystal, colorless, crystal;
closer in, sugar-like sand,
and coconut palms with coconuts in the foreground.
And the female bather saunters towards us
dripping wet.
Life came out of the sea. Venus gushing water.
That's why our blood is salty like the ocean
and the proportion of salt is *the same.*
And likewise the sodium, the potassium in our veins

come from the primeval ocean.
Gushing blood and tears.

Clay began to live.
That's to say, the glutinous mud converting into organism.
"Clay has an innate tendency to evolve."
The earth molecule became a virus; later reproducing.
Clay from which the human body was shaped
like an amphora.

A perpetual night. Only
the blaze of lightning and eruptions.
Searing acid rains
            upon black rocks.
      Then it rained less. A cloud parted
and above the ocean the first day
shed its light.
As soon as the earth had cooled
life at once burst forth.
(A most telling sign
to say the least.
If it was the product of highly improbable chance,
how did it come to be born at the first opportunity?)

Life came from the water.
      Medusas appeared first.
Then the transition from worm to fish.
Then onto dry land. Where
ocean eyes gazed at non-aquatic images.
Two hundred million years later came the saurians.
Another hundred million
the invention of warm blood.
Homo erectus set apart from the animals
because of fire.
From the physico-chemical to freedom.
Inanimate matter became spiritual.

"What's your understanding, general, of that first force?"
The journalist Belausteguigoitia asked.
        Sandino replied:
"As a conscious force. Initially it was love.
That love creates, evolves. But everything is eternal.
And we are moving towards life being
not a passing moment but an eternity,
through the multiple facets of the ephemeral."

Our teeth have their origin in sharks
but later as mammals we acquired lips that could suck
and because of those lips that could suck we acquired kisses.
The opening of the mouth 1,000 million years ago,
in those waters,
400 million years ago teeth,
red lips merely two or three million ago.
Having climbed out of the trees
    the tall grasses forced him to stand up.
In Aurignac, at the end of the last ice age
a being no longer simply a scrap of nature, but
    carved ivory, wall-paintings, myths.

Beyond the village with its chapel and the pitch
where Greek boys played soccer:
    a blue deeper than any blue,
amid the dark-green olive groves and cypresses darker still.
The mountains a pallid blue,
                the sky merest hint of blue,
calcimine cliffs, down below barren white keys,
    limestone no doubt,
all of this to further enhance that sea-blue.
And catching sight of that sea
        quite suddenly
at a road-bend in the Peloponnesus, just outside Corinth,
            (only a glimpse of the sea:
                the car tearing along)
I imagined I saw in a flash Aphrodite completely naked.

Or to see nothing, and be blind, and perched on a step
imagining Odysseus under sail.
Melina Mercuri was Athenae Minister of Culture,
and at a restaurant on the terrace of a tall Athens hotel
she showed me the Parthenon lit by night, high above the hotel.
She bemoaned being a Minister and no longer able to make films.
Athenae Mercuri also paid our way for a trip on the Aegean Sea.
Excursion to the island of Hydra by Hydrofoil.
And to the island of Aegina, where the beach was full of naked flesh,
people with nothing more than their bodies
                    and their tangas,
on sands much warmed by Apollo,
      or in the water,
            or under sun-shades,
or emerging dripping wet. And I thought how those bodies,
      with nothing more than their bodies
made sunshades,
            folding chairs,
                    the cans of beer they sip,
spectacles, cameras,
      the newspapers and books that they read in the sun,
the boats and yachts bobbing in the bay.
Hydrofoil, Parthenon, etc.
Life came out of the sea.
Bacteria after three thousand five hundred million years
now gazing on 100,000 million stars in the galaxy.
We listen to the microwave music of hydrogen atoms.
            We have weighed the stars.

Strange body is this: head, trunk, limbs.
Elongated trunk and limbs even more so,
but not just another vertebrate or another mammal,
biped with chest extremities ending in hands,
not merely that, but rather
            a harmonious god-befitting composition.

The step to land.

The step to land in the Devonian.
Great intelligence was born in the oceans
but technology needed to be land-based.
There've been about 40 evolutions of eyes on earth
but only one of consciousness.
Hence our importance, Luz Marina.
Eyes are to see with.
The *other*, what can the point of that be?
A touch more ammonia, a touch less,
and the planet would be vapors and boiling water,
or a ball of snow stable and dead.
The seas had to have the correct salinity
(that of our blood).
Coincidences really?
Venus's night is very long or never ends.
Merely products of an inconceivably improbable event?
The necessary conditions for stars and galaxies
and their observers.
This my astrophysical epic has but one purpose:
to proclaim that the universe makes sense.
Consciousness slowly forming itself for aeons.
For WHAT? For WHOM?
Or as Dyson said:
It appears that the universe was expecting us.

In the totality of space and time
the universe in its total evolution.
The organic born of the inorganic.
Life as the flowering of matter.
A single-celled bacteria is more complex
than an entire Apollo space ship including
its earth station.
Life an error of the universe?
The earth revolved for five thousand million years
until it acquired consciousness.
A mere five thousand million years.
Until the rivers and winds found a voice in man,

and we became the consciousness of basalt and poplars.
Suffering consciousness.
Born a tiny sphere of
blended proteins and liquids.
Taking into account also the close kinship
between the human hand and a whale's fin.
From a tenuous cloud of gas
to you and I.
Evolution
down the cosmic ages
like the evolution of freedom.
Or matter increasingly more conscious.
The appearance of the first cell
a revolution within the universe.
Something individualized and free emerged.
The dialectical evolution of the universe
towards the Kingdom of Heaven.

And Sandino in his misty camp:
"Let me tell you: spirits also struggle in the flesh
and outside it... Ever since the world began
the earth has been in continual evolution.
But here, in Central America, is where I see a tremendous
transformation... I see something which I've never mentioned...
It's as though one sea had emptied into another...
I see Nicaragua surrounded by water...
The volcanoes above only..."
Sandino, first-born of murder victims.

It represents a tiny proportion of the universe's matter
organized matter.
Water sparked off the organization.
Molecules tossed about by the waves,
intermingling with the surf and feeding upon
solar photons.
And life began: liberty began.
Until we appeared, the earth's language.

And we named the rock rock and the poplar poplar,
we being matter gazing upon itself.
But are we the observers of the universe by pure accident
or is the entire universe an evolution towards an observer?

CANTIGA 13

The Tree of Life

In the beginning was the big grandfather
who has no beginning nor end.
He taught them to produce fire by friction after the flood.
He taught them to govern themselves.
A girl he taught how to sow manioc.

As for the Tucano: they ate the fruit of the star-apple tree.
He said to them: "You have no respect for me."
And he told them they would die.
And he told the Tucano:
"You will have riches in this world:
feathers, arrows, blow-guns, sticks to kill people.
Your riches will remain in the Tucano's huts."
And there are all their riches. Which are few.
And he said later to the Germans:
"You will have armaments, muskets, knives, papers.
And you, German, will never be able to remember things by memory alone
but will have to write it down on paper. The Tucano
will remember by memory alone everything that goes on in the world."
And he also said to the German: "Your riches will bring power.
Your factories will have planes, automobiles, ships, submarines.
And you will also die."

We began as tree creatures until later we became *Homo sapiens.*
The Tree of Life
which is the tangled tree of evolution.
The history of evolution is of creation, and of invention.
            Insects don't try new things.
      Ants: well organized; but they don't learn.
                  The step from the monkey's brain to metaphysics!

Note, in France they adorned their villages with skulls.
            Herodotus tells of head-hunters
in the Danube.
Can ideas be merely a process of inanimate matter?
And is love merely physical and chemical?
Certainly
we are interactions of electromagnetic fields.
But how is this mystery that we humans are?
            Computer designers would love to know!

A mutation which was that of thought,
says Teilhard.
And when man appeared
all other branches of the Tree stopped growing.
We have not, like birds, inherited what has been learnt
but the ability to learn.
      Man, a learning animal/
The oyster of 150 million years ago identical to the one in the restaurants.
Antelopes haven't changed in two million years
but those who hunted antelopes have.
            Learning came to be evolution.
Oh that in the White House they might learn!
Child Cro-Magnons learnt from old Cro-Magnons.
            Thus, gradually: Cro-Magnon.
For whom evolution, more than biological,
was cultural.
      The invention of the needle
spread throughout Europe more swiftly than a galloping bison.
First only bodies were beautiful.
Naked bodies of course.
Then clothes, paintings, flowers, a twilight.
And also bodies, naked or dressed, of course. And so
                  you may find her at the foot of a traffic-light:
a beauty such, as we have painted the gods and the angels.
            At the beginning of the Mousterian
            signs appear of belief in immortality.
And the rapid transition from hunter-gatherers

to industrial society.
(It seems that the Australopithecos, who hunted and gathered,
did not compete for money and social position..)
"Like the stars in the sky
and the sands in the sea."
A tree creature and now he makes skyscrapers.
We are chemical substances which we develop for aeons
until thought and dreams.
Metals, of short evolution, preferred to remain fixed.
Although the chemical of holiness or heroism does not exist.
And faced with something very new now
as when the invention of fire occurred.

When those animals returned to the ground
they had been perfected in the trees.
Their manual skill, binocular vision,
more advanced than any animal on the ground.
The *Sinanthropus* was already making fire and sharpening stones.
There was much time for art in the ice age.
With no more than thirty hours
of gathering and hunting needed a week.
Later the cultivation of grasses: among them, wheat.
Afterwards the divinity ceased to feed on human flesh
and ate only that of ruminants.
Pay no heed to the dreams they have,
Jeremiah said of the false prophets:
Who supported views held today:
the poor are poor because of biological inferiority.
What the fabulous Reagan believes, "fabulous"
in the strict sense of this word
as used in Hollywood.
Simians descended from those that preferred
to remain in their surroundings. Those afraid
to come down from the trees.
The others: the zoological group of humanity.
Humanity whose activity is political
like that of the earth to produce plants,

according to the grandson of Confucius.
"While there are poor, a religion"
said Roque Dalton (the Revolution). And also:
    "sole valid fanaticism."
Christianity is the *phylum* of evolution to Chardin
(but I say not all Christianity only that of the revolution).
Nobody knows what percentage will enter the kingdom.

But the hesitant steps of life.
Animals that proved to be inefficient
and ceased to exist even before the Cambrian.
And following error after error we became conscious mammals.
Turtle hunters in the Galapagos told Darwin
they could identify from which island each turtle came
and Darwin inferred that they all came from the same species.
And later, that living beings were all one single family.
    Let us consider it scientific to say
that the evolutionary cycle doesn't end with consciousness
and there will be something else ahead.
    Humble little warm-blooded animals
    fleeing from enormous cold-blooded dragons.
Trying to move about undetected. Stealing the odd egg from them...
Dinosaurs and their allies were at their peak.
Perhaps we robbed too many eggs from Goliath
says Prof. Barach. Descendants of the shrew
we climbed the trees. And then we gazed at the stars.

        "Descendants of apes?"
the Bishop of Worcester's wife exclaimed horrified.
From chaos to cosmic intelligence.
The thrust of evolution is unswerving.
The mineral, vegetable and animal kingdom
            and the other kingdom.
Harmonized collectivity of consciousnesses,
or Chardin's super-consciousness.
The planet with a single thinking envelope.
The plurality of individual reflections

in a single unanimous reflection on a sidereal scale.
What name shall we give you mata tiru tiru la?

Birds: 8,500 species.
Insects half a million.
Man: a single species.

The difference between the human species and other species
is that it did not fragment into different species.
The further it has spread throughout the planet more and more
it has come together as a single species.
And all because it is round.
Gaia, the earth, being round.
We scatter throughout it so as to be united on it.
As meridians draw apart and converge again
on every sphere.
Or Planetization (Chardin again).
Roundness is
unification.
Hominization.

This earth which is always in the moon's sky
(the part of the moon that always faces the earth)
the moon having neither earth rise not set.
Sun rises and sets. But the earth is there always.
The moon's sky always black, black even with sun
and even with sun, with stars. And the earth, enormous,
four times bigger than the moon to us,
spinning round and round, with Europe, China, the Third World,
it shines always serenely upon the moon.
Pliny on the moon would have confirmed the divinity of the earth.

Knowledge is not what's human,
brother chimpanzee knows, sister whale,
knowing oneself, knowing knowing,
knowing one knows oneself, that's being human,
in depths within oneself deeper

than those outside that the whale or dolphin knows.
Reflection is knowledge reflected in oneself.
To be conscious of being conscious.
Not merely to be conscious, but of being conscious,
highly conscious, which can entail much suffering.
Non plus seulement connaître, mais se connaître;
non plus seulement savoir, mais savoir que l'on sait.
Which signifies abstraction, logic, anxieties, dreams.
The dolphin knows in those deep depths where it swims and doesn't know that it knows.
Darío envying stone even more:
"and hard stone even more because it feels nothing at all."

From the most simple to the most complex,
from lesser to greater organization.
Life evolved from non-life.
Fed in the primeval waters
on energy from volcanic eruptions and electrical discharges.
Poisonous volcanic eruptions and chilling flashes of lightning.
Cells began to eat light,
extracting sugar from the sun.
From sterile rock, sources of photosynthesis sprang forth,
the abundant sources of energy from solar radiation.
We are still born in the sea,
in the salt water of the amniotic sac.
First there were soft and gelatinous eggs in the water.
Then on land, with a hard shell and water inside.
We humans still gestating within water
and carrying within us the sea called blood.
The God-human died on the cross asking for water.
DNA our ADAM.
We began to walk upright
and gazed at the sky.

3,000 million years
since the primeval mire to the human being.
Animals that speak.

And now trying to listen in
to radio transmissions from distant planets
hoping that we operate in the same geological time.
Part of a process that began in some archaic pool
        (recording on the tablet of baked clay:
                "In the beginning...")
On the threshold of a new evolution
like when life emerged from matter.
From the most simple to the most complex,
from lesser to greater organization.
The laws of evolution are the same as the cosmic ones.
'Today [1918] Resurrection is Revolution' (Karl Barth).
And shall be so while the life of the sun permits it.

On the planet it is once again July 19.
            Once again after the triumph.
That is:
July 19 is going round and round the entire planet
and daybreak is going round and round the entire planet,
or rather, the planet going round and round the daybreak,
        this daybreak of July 19,
and our Nicaraguan bit heads towards midday
with the July 19 Square crammed with people under the sun
all the colors in it as though teeming with flowers
and it is travelling on, towards the cone of darkness,
            the starry cone of night,
and now the first stars are shining
                above July 19 Square,
in company with other dates from other calendars from other orbits.
Could there be a planet there under unending rain?
        Or could there be dinosaurs still?
            Or could the Kingdom of Heaven have arrived already?
And what will we look like from there?
        Like one of those stars!
How beautiful our Earth will be seen among them.

CANTIGA 14

The Hand

Our first parents in the trees
ate all kinds of fruit
including the fruit of Good and of Evil, their arms and legs
stretched by those trees.
Gripping onto the branches perfected the hands.
The body became upright to better survey the surroundings,
and judging the distance between branches
developed binocular vision,
and the complexity of tree-top activity
made the brain agile.
        Trees three-dimensional (unlike the ground).
Which brought their eyes forward,
with stereoscopic binocular vision,
eyes together on the same plane, the long
mustachioed snout shrinking.
A prehensile hand was more useful than claws:
To the branches we owe the thin fingers with opposable thumb.
        First came fins.
                Branching off on one side into wings to fly
                and on the other into the human hand.
Five fingers was perfect and that never changed.
Fins could caress but not play the piano.
One finger separated from the rest gave a better grip to branches.
The prehensile finger produced inter-space flights.
Spirituality included—due to the prehensile finger.
        You had to grasp on tightly so as not to fall.
Which is why babies clench their tiny hands like small monkeys,
and we are so often woken by the dream of tumbling into the void.

                The hand of man,
man made it. Like saying, shaping it.

The part of the human body that reaches farthest.
Being perfected in the branches of trees
becoming more and more dexterous until able
to work, to transform (transforming
transforms us)
and also caress better
than the fin, the wing, the claw.
Which is why we began to lose the sunken forehead,
the prominent jawbone.
Claw became hand, talons soft fingers.
Called to be passionate about change,
by an Evolution irreversible
and incompatible with the hypothesis of total death.
Which is why the human face became flat.
The most human thing about man is his hands.
Dolphins are brilliant, but without hands.
And one looks at them beautiful, for a second, breathing,
and sadly plunging once again into their deep shadows.
Smell was of little use up on high with the winds.
That's why afterwards we didn't walk around sniffing the ground head
down
(and upright it is more important to see than to smell)
but looking forward head high through the grasslands
and to the heavens.
And we gazed at the stars.

We don't know what or who brought them out of the trees.
The hands for grasping branches and fruit
were for grasping everything.
No longer for walking but for making and communicating.
The liberated hand Engels spoke of.
The hand made work, as work made the hand.
And through work and the hand the evolution of the mind
and consequently the enlarged human brain.
The thinking hand.
Not like the monkey's hand
only for grasping and holding on, scarcely

much more than the feet.
    Differentiated from the foot it evolved into tool.
Hands excavated caves, lit fires.
Hand and tool approximately at the same time.
Together with the first conscious thought.
    The faculty of making thought a reality.
        Many defective pieces cast aside
            demonstrate that there was much struggle.
Our teeth and nails were no longer weapons.
Product of the work of man was man.
The first product of work was the hand
and man is made by the hand of man.
And work made of man society of men
and making him society made him talk.

In Aurignac, Aurignac period,
simultaneous with the first appearance of art:
symbolic hands on the cave walls.
In relief on clay,
or painted with colors in positive or negative.
First appearance of color in the history of art.
A great leap forward for humanity.
    It's the start of the art of painting.
And the first thing painted was the painting hand.
    The hand daubed with red or black paint
    and flattened fingers spread against the stone.
Red ochre and blue-black manganese in cave crevices.
Or the hand placed open against the stone, and the color
around the outline. Without a brush.
This with greater visual impact, and most widely used, the color
fading away with a magical, invocatory force.
Characteristic of the Aurignac plastic period
rows of hands surrounded by color
rising up from the ground across the rough rock.
There is a long refined hand in those semi-darknesses,
left hand, with delicate fingers separated upon the rock
as though caressing or laying a spell on a body,

with a most beautiful curve between index and thumb,
now no longer like the result of a simple impression
but refined and stylized with paintbrush.
The most charming prehistoric human image, they say,
is this hand, and as though
        already a spiritual revelation of *Homo sapiens*
using Art to externalize his inner-self on the cave wall.
Hand that is action,
                which grasps and makes
                        and appears to think.
The interior on the exterior crystallized in symbol
that hand.

At the revolutionary float competition
        —me one of the jury
                on a raised platform, next to
Comandante Tomás Borge, watching
the floats go by, and the tide of people
the majority waving, their hands aloft,
                shaking their palms,
                or tightly clenched fists:
        suddenly I saw
                a hand.
Everything else eclipsed, I saw only that raised hand
as when the camera draws in to focus on a single detail
a palm and the five separated fingers
and what was that hand telling me?
It was showing me that most human of human organs
which transformed us from ape to human,
and the most perfect member of the human body.
A flat space with five cylindrical agile prolongations
like acrobats.
                The hand was waving.
That which made the first flintstone
which made skyscrapers, books, fabrics, tractors and violins
and also these floats,
a palm and five fingers,

that which made the homonid think and speak,
discover fire,
make these revolutionary floats,
make a Revolution.
The hand that also clutched a weapon on the barricades,
the rifle raised to the sky in stylized silhouette.
        All that is made,
everything human on the earth is hand-made.
I couldn't tell whether it was a male or female hand
but it was a hand to clasp other hands, or
            another hand,
and to caress also another human being.
        Nothing more human than a hand
                brother give me your hand
we were also given hands brother to walk holding hands
        hand in hand
                holding hands.
And that hand disappeared
and more hands held high kept on waving...

FOUNDATION OF THE LATIN AMERICAN ASSOCIATION
                FOR HUMAN RIGHTS:
The conference hall in the form of functional
                        amphitheater, genuinely
style-free,
    typical intercontinental architecture,
        delicately covered
with a rough creamy material, a texture stimulating to touch,
and where the brown plywood gleams under the golden light
shed by silvery cylinders set in the white plastic ceiling
and still more
by blinding spotlights, and photographers' flashguns;
where the rows of Latin American flags
form a single borderless pot-pourri of national colors
behind the raised platform on which stands the main table
with gleaming glasses of sparkling water

and the podium with nickel-plated microphone shining beneath the
spotlights
this hall in Quito,
today I see it, from my place on the platform
strangely, full of animals.
There are ex-presidents. Important personalities.
From the iguana slowly we arrived at this species
which is seated in this conference hall
and from the microphone denounces the fascist regimes.
Article 16: The Executive Committee has the following functions
We are animal, each one separate, individuals.
Animal just like the iguana.
Although we're called a rational animal.
But together we are NOT animal, we are man:
man, for example, in this hall, defending man,
his human rights.
We are a strange species, with spectacles, with ties, with hairstyles.
From life in the trees to these talks—a great advance.
We're strange beings looking at each other, smiling together, talking
together
in this hall:
a diverse being and one.
In the hall there is only One
in many seats, that one getting to his feet,
the other taking out a cigarette,
this other one photographing the rest.
The Arhuacos gave themselves that name,
arawak: which means "man"
"people."
Ruth Benedict says that the Zuni, the Dané, the Kiowa
gave themselves those names, which mean: "human beings"
although they were surrounded by other peoples.
The Colombian Kogi: their name is "people."
My Yaruro friends: their name is "people."
And in Antioquia, in that Indian boarding school
a young Páez told me that their name is not Páez but Naza
"which means people or person."

Animals adapt biologically
to the environment, and their adaptations are hereditary.
(Whence the species.)
Man's adaptations are cultural,
not subject to heredity. Which is why Paul said:
"there is no Greek or Jew."
For a long time I continue to gaze at my species
although the flashes and the spotlights dazzle me.
Gentlemen: solidarity with Bolivia, with El Salvador
is a human impulse which has its origins in brother iguana.

But there was something that made us human:
the hand no longer suited to climbing.

CANTIGA 15

Nostalgia For Paradise

In the beginning, they tell, there was only water and sky,
everything was empty,
            everything a huge darkness.
They tell that one day Tupana descended in the midst of a mighty wind
and from the depths of the water brought out a little earth.
He kneaded it in his palm and formed a human figure.
He blew a dense smoke into its mouth and then, they tell, it spoke.
      (It spoke, yet missionaries have now forbidden them
      to utter the name Tupana.)

Through song God made man in Arizona.
He infused life into the mud body with a song.
      According to the Fon, clay with water
      like the walls of their houses are made.
"Clay men, very deficient,
never ate nor spoke..."
            (The Sumerian text breaks off.)

Two negative electrical charges repel each other,
two positive electrical charges repel each other,
but negative and positive attract.
      (The love-hate of atoms said Democritus.)
A heavy nucleus of positive electricity and around
spin the electrons, negative electrical charges.
The hydrogen atom was the first,
            the simplest of all:
a single negative electron around a positive nucleus.
Adam and Eve who engendered the rest of the atoms.
Helium first
            (now a nucleus with 2 protons)

and then the rest.

The universe isn't only atoms and chaos.
And it didn't come about simply by chance
but by laws which guided chance.
"The atmosphere, such as we have it, is highly improbable."
The unity in the diversity
is because the whole of creation stems from a single creator.
Einstein's theory of relativity is
that different observers see a different thing
but the thing is the same
and the law which governs that thing is universal.
Matter appears a thought
but with someone thinking it.
Or like a dream, with someone dreaming it.
Or like someone's love...
Who is the one that loves?
Not merely a journey from nothing to nothing.
In any case, there's a purpose.
In the universe, an energy
directed towards a progressive concentration.

The hand made man, but also language.
Or they made him together, hand and word. Or
work made man with the hand and the word.
Is God communication and we his grammar
as the Sanskrit text says? Communication
itself included in the Sanskrit text.
The Campas—Peruvian jungle—distinguish 27 greens.
Miskitos on the coast, such good sailors,
have 25 words for the wind.
Eskimos twenty-plus colors for snow.
Lapps more than 60 words for reindeer.
Tupana showed them the words in paradise
yet in Amazonia they forbid them to mention Tupana.

Also widespread the business of the great tree

that joined the earth with sky.
"Cosmic intertwining" of the Pseudo-Chrysostom
which for him was the cross. Tree that rises from the earth to the sky.
That was on Quetzalcoatl's clothing.
Huge solitary tree of the Pampa
which Darwin saw being adored:
úúúúúúúú úúúúúúúú
In ancient times, say the Kogis,
they went to visit the lands above.
Now that's not possible.
The Peruvian land was blessed by Con.
Sins laid it waste
as the Puno wilderness has remained.
Ever since, it never rains there.

Bohemia: the young with fir cuttings.
Saxony: the brides' fresh conifer.
Alsace: from house to house singing.
In Swabia: holding hands beneath the tree.
Crowned with sprays of wheat in Bavaria
and crowned with flowers in Westphalia.
Silesia, Franconia, etc...

Tree of Life. Or Tree of Love, like the one they gave me
(in bronze) in Bhopal, India, with courting couples in the branches
like fruit, two making love.

The tendency of atoms to combine
—did they come together by pure chance?–
has produced life.
(Life, an organized form of matter.)
The stars and life.
From hydrogen to man
there's a purpose.
We can say: life is inherent to matter.
And also love.

The multiplication of life by division
and suddenly in reverse: union. We don't know
when nor how, in which microscopic, nigh invisible
paradise
two ordinary cells came together
amid thousands of millions of others.
Greatest revolution the earth has seen.
Three thousand five hundred million years ago
there were already cells which had experienced sexuality.
With sexuality and death, mass-produced life
gave way to the diversity of life.
Each different one from the other.
Death making life increasingly more varied.
A change of chromosomes in each new generation.
Each one a product of the union of two
and each one different from the two.
—A taking away in order to increase.
Variation between individuals ever greater.
And in this way sexuality and death became accelerators
of an evolution until then so very sluggish.

Love alone unites without destroying.
The fusion which brings not death but yes, life
is only that of love.
We don't believe it
despite the experience
of human reproduction.
So it is that nothing is still.
From gas come galaxies,
from them stars spring like flowers,
atoms become molecules, molecules cells
and from cells flowers emerge, animals.
And the point that everything is rotation.
Dance chorus.
Harmony, but of jazz.
Dance from the atoms to the stars.
According to Rowland the hydrogen atom

is like the vibration of a single guitar string
and that of mercury like a grand piano.
The sun and the moon are circles, the horizon a circle,
their tents are circular and they make camp in circles,
in their ceremonies they sit in circles,
day and night form circles, the year is a circle,
and in a circle the sacred pipe is passed around.
The same ones who invoke "The Force that moves," and say to him
in their soiled buffalo-skin tents:
        "The fragment of life you have given us..."
And they also say: "What is life but love?"
According to Dirac it is more important to have beauty
in one's equations than to have them fit the experiment.
Creation you made too beautiful
and we fell in love, but not with you.
And in eroticism, Lord, you got carried away.

With gigantic forces the stars attract each other. Similarly
the magnetism that beats in the heart of atoms.
And in me.
            "Unquiet is my heart..."
and similarly the sexuality of molecules, this is
the internal propensity of the molecule towards union.
The urgency of corpuscles to come together
                                    is that of my heart.
The pressure the stars engender
                              is that of my heart.
Heisenberg's uncertainty principle
is also in my heart.
And the attraction of matter,
                        my crucifixion.
        The condensation of corpuscles.
        The dances and courtships of atoms.
        The wedding of spermatozoa and ovum.
Shoots stir from their sleep,
young pigeons chirrup,
a couple hug each other in the park

and the park keeper looks away.
Spring arrived in monokini.

"We are crucified in sex" said Lawrence (D.H.)
I don't know in which context. I have my own.
St. Augustine spent nights crying
over what he would never again enjoy.
Ancient Jerome: the Roman dancers
which he saw in his youth. Which is why
he set about furiously translating books of the Bible.
Book of Ruth in a night.

Those eyes which to see again
would be as though light were to travel backwards.
Together in my sad canto, astrophysics and love.
Eyes the color of gold were Mireya's.
Mireya my childhood love on the beaches of Poneloya.
She was my Beatriz. With Dantesque eyes
for the Dantesque is not merely a bombardment, an earthquake,
Dantesque is also Paradise.
And my Mireya, Dantesque.
Pius XII was for me what Stalin was to Neruda.

Faces in which we have seen heaven,
a radiance of heaven to be more exact.
Occasionally as the car passes swiftly by
the unknown woman waiting at the light seemed of a beauty
impossible for her to be in reality.
That girl, Cha, in swim-suit,
me 18 years old, she stretched out in my canoe
on a picnic, did she not hail from Olympus?
Now would seem a good time to mention her. For
it's not that she "was beautiful," she was of course, but that she was
much more than that.
The beautiful were many. They were *the* others.
She was perfect. And even more than that,
the only one.

If through some scientific break-through,
yes, if through some scientific break-through it were possible
to choose one's dreams, I'd always dream like the other night
the long dream in which we were so long together,
finally so united, at least I dreamed it was a long dream,
but what if that pain which once was real
were to recur in my dreams.

Fire it is.
And the production of fire by friction
was learnt from that friction.
Rose-petal skin. Its chafing
the chafing of kindred corpuscles.
Essence of the universe. Body plenitude of the cosmos.
Ah, tiny cosmos.
There's something oneiric in woman, something seemingly born
from the male dream.
Her sex, that little infinity.
Attraction of that nook of woman.
Cave of Mysteries.
Whence so many of us in the world.

But also the question of entropy again.
Perpetual process towards disintegration and chaos
of the second law.
The car rusts away. The childhood country house stands derelict,
stars go out, Melba died.
How did the cosmos begin against this natural tendency?
Against the second law of thermodynamics
beautiful order, Venus, skin color of pearl, emerged from chaos.

Demographic explosion of beauty. Pity
that youth is not so long in the lasting
and once it's passed has lasted nothing.
Alone You are unending youth.
Paradise is not in Paria
as Don Christopher Columbus believed

"...most beautiful, indeed luscious and green lands
like the gardens of Valencia in March..."
"...most clement temperateness and the lands and trees
as in April in the gardens of Valencia..."
Neither
in Antigua where the temperature never goes above 80°
and bathing conditions are almost perfect, and there's electricity
and no malaria, and there are three golf courses
nor in St. Lucia
painters' and photographers' paradise
nor in the Cayman Isles (with no income tax)
where you can still hunt for pirate treasure
—and live in a hotel for $6.00 a day—.
You can't get there through Tourist Agencies.
And it's not Tobago
a mere 7 hours from New York
A TROPICAL PARADISE AT REASONABLE PRICES
where on $2,000 a year a couple can live
in a bungalow by the sea, with electricity and TV
amid mangoes coconuts guavas exotic flowers
and the rum's cheap and you spend nothing on clothes
because you can live in shorts and sports shirt
nor in the Virgin Islands (English)
"a perfect paradise
were it not for the nuisance of there being no dentist."

The kisses you were unable to bestow shall be granted.
The union that never was, I swear to you by God...
"Who there is in our eyes, he does not die."
That was said
in front of their villages of rotting palm in Amazonia.
Or are we humans the failure of the universe?
Because animals they do have their fill.
Who am I in my most intimate face
that no one has seen
but a cry that the universe hurls at you.

The lakes that you gave me. Never till now have I revealed
my obsession with lakes. Fixation!
What it cost me to renounce my tropic
and even more my lake. Shall I reveal it now?
        Lake as fixation.
Not understanding how anyone can live without a lake nearby,
or a sea, or a big river at least.
The gentleness of that blue, to what shall I compare it?
To the heavens.
                Reflection of the kingdom of heaven.
In the Yankee Trappist monastery there were
only man-made lakes:
they *called* them lakes.
And a dwarf banana tree, skeletal, unable
to bear fruit in its exile
(like me: I thought).
And now the film cuts to Solentiname
focusing
            on a rainbow above an island
            and duplicated below in the still water
or another shot:
                    the dark lake, and flashes of lightning,
                    for a moment the lake golden,
                    again dark, then gold again.
My lake greets the day like a dream. Only
the wave on the shore like a kiss,
sounds on the sand like a kiss.
        Only
                that wave alone.
                        A tiny bird on a branch
                                    sings and shits.

Beauty the supreme creator of the world;
        this was a way of saying it,
and THEOLOGY is a word invented by Plato.
But those to whom reproduction has been denied,
envying the insects, the Batrachia, the mammals,

that reproduce, and the stars that reproduce,
we bear testimony to the void,
to the unfulfilled fullness,
of the future paradise.
Touchable arms, those exchanged
for another embrace.

Against nature, to have your arms on a cross.
Stone embraces in Khajuraho
(Tantric Hinduism)
stone embracing stone
passionately,
in human embrace,
not of flesh but of stone.
The ineligibility to unite with someone from one's species.
We are sinking a canal in dry land
for when the floods come.
For when the floods come.
Beautiful girls with their internal flower between their legs.
The suppleness of the human body greatly facilitates coitus
says Remy de Gourmont
(comparing it with other animals).
It's the solitary ones who will enter the Nuptial Chamber
says Jesus in the Gospel of Thomas
which bears no trace of being apocryphal
but merely more revolutionary than the Synoptics.
Sierra Leone, bride of God.
Nigeria, bride of God.
The loving earth longs to be wed with the sky says Aeschylus.
"That your Self may separate my self from us two"
I don't know whether between quotes "Self" and "self" in Arabic,
if they use quotes in Arabic.

Some of them so beautiful
that to us it seemed we were in the presence of eternity.
Bodies on their surface reflecting the sky.
But fleeting they were

like the iridescence of diesel on water
in a port we are leaving.
They flew off like frightened larks
and never returned.

The words below written in a sterile corner of paradise
—it is not appropriate for man to be alone—
with enforced solitude. Or, if you want, voluntary.
Like that emaciated banana plant in the monastery
next to the refectory.
With the man-made lakes. So-called "lakes."
Seems the banana was the fruit of Adam and Eve
and not the apple. Primates are from the tropics.

Paradise, but a sterile corner of paradise.
This May night with rain. Alone but with the people.
Better that love like love amongst flowers,
among them there's none who loves more or who does not love,
love is by force major, that of chance,
some it unites, others are excluded,
but it's love without the pangs of love,
without the pain of pollens without an ovule
or the ovule alone without its pollen.
Or if our love were like that of the sexual cells
that are irresistibly attracted to each other after copulation,
whatever the manner of that copulation.
Already the May rains are upon us.
Tropical winter with gentle dawnings.
For us winter means rain and it starts in May.
The May rains are here with their smell of childhood, and a smell
as of being twenty years old again and being in love.

"A secret that his creatures are unaware of"
(Egyptian hieroglyphs)
The uncreated which we carry within us
in the language of Eckhart in the XIV
on which basis a Princeton undergraduate today would say in the XX

Are you serious, Mr. Feynman?
Surely you're joking, Mr. Feynman!
I sought total happiness when I entered the monastery
and a friend told me her ambitions were modest,
complete happiness for her could consist in nothing more than
a beauty salon.
Did Haydée ever get her beauty salon?

The ad's in full color.
The photo's of an emerald sea.
On the beach Adam and Eve stroll in swim-suits.
The vegetation, as they say, luxuriant.
In the background the yacht...
Beneath the photo runs the legend:
Our island's as it was an aeon or two ago.
The water still crystal pure.
The beaches are pristine.
Just picture yourself on a picture-postcard beach.
In fact we've printed such picture-postcards. And
although we have all the comforts of civilization
our island is virgin, sparsely inhabited and beautiful.
(Visit your Travel Agency.)
Come see the world as it was when it was new.
Our island's called "The Best of the Bahamas."
(Or ask for a free BROCHURE.)
Taste the finest cocktail under the shade of our palms.
And have no fear, here there's no revolution
nor will there ever be, not in an aeon or two.

The dove-song from the *Song of Songs.*
"Mourning dove," "Mourning dove"
which sang to me in Kentucky so lovingly at daybreak,
dove of the Song of Songs for me
is this same St. Nicholas dove here, in Solentiname
gentle dawnings and dusks. Coo of the St. Nicholas dove,
say the peasants.
Blue earth upon blue water, and sky.

The clouds trail stains in the water.
In the deep blue some a deeper blue
(the stains) or green.
Keys,
waters all around
mother-of-pearl hue.
Here we have seen love. All this the work
of such a sexual creator. We've seen
on the island of Ometepe the kingfisher
with long beak and ruffled crest, the
veteran with plucked neck like an old duck
though still young.
The fin of a young shark
cleaving the wave like a machete.
Two chirrups on this key
and another identical chirrup replies on another key.
Moyogalpa under moonlight:
a single wave in the lake
(on the shore)
that dies in the sand and shines beneath the moon,
is born again and dies and shines beneath the moon.
The shadow of a launch in the milky night,
and there in that spot
a tiny light in the water:
a launch
star or thatched hut.
Not a launch. It's
a star or a humble thatched hut.
Star or hut?
And the tenuous sound of the moonlit wave
and that of the generator motor.

Hydrogen, the most abundant element in the universe.
And in our body the same abundance of hydrogen
(especially in water).
Hydrogen that we reflect a universe of hydrogen.
The sun so distant from the earth and simultaneously

right here in the gull's wing and in the wave.
            Kleenex clouds.
      The grey-green water wavy,
above it the black crag,
and upon the crag the heron
with its neck curled backwards.
Girl and boy with dog between the rocks
hunting crabs.
            Neck of duck like snake emerges
            with silver-plated fish in beak.
Oscar drifts by whistling in his boat
and firm as ice
the wake remains still in the lake.

Merely albumin, salt and water make an eye.
Two eyes really, precise for a single image.
And 80% of the eye is water.
Lenses created in womb-darkness, for the light.
Lenses from skin cells turned transparent.
In practice we see through water.
Along one of the old lanes of the Storgtorget, behind
the Royal Palace, in a pair of eyes
I saw the transparency of flesh,
            where the flesh sees and is seen,
            crystalline flesh
(the rest smooth skin but opaque
fresh tissue but opaque)
      seeing there very deep, down to the bottom
            —perhaps there was no bottom—
and I saw there the immateriality of the soul.
I didn't take her to my hotel.
I never saw her again.
They say the eyes emit no light, rather
they receive the impact of light quanta.
But where does the eyes' light come from?
And how can one see there so deeply
as in the clearness of Corn Island where

even at thirty meters the barracudas can be seen.
The world is brimful of beauty
but none is greater than human beauty.
Puddles in the night inlaid with moonsilver,
from a full moon in turn inlaid by the sun.
All the frogs singing in the muddy light
or the luminous mud. This is how we reflect you:
puddles in the night made to shine very brightly by the sun.

By the lake a small bird sings on and on,
a song about and for whom I don't know. Song gone now
and I guess I know why.
Next a pigeon sings, much less musical
like if I were to sing. And its song ceased and it has to be
because it went off with someone. Me left alone.
Half-moon impaled amid the blossoming Silk Cotton.

Silent lakes green from the green
silent woodlands reflected in them
formed the frontiers of the Beyond in Ireland.
Which one could not reach by boat on those lakes.
In Australia they say it lies to the west,
the island of souls.
            Island of music and sport for Pindar.
      "It seemed such that we were in the Earthly Paradise."
(But Captain Cook later admitted:
      "For them it would have been better
      never to have known us.")
            The lakes like a fixation.
That sudden delight on the Mexican plain,
bone-dry Mexican plain bordered at the end
there, way in the distance, by lilac mountains, and all of it
beneath a patina of silvery mist, so flat
that it seemed like a lake. Unconscious delight.
            Believing myself to be in Nicaragua!

Ducks' wings thrashing in the water.

The whole group thrashing their wings in the water
simultaneously as though a scaly dragon
were approaching. Could that explain dragons?

Water, sky, keys and
        a boat alongside a key:
this is the scenery.
But the water is a mirror reflecting
boat, keys and sky
and it renders every thing two.
            Suddenly a duck. And
            the duck also is two.
And I wonder if in turn this scenery
isn't also, all of it, like another mirror
reflecting God.
            Lake Nicaragua, my sacrament.
I ask for a glass of water in Cologne
in the restaurant overlooking the God-knows-what-green Rhine.
Hermann tells me: "The water in Germany's bad.
            It's not like Solentiname water.
                        It's lavatory water."
I sip it, it's true.
            Colorless, tasteless and without smell, sterilized
                lavatory water.
It's been recycled at least ten times.
Has passed through the human body. Out in urine and fecal waste.
Drunk by animals and urinated and shitted by them.
Purified and sterilized.
        Passed once more through the human body.
Passed once more through toilets and urinals.
Hospital and brothel water
flowing again through the sewers
        to the world's largest sewer which is the Rhine,
with arsenic, mercury, sulfuric acid,
purified again.
        Put into this glass.
I think of a glass of Solentiname water, fallen from the sky.

"Out of Eden there flowed a river which watered the garden
and thereafter divided into four branches."
In other words, all the world's waters residue of Paradise water.
    Paradisians?
The hot and humid nights with idyllic frogs.
Silhouettes of black islands in the night with moon.
Three stars,
and with the moon, an almost perfect quadrilateral.
All so clear that you can see
on the far shore the volcanoes of Costa Rica
(three).
Smell of the *sacuanjoche* flower like a girl's smell
    —between the little church and the jetty—.
Flower also known as "nicaraguanita" (red *sacuanjoche*)
of this Nicaragua which Fray Bartolomé de las Casas
called "most felicitous" land.
And wanted to found a peace community in this lake.
    Paradisonians?
You, from the international jet-set, yet *nica*,
nicaraguanita, with smell of *sacuanjoche*
that night. Shortly after, or not long after the Triumph.
Your atoms and mine
had never drawn close to each other
in the 15,000 million years
                more or less
of the present universe
and never again will draw close
            in the present universe.
I didn't go up to your room in the Intercontinental.
It was merely the brush of a kiss on the cheek.
But I believe in the dogma that in another way we'll be united.
The Law of Gravity was felt between us.
In this "most felicitous" land of Nicaragua.
    "This Nicaragua is a paradise of the Lord.
    It is many delights and joy for the human kind.
    So much fertilitie, so much abundance, so much amenitie

and freshness, so much healthyness, so many fruiting plants,
laid out like the gardens of the cyties of Castylle."
And he wanted to found a peace community in the south of the lake
(region of Solentiname)
"a fresh water lake which descends one hundred and thirty leagues
with a river which emerges from it like the river of Seville...
believe me your majesty..."
Which explains that decree which forbade the Spanish to enter there
"unless so licensed by said Fray Bartolomé de las Casas
under pain of being perpetually banished from that said province
and from all the islands and Indies of the Ocean Sea./I THE QUEEN."
To the south of the lake, region of Solentiname.
Which in Nahuatl is *Celentinametl* ("Place of many guests")
("Place of hospitality").

I learnt from the Solentiname peasant woman
that previously the scenery gave them no pleasure.
Three stones in the calm lake
and three ducks, one on each stone,
black like them and like them motionless
but tremulous their reflection in the water
and that of the ducks. The ducks by now not hungry
since they're not scouring the water for fish
but it's still early to go to sleep.
The ducks not looking anywhere in particular
merely globally taking in the immense afternoon,
the rose-hued vastness of lake and sky
absorbed in the scenery and part of the scenery.
But for the peasants it was only a place of misery
from which they longed to escape.
Later they learned to love the scenery
with their primitivist painting.

My fixation with this lake.
And that non-stop flight over my country:
First there was the lake, calm.
And in it

my place, what was my home, Solentiname.
        All the islands in a cluster; they seemed a single one.
But from a distance I could pick them out, name them.
The spot where the community stood. All razed.
The library burnt. That hammock under a palm roof
                                                    overlooking the lake.
Elvis and his guitar. Where did the guardia bury them?
        Nearside, La Zanata, alone in the midst of the lake.
Where we went to fish *guapotes*.
        Virtually beneath the plane but unreachable.
From the string hammock I'd now see this plane.
The air hostess offers drinks. I ask for whisky on the rocks.
I drink it, eyes glued to the glass that separates me.
Nobody on the plane has a hint of this tragedy.
                                        The exile looking at his country.
There through the glass.
                But between me and my land lies an abyss.
My land at war. It was after the September business.
Me flying to a Socialist International congress in Lisbon
to cry out for the beloved blue I could see from the clouds.
I want to see the sites of huge demonstrations. The places
of night meetings by the light of campfires,
the shots at jeeps which patrol the streets, the children in masks,
the contact bombs, exactly where they are operating in the hills,
the mothers crying, Monimbó, where they dumped the murdered.
I want...
        That for which it is beautiful to die, all blue and clouds.
The beloved geography denied to me.
I couldn't see the cities. Only blue mountains.
                                                    And suddenly

        I saw Estelí,
to my chagrin, I knew that that was Estelí:
                A grim and blackish quadrilateral
amid green fields.
Not the white and multi-colors of tiny houses:
        but a carbon-colored, ashen stain
like a charred body.

No one else has noticed anything... And the stewardesses
begin to serve the plastic food, quite oblivious.

Unbroken flight over paradise,
"and because Fray Bartolomé de las Casas has offered
that he alone or with other religious disposed to whatever martyrdom
/I THE QUEEN"
(Doña Juana the Mad)
"very fertile with much diversitie of fruits" said Las Casas,
the land where he wished to settle.

In the new Eden (was there already one? I doubt it)
there'll be no forbidden tree.
All trees trees of life.

CANTIGA 16

The Darkest Before Dawn

I'm going to tell you now about the screams from the Cuá
screams of women as though in labor.
María Venancia, ninety years old, deaf, one foot in the grave
screams at the guardia I've not seen the muchachos.
Amanda Aguilar, fifty,
with her little daughters Petrona and Erlinda
I've not seen los muchachos,
as though in labor.
—Three months imprisoned in a mountain barracks—.
Angela García, aged twenty-five, with seven young children.
Cándida, sixteen, breast-feeds a little girl
so small and malnourished.
Many have heard those screams from the Cuá
the Nation wailing as though in labor.
Upon leaving jail Estebana García with four youngsters
gave birth. Had to give away her children
to a landowner. Emelinda Hernández aged sixteen,
cheeks glistening with tears
tresses wet with tears...
Captured in Tazua while on their way from Waslala
the corn field in flower and the yucca by then high
patrols going in and out with prisoners.
Esteban they took up in the helicopter
and returned a short while later without him...
Juan Hernández was snatched by the patrol
one night, and never returned.
Another night they snatched Saturnino
and we never saw him again...they also took
Chico González
(it was like that nearly every night

around the time the *cocorocas* sing)
with people not known to us too.
Matilde miscarried where she sat
as all night long they grilled us about the guerrillas.
A guard summoned her, Cándida,
come and wash these pants
but it was for something else
(Somoza smiling down from his picture like an Alka-Seltzer ad).
Worse ones arrived in an army truck.
Three days after they left Cándida gave birth.
This is the story of the screams from the Cuá
sad like the *cocorocas*' song
the story told by the peasant women of the Cuá
who in tears tell,
as though peering through a haze of tears, of a jail
and above it a helicopter.
"We women know nothing of them."
But Yes they have seen
their dreams are subversive
men with beards, blurred in the mist
swift
crossing a stream
hidden in the corn field
taking aim
(like pumas)
springing up out of the cane fields!
giving the guardia a fucking hiding
calling in at the hut
(smothered in dirt and glory)
Cándida, Amanda, Emelinda
in their dreams, many nights
—with their rucksacks—
climbing a mountain
with songs of *dichoso-fui*
María Venancia aged ninety
at night they see them in dreams
on strange mountains

night after night
                    the muchachos.

We leave the plane and head, Nicaraguans and foreigners,
pell-mell towards the large lighted building—first
Immigration and Customs—and I'm thinking as we get closer
passport in hand: my pride in carrying
the passport of my socialist country, and the satisfaction
of arriving in the socialist Nicaragua—"Compañero"...
they'll say to me—a revolutionary compañero welcomed
by the revolutionary compañeros of Immigration and Customs
—not that there's no control, there should be
so capitalism and Somocism never return—
and the thrill of returning to the country in revolution
with ever more changes, more expropriation decrees
which they tell me about, ever more radical transformations
many surprises in the short time you've been gone
and I see joy in everyone's eyes—those who remained,
the others have now left—and now we're into the light
and they ask for the passports of nationals and foreigners
but it was a dream and I'm in Somoza's Nicaragua
and they take my passport with the cold courtesy
with which they'd say to me in Security "this way"
and they take it inside and don't bring it back (you can bet
they're on the phone—you can bet to Security,
to the Presidential office or who knows where) and now
all the passengers have gone and I don't know if I'm to be arrested
but no; they return with my passport after an hour
the CIA must know that this time I didn't go to Cuba
and was only a day in East Berlin
finally I'm allowed through to the Custom's check
me the only traveller in Customs with my old suitcase
and the young man checking my bag goes through the motions
checking nothing and in a low voice has called me "Reverend"
and he doesn't dig deep into the case where he'd find
the recording of Allende's last call to the people
from La Moneda punctuated with the sound of bombs

which I bought in East Berlin or Fidel's speech
on the overthrow of Allende which Sergio gave me
and the young man says to me "Eight o'clock and we've not eaten,
Customs workers also get hungry"
and me: "When do you eat?" "Not till the last plane's in"
and now I travel on towards the gloomy devastated city
where everything's the same and nothing's happening but I've seen
his eyes and with his eyes he called me: "Compañero."

The blood-stained moon rises on the horizon.
That is, it appears to rise on the horizon.
The countryside a single vast cotton field as though it had snowed.
And what did they once sow?
They once sowed their maize
and beans and pumpkins and *pipianes*
but now someone has a cotton plantation.
The plots ploughed by those beautiful oxen—back and forth—
are gone
and the carts that clattered along loaded with maize
at harvest time, are gone.
And there are no more trees. Just the sun over the cotton field.
Cotton's been sown up to the foothills.
They head into the hills with dogs to hunt for garrobos,
pigeons, armadillos, but populations have declined
and now it's hard to catch a rabbit, pigeons are few and far between.
When there's nothing to eat they go into the brush to look for guavas
go to someone else's land to cut green mangoes.
In these pastures there used to be tree after tree of hog plum
providing fruit and shade in the pastures
and now there are no plums and there are no pastures
just cotton field after cotton field and clouds of dust
from tractors and trucks laden with cotton.
At midday they set out with dogs to hunt quail
hoping to catch them on the foothills.
There on that hill in their palm hut
the Martínez family dine nightly on maize tortillas and salt.
The fresh-tilled lands my friend no longer exist

saddlebags full of young ears of corn are unknown
the cattleherd's cry is no longer heard
nor is there the early morning bustle bringing the oxen
to their land to sow maize beans pumpkins ay
        my friend I'm telling you their lands have gone
leaving files of men and women and children and old people
every morning amid clouds of dust
carrying water-filled gourds and bundles of sacks
        to the cotton field.
At night you see their feeble lights in the hills
like stars. They go out and only the stars are left.
The moon sets behind the hills.
That is, seems to set behind the hills.
And now the stars have gone.
Then the September repression. The so-called Black Friday.
The darkest point of night before the dawn.
I gave a speech in Bogotá to the Congress, Plenary Session,
October 25, 1978 (it's in the Congressional Records).
        Mr. Senators and Deputies...
And not only congressmen but some thousands in the galleries.
To whom I spoke of the old narrow streets of León
where tearful eyes peered from doors and windows.
Shyly they began to come forward, saying to the reporter:
        "In that house lived two."
                "One lived there."
        "On that corner only the women and children were left."
Two girls told what happened:
They discovered a pistol on a boy from the neighborhood,
and they didn't search anymore.
They pushed the women, children and elderly to one side.
Made the boys lie on the ground.
Three of their brothers were on the ground;
a guardia ordered them to look away.
After the shots they saw the bodies writhing on the ground.
They drove a tractor over the bodies.
The tractor then piled them up, a single red mass.
        They were the boys of the "Dead End."

Aged 21, 20, 19, 18 and 17.
They met there to play baseball or to chat.
Boys who'd never again meet in the Dead End.
The female reporter from the *Times* saw the boy taken from his house,
a guardia holding a rifle to his head.
His cheeks streaked with tears. He knew he was going to die.
They ordered the *Times*' reporter to clear off.
        Senators, Deputies, sirs:
they took 21 boys with their mothers to the outskirts of León.
They pushed the women aside, and killed the boys on the road.
They stole their watches, forcing their mothers to wash them.
Dogs tore off pieces of badly buried arms and feet.
The mothers buried what was left in a cotton field.
Or there's the case of Doña Socorro de Martínez, in León,
with a few tatters of her husband's and her son's shirts.
Or Josefa Pérez who's lost her mind: eyes turned to the void, she rants:
"Roger, my love, Roger, come... Where is Roger?"
In Subtiava's Indian quarter seven were playing baseball in the street,
            ages 24, 22, 20, 18, 17, 16, 14,
a patrol arrived and they started to run,
and there they died right in the street where they played.
A boy leaned out into the street wearing a red cap,
they seized him, and broke both his legs before killing him.
The neighbors heard him begging for mercy,
and the guardia: "Fucking red-and-black son-of-a-bitch."
In Catarina they'd shoot two young people every night.
        Killed in pairs.
Imagine the mothers' dread as night drew in.
        At the risk of boring you:
In Managua three truck-loads of boys,
taken to a police station and never heard of again.
The pregnant woman with her belly rent by a bayonet,
the child coming out alive. The bayonet in the child.
            "One Sandinista less!"
Senators and Deputies sirs:
        Night falling in Masaya
not knowing who'd be dead by dawn.

In many parts of the country the killings would start at sunset
after the curfew.
        The wait for curfew time.
High on dexedrin they fought women and children.
Orders were issued in English, translated into Spanish.
        And in Estelí the Butterflies of Death phenomenon.
The code name for their planes was "Butterflies."
Hovering around from first light until nightfall.
And at night the tanks came in.
        Not wishing to go on too long.
They told of a sudden flash of light as though platinum-plated.
And they heard their radio-call for more white phosphorus.
There were no prisoners in the big insurrection, just murder victims.
Let me end with what a woman selling clothes in Chinandega market
told the reporter from *La Prensa*:
"My boy, let's hope all these deaths have not been for nothing"
and the reply of another female stallholder:
"Rest assured, lady, better times are on their way."
    My speech over. The session over.
With a huge ovation in the galleries that night.

"Eed it!... Eed it!... Eed it!", the Chinaman was saying.
He was cutting off chunks of flesh from the peasants,
frying it and making them eat it.
(The Chinaman maybe wasn't Chinese but Vietnamese or Korean.)
"Once the hole was dug they got them on their knees at the bottom
and there the sound of bullets."
        Night after night the sound of bullets.
"Helicopters would fly into the camps with peasants.
They all emerged trussed like garrobos."
Black Macho called over the radio from the mountains asking for bags.
They all knew they were plastic bags for the dead.
"To the trained dogs they gave raw meat, never cooked.
I once saw the Chinaman give them flesh from the prisoners themselves."
Night of bullet-sounds and Black Macho saying "send me bags."

Now the cocks are crowing.

Now your cock has crowed, dear Natalia
yours has crowed now, dear Justo.
Rise up from your straw beds, from your sleeping mats.
I think I hear the Congo monkeys awake on the other shore.
Now we can blow on the embers—empty the chamber pot.
Fetch an oil lamp so we can see our faces.
A dog barked in a hut
and from another hut another answered.
Must be time to light the stove dear Juana.
The darkness grows darker but because day is coming.
Get up Chico, get up Pancho.
There's a colt to mount,
there's a boat to be paddled.
Sleep kept us apart, on cot beds
straw beds and sleeping mats (each one with his dream)
but waking brings us together.
The night is receding pursued by its demons and haunting animals.
We'll see the water deep blue: right now we can't see it.—And
this land with its orchards, which we can't see either.
Get up Pancho Nicaragua, grab your machete
there're many weeds to be cut down
grab your machete and guitar.
A barn owl at midnight and another at one.
No moon had the night nor any bright star.
Jaguars were roaring on this island and those on the coast answered them.
The night-bird has gone that says: Fucked up, Fucked up.
Later the skylark will sing in the palm tree,
will sing: Compañero
Compañera.
The shades fly off like a vampire before the light.
Get up you, and you, and you.
(The cocks are now crowing.)
God speed your day!

CANTIGA 17

Journeys in the Night

The sky pitch black with all its stars
and me gazing at them in the middle of the lake from an old launch
—the "María Danelia"—
lying in the stern on some bags of rice.
I've just come from being interrogated by the Military Court
and I think of the immense worlds above us
a single galaxy
(if the Earth were like a grain of rice
the galaxy would be like Jupiter's orbit).
And I think of compañero "Modesto" in the mountains;
of peasant origin; his real name's not known.
They are fighting to fulfill our destiny in the galaxy.
And about the peasants hung by their wrists
dragged by their balls.
A boy of eight beheaded, say the Capuchins.
Prisoners kept in communal latrines
one on top of the other, women, children, old people.
And those luminous worlds
the society of the stars
all around us.
The Kingdom of Heaven radiating light-years.
("...Which was prepared for you from the beginning of the world")
Ever since the primordial gas
emerged from the black and cold interstellar spaces
and as it condensed
grew hotter and brighter
hotter and brighter.
Will we ever return to the interstellar spaces?
And life,
might it not be as characteristic of the universe

as light?
        So distant in spacetime!
        Worlds that reach us only as light.
But we do not see all of the light. In the rainbow
beyond violet there's invisible ultraviolet.
        And there's another ultra beyond ultraviolet
        now it's the zone of love.
I gaze from the "María Danelia" and the dark waters of Nicaragua
        at the universe of light. The curvature
of light. Like flying by night over New York.
Or rather:
        the stars in the galaxy holding hands
        like a chorus of dancers around a bonfire
        and Pythagoras heard the maracas.
Yet the center of the Milky Way isn't a major star
but a cluster of stars
        (out there by the Sagittarius constellation).
They're something like 1,000 worlds I'm looking at
but astronomers can see about a billion.
        'To love evolution'
In Cuba schools, health centers, nurseries
proliferated like mushrooms after the rains.
Gravity is nothing more than the curvature of the universe
        that is, its desire for union.
        We have a common center and it lies before us.
Many are in prison, others in hiding.
They throw peasants out of helicopters.
        To give your life is to offer yourself to the future.
So as to be a single body with a single mind
and wanting the same thing all together.
The president of the Court said:
        'Do you have evidence that they are fighting for the poor?
        answer yes or no.'
To transform yourself into something greater than you.
Everything is movement: galaxy, solar system, planet
with the "María Danelia" the Lorío family's old launch
        everything sailing through spacetime.

'I believe they are fighting for the poor.'
I was summoned to the Court
and I fulfilled your will.
I gaze at the stars and say:
I have kept your commandments.
In our small corner, the planetary revolution
a humanity without classes
that
for which the planet revolves around the sun.
The unification
of the universe!
And the "dark outer depths:"
the interstellar spaces?
Everything is movement
thy will be done
on the planet as in the galaxies.

Waking up at midnight next to the small oblong window
of thick transparent plastic
only blackness and stars, like in a telescope lens,
small ones, tiny ones, bigger ones,
the Plough among them,
we're half-way across the Atlantic,
surely the Sargassos, en route to Czechoslovakia,
the nearby passengers asleep,
(like lights of a village in mid-Atlantic,
Bermuda... the Azores...
yet not below but above,
a village of worlds).
And thus Giordano Bruno in his window:
Worlds!
Whether there are more planets?
As though there aren't more birds than those seen from my window.
Brother Celestino, Giordano's cell neighbor in Venice
has informed: He said that a multitude of worlds exists
all the stars are worlds. The same witness
upon interrogation:

He insisted that there exists a huge quantity of worlds
and whatever stars can be seen are worlds.
Brother Giulio mentioned above: I've heard from him
that everything is world
          every star is world
and that above and below worlds exist. He was not
interrogated again. Francesco the Neapolitan:
That he said that many worlds exist,
there is a great confusion of worlds, and all the stars are worlds.
Francesco Graciano, cell neighbor in Venice:
That in his conversations he affirmed that many worlds exist
that this world is a star, and thus resembles other worlds
just as the heavenly bodies, worlds too, shine on us like stars.
He himself, interrogated: Once one night
he brought Francesco the Neapolitan to his window
and showed him a star saying that it is a world
and that all the stars are worlds...
     Which is why he was burned in that Roman square.
In the Campo di Fiori, in chains, wood piled around
     "We cardinals inquisitor generals signatories..."
     (pursuing the future of an idea like a dog on the trail).
Like Hus burned in a flowery meadow among vine groves,
the smoke of his body like a cloud over Lake Constance.
Some ashes were left, for the waters of the Rhine.
     For making Czechoslovakia Bolshevik.
The blood of Christ like a flag
          —red chalice embroidered on white—.
Communion under both kinds
like a symbol of the communism of the early Church.
                    The clergy were the theoreticians
of a mass movement of lay peasants.
     Communism as important as the religious reformation.
The Taborites.
The village of Tabor Hill, on a mountain, fortified,
ringed by a ditch—the ditch is still there, I saw it—
and there the classless society proclaimed.
Peasant tools were their weapons.

Fierce long scythes,
covered wagons for transporting crops:
weapons that required no training.
A barricade of covered wagons impassable
to the traditional feudal army,
mobile barricade.
A movement above all from the villages.
A community of brothers and sisters.
social equality and suppression of all domination.
Against international reaction and foreign intervention.
In Southern Bohemia a Kingdom of Heaven.
And there on the other side of the plastic
—while here the passengers sleep in the darkened aircraft
of the Cuban Air Line—on the other side of the plastic,
with the Plough, the celestial village.

Midnight, in a launch, in the middle of the lake,
between San Miguelito and Granada.
You still can't see the lights of Granada
and the lights of San Miguelito can no longer be seen.
Just the stars
(the mast pointing up at the Pleiades)
and the moon rising over Chontales.
Another launch sails by (a red light)
and sinks into the night.
Us to them,
another red light that sinks in the night...
And me lying down on deck gazing at the stars
among bunches of bananas and Chontaleño cheeses
I think: perhaps one of them is another earth like this one
and someone is looking at me from there (gazing at the stars)
from another launch in another night in the middle of another lake.

That clandestine night flight.
With the danger of being shot down. The night serene.
The sky full, really full of stars. The Milky Way
so clear through the thick glass of the window,

whitish and gleaming mass in the black night.
With its millions of processes of evolutions and revolutions.
We were passing over the sea to avoid Somoza's air force,
but following the coast.
The small plane flying low, and flying slowly.
First the lights of Rivas, taken and retaken by the Sandinistas,
now half under Sandinista control.
Then other lights: Granada, controlled by the Guardia
(it would be attacked that night).
Masaya, completely liberated. So many fell there.
Further on a glow: Managua. Place of so many battles.
(The Bunker). Still the bastion of the Guardia.
Diriamba, liberated. Jinotepe, battle raging. So much heroism
shines forth in those lights. Montelimar—the pilot points out—:
the tyrant's ranch by the sea. Nearby, Puerto Somoza.
The Milky Way above, and the lights of the Nicaraguan revolution.
I seem to see further off, in the North, the fires of Sandino.
("That light is Sandino.")
The stars above us, and the smallness of this earth
but also its importance, the importance of these
tiny lights of mankind. I think: everything is light.
The planet comes from the sun. It is light made solid.
This plane's electricity is light. The metal is light. The heat
of life comes from the sun.
"Let there be light."
The deep darkness also exists.
There are strange reflections—I don't know where they're coming from—
on the transparent surface of the windows.
A red luminosity: the tail-lights of this plane.
And reflections in the calm sea: they must be stars.
I look at the tiny light of my cigarette—it too comes from the sun, from a
star.
And the silhouette of a large ship. The U.S. aircraft carrier
sent to patrol the Pacific coast?
A great light to our right startles us. A jet against us?
No. The moon rising, half-moon, so serene, lit up by the sun.
The danger of flying on such a clear night.

And suddenly the radio. Confused words filling the small plane.
The Guardia? The pilot says: "They're our people."
Those waves are ours.
Now we are close to León, the liberated territory.
An intense red-orange light, like the glow of a cigar: Corinto:
the powerful lighting on the wharf glimmering in the sea.
And now already Poneloya beach, and the plane heading inland,
the cordon of coastal foam radiant beneath the moon.
The plane dropping down. A smell of insecticide.
And Sergio says to me: "The smell of Nicaragua!"
It's the moment of greatest danger, the enemy air force
could be waiting for us above this airport.
And now the airport lights.
We're on the ground. Out of the darkness olive-green comrades emerge
to embrace us.
We feel their warm bodies, which also come from the sun,
which are also light.
It's against the deep darkness this revolution.
It's dawn on July 18. And the beginning
of everything that is to come.

CANTIGA 18

Flights of Victory

It was like a trip to the moon
with the complexity and precision of all the details
reckoning on everything foreseen
                                        and also the unforeseen.
A trip to the moon in which the slightest error could be fatal.
"Workshop here" "Hello Asunción" "Hello Corn field".
"Workshop" was León, "Asunción" Masaya, "Corn field" Estelí.
And the calm voice of the young Dora María from "Workshop"
saying enemy reinforcements were dangerously
closing in on them,
her calm sing-song voice,
      "Workshop here. Do you read me?"
And the voice of Rubén in Estelí. The voice of Joaquín in "Office."
"Office" was Managua.
"Office" would be out of ammunition in two days ("Over").
Precise coded instructions, where the plane would land...
And Dora María: "Our rear-guard is exposed. Over."
Serene voices, calm, back and forth on the Sandinista frequency.
And there was a time when the two forces were evenly balanced
and nothing would shift, and it was becoming very dangerous.
It was like a trip to the moon. And without any mistakes.
So many working in coordination on the big project.
The moon was the earth. Our piece of the earth.
And we made it.
Now it's starting, Rugama, to belong to the poor; this here earth
(with its moon).

            It was a task for everyone.
Those who left without kissing their mother
so she wouldn't know they were going.

He who kissed his girlfriend for the last time.
And she who left his arms in order to embrace a Fal.
He who kissed his grandmother who was a mother to him
and said he'd be back soon, took his cap, and never returned.
Those who spent years in the mountains. Years
undercover, in cities more dangerous than the mountains.
Those who acted as couriers along the dark paths of the north,
or drivers in Managua, drivers for guerrillas each day at dusk.
Those who bought arms abroad dealing with gangsters.
Those who set up meetings abroad with flags and shouts
or trod the carpet of a president's reception room.
Those who attacked barracks to the cry of Free Country or Death.
The boy standing guard on the corner of the liberated street
a red-and-black scarf over his face.
The children hauling blocks,
                tearing up the blocks that paved the roads
                        —the blocks one of Somoza's businesses—
and hauling more and more blocks
                        for the people's barricades.
The women who brought coffee to los muchachos on the barricades.
Those who carried out the most important tasks,
                            and those who did the least important ones:
This was a task for everyone.
The truth is we all piled blocks on the great barricade.
It was a task for everyone. It was the people united.
                        And we did it.

It was a week after the triumph.
We were returning from Cuba
                from the July 26 celebrations.
I was mulling over Fidel's speech
and Martí's phrase "Everything is glory in July."
And suddenly there's Momotombo, blue on blue,
free for the first time since the age of the Indians.
The squared fields, soft green, at daybreak.
                Lake Managua pinkish in that daybreak,
tiny Bird Island close to Managua

(it too was Somoza's,
the first Somoza wanted to change its name to Love Island)
and I realize that the country seems more beautiful now.
And I say so to Dora María who's sitting beside me
gazing ecstatically at the liberated country
this dream we are all living and from which we'll never awaken.
        Before this beauty was kind of withered...
How beautiful the country now seems.
        How beautiful our nature without Somoza.
And the thrill of hearing over the rose-dawn lake
the Cuban Air Line stewardess announce
that we are about to land in the "Augusto César Sandino" airport.
        The plane full of guerrilla commandants.
And now getting off without any fear
            (and incidentally we weren't carrying passports)
and arriving at Immigration, and arriving at Customs,
and for them to call you: "Compañero."

We're all very busy
the truth is we're all so busy
in these difficult and jubilant days, that will never return
                        but which we'll never forget
we're very busy with confiscations
                  so many confiscations
so much land distribution
everyone removing barricades from the streets
                  so cars can get through
        the barricades in every neighborhood
also changing the names of streets and neighborhoods
                            those Somocista names
disintering those murdered
repairing the bombed hospitals
        —this hospital will be called such and such—
now setting up the new police force
taking a census of artists
bringing drinking water to such and such a place
and these others are asking for electricity

the electricity Somoza had cut off from them
quick, quick repairing the installations
water and power for Ciudad Sandino
—their choice, to call their neighborhood Ciudad Sandino—
we are very busy, Carlos
the markets have to be clean, have to be well-ordered
more markets also have to be built
we are creating new parks, and of course already new laws
rapidly we ban pornographic ads
the price of basic grains under tight control
it's time also to make lots of posters
quick, quick new judges have to be appointed
quick, to repair the roads
and how beautiful, also we have to lay out new roads
the election of local government steering committees
it's time a million people learned to read
you go to your cabinet meeting, you go to your trade union
the country-wide vaccination of children
and right now plans for education
power shovels clearing away the debris
—Monimbó once more with marimbas—
fields humming to the sound of tractors
the association of field-workers organized
seeds, insecticides, fertilizers, new consciousness
and quickly, we have to plant seeds right away
it's also the time for new songs
the workers returned to their noisy wheels happily
brother, all the urban bus routes are running again
—and so many cultural festivals in the neighborhoods
politico-cultural events they now call them—
and also every day there are masses for the fallen compañeros
and there's a new word in our daily speech
"Compañero"
all this will be left in the old newspapers
for whoever wants to see it,
in yellow newspapers the beginning of the new history
poetic newspapers

there they'll see in beautiful headlines what I'm saying now
about these heady days which will never return
about these days in which we are so busy
because the truth is we are very busy.

Now everything is happy in Waslala.
        Waslala, lovely name.
(Before, the name alone struck terror.)
No more do peasants arrive blindfolded and tied up.
Nightfall no longer brings with it blood-curdling screams
but guitar sounds.
Free of those people who shouted:
        —"Long live the guardia, down with the people."
Girls have come down from the Cuá very happy, with flowers in their hair.
The nightmare's over now: "Waslala."
            Waslala's happy, the
capital of terror and death for peasants in the north.
It was the headquarters of the integrated counter-insurgency plan
for the strategic siege for guerrilla annihilation.
The worst of the "strategic villages" of peasant repression.
German shepherds no longer are used to hunt down revolutionaries.
            This light-hearted corner of the mountain
which was the darkest in Nicaragua's night.
They'd kill everyone in the hut.
                                        They'd burn them alive in the hut.
    Waslala now free of the beasts.
These lands meant for maize were silent cemeteries.
        Sometimes whole families buried.
Now Pancho is weeding the corn field with his machete.
You don't have to ask permission at the barracks to bathe in the river.
Waslala's school will have teachers, and not Security appointees.
Soldiers in olive-green play with the children.
            The fields are no longer concentration camps.
Helicopters no longer roar above the hills
with peasants, returning minutes later with just the crew.
            They brought people here from Dudú
                        from Kubalí

from Kuskawás
from Wanawás
from Zinica
from Zapote
Here were the jails, were the underground prisons,
were the pits with men, women, children and old people.
The mountain is now free of the wild animals in camouflage.
Peasants who come from elsewhere sleep in the barracks.
Five years the night lasted.
How beautiful the mountain is this morning,
the mountain where so many guerrillas moved among monkeys.
Outside the police station, children flitter like humming-birds.
Outside the CDS, women chat among flowers like toucans.
The red-and-black flags look like birds.
How beautiful is the green of the fields and the green of the compañeros.
How beautiful the river Waslala now slips by.
Suddenly the day came.
The coffee will be good this year.
How happy Waslala is.

When after two years you returned to Solentiname, Juan,
a child of five then,
I remember perfectly what you said to me:
"You're the one that's going to tell me all about God, right?"
And I increasingly
have come to know less of God.
A mystic, that is, a lover of God
called him NOTHING,
and another said: whatever you say about him is false.
And the best way for you to have knowledge of God
was perhaps for me not to be talking to you about God.
But once
I did talk to you about God, by the lake,
on the jetty,
one late afternoon all pink and glowing:
"God is someone who is in everyone,
in you, in me, everywhere."

"And is he in that heron?" "Yes he is." "And is he in the sardines?"
"Yes he is." "And is he in those clouds?" "Yes he is."
"And is he in that other heron?" "Yes he is."
A tiny boys naming your entire small paradise.
"And is he in this jetty?" "Yes he is." "And is he in the waves?"
Why do children ask so many questions?
And me
        why do I ask why
                like a child?
"And is he also in my mum and dad?" "Yes he is."
And you said to me:
            "But he doesn't go to the island of the wicked, does he?"
12 years old now
a member of the Association of Sandinista Children.
You go to rallies. You contribute voluntary hours.
You undertake revolutionary vigilance. You are in the militia.
                (Those on the island of the wicked have now gone.)
"And he's also in the tiny stars
the tiny tiny stars that are so big, isn't he?"
The numbers of the small
            are as big as those of the big.
Where did you come from?
And I was staggered, not only by your questions
but because in addition I thought that
out of three-hundred million spermatozoa
                        only you were, Juan,
out of three-hundred million Juans
distinct from the Juan that you are
but your twins
only you were, once.
And like you
three-hundred million were asking me from their non-existence
            where is God,
telling me to tell them all about God,
            whether he is also within them?
(And with them all the infinity of those non-existent
infinitely greater than the existing one.)

As though I were suddenly being interrogated by
three-hundred million stars but non-existent ones.
Although out of all those millions,
in which God is also,
only you were, Juan,
the one who was asking me questions that evening by the lake.
He who one day believed I'd tell him all about God.

In the little round window, everything is blue,
earth bluish, blue-green, blue
(and sky)
everything is blue
blue lake and lagoons
blue volcanoes
the more distant the earth the bluer
blue islands in blue lake.
This is the face of the liberated land.
And where all the people fought, I think:
for love!
To live without the hatred
of exploitation.
To love each other on a beautiful earth
very beautiful, not only in itself
but because of the people on it,
above all because of the people on it.
That's why God gave us its beauty
for the society on it.
And in all those blue places there was fighting, suffering
for a society of love
here in this land.
A patch of blue has greater intensity...
And I seemed to be seeing there the places of all the battles,
and all the deaths,
through that small round glass,
blue
every shade of blue.

Boys whose pictures appeared daily in the newspaper
        lying down
    eyes half-closed, lips half-open
    as though they were laughing, as though enjoying themselves.
The young people from the horrendous list.
Or otherwise they appeared serious in tiny ID or passport shots,
perhaps deeply serious.
Boys who daily swelled the horrifying list.
One took a walk in the neighborhood
and they found him dumped on a piece of rough land.
Or he left for work, from his house in the San Judas neighborhood,
and never returned.
    The one who went to buy a Coca-Cola on the corner.
The one who left to see his girlfriend and never returned.
Or taken from his home
    and carried off in a military jeep that sank in the night.
And later found in the morgue,
or by the roadside on the Cuesta del Plomo,
or on a rubbish heap.
        His arms broken,
his eyes gouged out, his tongue cut off, his genitals ripped away.
    Or they simply never turned up.
Those taken by the patrols of "Black Macho" or "Lion Face."
Those piled up on the lake shore behind the Darío Theater.
    The only thing left to their mothers of their physical form,
the flat shining gaze, the smile, on a piece of paper.
Pieces of card their mothers held up like treasures in *La Prensa.*
(The image engraved in their entrails: on that tiny card.)
        The one with the unkempt hair.
        The one with the eyes of a frightened deer.
        This one smiling, roguish.
        The girl with the sad look.
        One in profile. Or with the head to one side.
        Thoughtful one of them. Another his shirt open.
        Another with curls. Or with hair in his face. With a beret.
        Another out of focus, smiling beneath his moustache.
        Wearing his graduation tie.

The girl smiling with a frown.
The girl in the photo her boyfriend carried.
The boy posing in the photo he'd give to his girlfriend.
Aged 20, 22, 18, 17, 15.
The young ones killed for being young. Because
to be between 15 and 25 years old in Nicaragua was illegal.
And it seemed Nicaragua would be left without young ones.
And after the triumph I even was surprised sometimes, suddenly,
when a young boy greeted me at a rally
(me asking him inwardly: "And how did you escape?")
They were feared for being young.
You, those taken by the guardia. The "beloved of the gods."
The Greeks said that those whom the gods love die young.
It must be, I think, because they will always remain young.
Others might grow old but in their minds
those will always be young and fresh,
the smooth forehead, the black hair.
The blonde Roman girl who died remained forever blonde in the memory.
But you, I say, are not those who never grew old
because you remained young (ephemerally) in the memory
of those who will also die.
You'll be young because there will always be young people in Nicaragua
and Nicaragua's young will now all be revolutionaries, because
of your deaths who were so many, those killed daily.
They will be you again, in lives forever renewed,
new, just as each dawn is new.

In September more coyotes were seen around San Ubaldo.
More alligators, shortly after the triumph,
in the rivers up by San Ubaldo.
On the roads more rabbits, raccoons...
The bird population has tripled, they tell us,
especially that of the *piches*.
The noisy *piches* come down to swim wherever they see shining water.
Somoza's people also destroyed the lakes, rivers, and mountains.
They diverted the course of rivers for their farms.
The Ochomogo had dried up last summer.

The Sinecapa dried up because of the big landowners' deforestation.
The Río Grande in Matagalpa, dried up, during the war,
down by the Sébaco Plains.
They placed two dams on the Ochomogo,
and capitalist chemical wastes
flowed into the Ochomogo and the fish floundered in the water as though drunk.
The Boaco River with sewerage.
The Moyuá Lagoon had dried up. One of Somoza's colonels
stole the land from the peasants and built a dam.
The Moyuá Lagoon which for centuries had been a beauty spot.
(But soon the little fish will return.)
They deforested and built dams.
Few garrobos sunning themselves, few armadillos.
Somoza used to sell the Caribbean green turtle.
In trucks they exported *paslamas* eggs and iguanas.
Making the *caguama* turtle extinct.
José Somoza wiping out the saw-fish in the Great Lake.
Near to extinction the jungle wild cat,
its soft pelt the color of jungle,
and the puma, the tapir in the mountains
(like the peasants in the mountains).
And the poor Chiquito River! Its misfortune,
shared by the whole country. The Somoza era reflected in its waters.
The Chiquito River in León, fed by springs
from sewers, waste products from soap factories and tanneries,
white water from soap factories, red from the tanneries;
plastics on its bed, chamber pots, rusty irons. That's
what the Somoza era left us.
(We have to see it clean and pretty again singing its way to the sea.)
And into Lake Managua all the sewerage of Managua
and the chemical wastes.
And down by Solentiname, on the island of La Zanata
a huge white and stinking tip of saw-fish skeletons.
But now the saw-fish and the freshwater shark breathe again.
Tisma is once more full of royal herons
reflected in their mirrors.

It has many starlings, *piches*, *güises*, widgets.
The plant-life has also benefited.
Armadillos are very happy with this government.
We will reclaim the woods, rivers, lagoons.
We're going to decontaminate Lake Managua.
It wasn't only human beings longing for liberation.
The entire ecology was crying out. The revolution
is also for lakes, rivers, trees, animals.

And women from the Cuá also attended the huge rally.
The wife of Jacinto Hernández who fell in Kuskawás.
The wife of Bernardino.
Amanda Aguilar.
A delegation from the Cuá.
They brought children along too.
They remembered the sufferings, the "Events in the Cuá."
From the Cuá where they wouldn't say where the guerrillas were.
Amanda Aguilar knew a poem about the Cuá.
(Amanda Aguilar was her pseudonym, her name's Petrona Hernández.)
They were taken with their children to the police station in the Cuá.
"Some of us were pregnant."
They lost their homes.
Angelina Díaz said:
"We drifted through the mountains from place to place."
And Bernardino's widow:
"Beaten and dirty, blindfolded, they took him away."
A story you never forget, said Juana Tinoco.
She told of the tortures on the little children.
The little children screaming in that police station.
"It was so they'd tell which of us gave food."
And Bernardino's widow:
"He had a sick child, and he was comforting him in the loft.
The guardia arrived. And they shouted at him to come down.
He said: I'm tending my son!
The lieutenant said to me:
Say goodbye to your husband—you ain't gonna see him again.
I walked out behind him."

Bernardino Díaz Ochoa, the one who said:
"We're not birds to live from the air,
we're not fish to live from the sea
we're people to live from the land."
When they took Bernardino away the corn was ripe for harvest.
And Bernardino's wife also told:
"They wrenched out his tongue with a cattle clamp.
They stuck nails in his ears.
They were asking him: How many guerrillas through here? You know Tomás Borge?
When they killed him, the *guardias* were drinking cususa."
Day and night nothing but night.
Until the lads' revolution triumphed.
Then it was like a hood had been removed from them.
Amanda Aguilar used to take food to the guerrillas.
These things were told by the women from the Cuá.
They came dressed simply
with a placard which said: The Women from the Cuá, Present!
This was the newspaper story
of the arrival of the peasant women's delegation from the Cuá.

Comandante, when we were with the Association of Sandinista Children
and you uttered a phrase in your speech,
a simple phrase
"now we are free"
(linked to other phrases)
just as you said that phrase I noticed
some children moving on the steps,
some going up and another tiny one, trying to get down,
one eating an ice-cream,
there was a lot of movement and even disorder in the happy gathering of children and adolescents
beneath your voice amplified by the microphones and its booming echo,
and I felt that all those children were free,
the seven-year old licking his ice cream, free forever,
would grow up free,
like the compañero who told me as we drove along the road

that he never thought he'd be able to drive along a road
that when he saw the guardia pass and the EEBI,
in the hills,
he thought he'd always be in hiding or in the mountains;
or like the peasant from El Jocote, beyond Palacagüina,
who said that now he went to parties at night without fear,
without fear of the helicopter which took away the peasants
and they never returned,
that before he felt like a caged bird:
all this flashed before me in a vision when you uttered that phrase,
and you were already on to other phrases, Comandante.

I remember Ernesto when you returned from your training
and were talking about the "most beautiful" weapons you'd learned to handle,
"...it's beautiful, mamá" you were telling your mother,
like someone talks about the beauty of a girl.
Later a sniper bullet struck you in the face
when you leapt onto the street in León
shouting, to encourage those of your squad following you:
A FREE COUNTRY OR DEATH!
Poet fallen at the age of 20.
I'm thinking of this Ernesto
now that children are kissed by soldiers
and the Police have their poetry workshop
and the Literacy Army in blue and grey uniforms
is scattered throughout the country, and Agrarian Reform's happening
and the child newspaper-sellers and shoeshiners are taken to play
and...well, truly those weapons were most beautiful
(and I remember the gleam in your eyes as you said it).

I was in Niquinohomo and there they told me a story of a young boy
who went off one August day to hunt garrobos;
he set out from the station over yonder, following the railway line;
where he met up with a friend;
it was midday and very sunny,
and there were some fat garrobos sunning themselves in the trees.

The boy shot the first garrobo with his pistol.
And suddenly the "Los Pueblos" train came along blowing its whistle
and the other garrobos took fright.
The train was crowded with people, all in khaki,
they seemed to be Nicaraguan soldiers,
but as they went past the boy saw they were Yankee marines
heading for Jinotepe,
and the boy was furious
and said that he'd like to hang every one of them from the trees.
The interesting thing about this story is that this boy
later was able to carry out what he wished.
They just told me this story in Niquinohomo
when we were turning the house where that boy lived into a museum.

Summoned to a cabinet meeting
knowing beforehand for a very important reason
but not what.
All the ministers and managers of state industries
around the big table.
And it was a serious matter:
The setting-up of a National Emergency Committee
to combat the danger of plague from the *Aedes aegypti* mosquito.
It breeds especially in man-made receptacles.
You recognize it by the silvery lines on its thorax.
It's the female which bites human beings.
It needs the blood for its eggs
which it deposits in any water-filled receptacle.
There has to be a preventative campaign in
flowerpots, cans, old tires, barrels, roof gutters,
the elimination of unnecessary objects
cleanliness in the patios,
land and air fumigation.
Dark and small
the disease it transmits
high mortality among infants,
dangerous to the elderly.
Very possible an outbreak may occur in Nicaragua.

Material resources. Financial ones.
An intensive public awareness campaign.
Contributions from every department: Health,
Transport, Education, Air Force...
The involvement of workers, students...
And I look at the serious faces around the huge table
where there are attaché cases, ash-trays,
and I think: how curious,
how curious. It's love:
The cabinet gathered together by love of their neighbor.

Combatant of the Frente Sandinista
in this photo with your pistol
aiming at the enemy
red-and-black scarf over your face
masking you to just below your eyes
taking cover behind a wall
with your gaze fixed and your weapon held tightly
trained on the enemy:
Many things happened in that battle,
which battle we don't know,
many more things went on to happen. We won.
July 19 came.
There've been many great things since then,
and there will continue to be great things.
New generations will come.
But you will always be like that, 18 years old,
behind a low wall, brave, tense, motionless
eternal
aiming at the enemy.

Sun and flags,
first the hymns,
sun and slogans,
placards and speakers,
applause and slogans,
sun and smiles,

eyes of every color,
        every shade of skin,
                all sorts of hair,
each smiling mouth different, each nose different
(the eyes: light of innumerable colors set in white),
long, short, straight, curly, afro hair,
young people, fat people, woman with child, wrinkled old woman, kids,
yellow trousers, red blouse, white T-shirt, red, blue,
white, olive-green, black, orange, pink, yellow.
And from the platform I suddenly saw a single face
with thousands of smiles and thousands of pairs of eyes,
A Face of faces, a Body of bodies,
like those photos in newspapers made up of tiny tiny dots.
        Face still blurred, but it had a kind of halo...
(Or a wide-brimmed hat, or a beret with a star?)
I saw that that united flesh was the triumph over death.
Photographers firing their flashes. The people squeezed together,
                and you could see the unity of everyone,
unity the guarantee of Victory.

My friend Michel is the commanding officer in Somoto,
        up by the border with Honduras,
and he told me that he discovered a consignment of parrots
which were to be smuggled to the U.S.
        so that there they'd learn to speak English.
There were 186 parrots, and 47 had already died in their cages.
And he sent them back to the place they'd been taken from,
and when the truck was approaching a place they call Los Llanos
close to the mountains those parrots came from
        (the mountains seemed huge behind those plains)
the parrots began to get excited and flap their wings
        and to press themselves against their cage walls.
And when the cages were opened
they all flew off like arrows in the same direction to their mountains.
The Revolution did the same thing for us, I'm thinking:
it freed us from the cages in which they were carting us off to speak English.
It handed us back the country they'd snatched from us.

Parrot-green compañeros gave the parrots their green mountains.
But there were 47 that died.

Who'd have told you, Colonel,
when you were dying in Cuba from lung cancer,
with the FSLN still a long way off from any victory,
that one day you'd be disintered in Cuba
and would enter Managua triumphantly
(where you'd been only once before, the time they murdered Sandino)
acclaimed by a square with more than 100,000 people,
on the shoulders of the National Directorate and the Government Junta,
all the ministers behind,
Sandino's flag waving all around,
and the 21 cannon salute, and so on,
the whole nation honoring Colonel Santos López,
the boy with no father who worked from the age of 8,
for 20 cents a day
—the Yankees then owners of the nation—
and began to fight alongside Sandino at the age of 12
in the children's platoon, "the Choir of Angels,"
never went to school
and afterwards said
by not knowing how to read,
he'd kept his mind clear so as to understand the intervention
for which reason Comandante Tirado has now called you
"an intellectual though he never wrote books
and an inexhaustible source of knowledge"
and seven times wounded
promoted to Colonel by Sandino at the age of 17,
and one of the few present at Sandino's midnight wedding
in San Rafael, withdrawing from San Rafael that same night,
the General saying:
"From now on the finches
and all birds will be the songs
that will accompany us in our mountain lives,"
a barefoot army, and almost without clothes,
plantain leaves your quilts and mattresses,

and those humble troops Sandino called
the Defending Army of Nicaraguan National Sovereignty,
with all the jungle diseases,
with only the medicines the jungle itself provided,
only moments of comfort, between battles, in El Chipote
with guitars and accordions,
and the air raids, Sandino gave the order
to fire on the planes, that
first plane shot down which was in Quilalí,
216 battles you fought,
that time for example, aged 18,
when with Umanzor you stopped all the trains,
and finally you accompanying Sandino on that fateful trip,
the only one to escape in Managua, leaping over the roof,
crossing an unknown Nicaragua, with your wounded leg
to Honduras, and starting work there
in Don Toribio's soap factory, in Choluteca,
always hidden in the soap factory, the endless exile,
and 28 years later a young man finds you, Carlos Fonseca,
and you prove to be a direct envoy from Sandino,
the link between the first Sandinistas and the new ones,
at once they put the new struggle to you,
and without hesitation,
you reply: "Let's do it,"
and you're back again with the Choir of Angels,
founding the FSLN in the forest depths by the banks of the Patuca,
you teach vigilance, guard duty,
how to move in the hills like a snake,
to carry a small branch of a fluorescent tree at night
so as not to get separated,
to leave no tracks as you travel,
how Sandino's ambushes worked
(three:
attacking in the middle
to finish them off as they flee, forwards or back)
your fondness for "Tapir" because like you he was a peasant,
unable to read,

and your advice, Sandino's,
peasants would still be the backbone
with the support of those who know more,
Modesto and Francisco quarrelling in front of you
over the leadership of a squad,
Modesto wanting Francisco to take command
and Francisco, Modesto,
now an old man with lung cancer, you fighting once more
in those rivers,
and later dying in a hospital in Cuba,
a death alone and battle-free, but for the battle with death,
so far from any victory,
when nobody knew when victory would come, nor whether it would come,
and now the homecoming, acclaimed by an entire people,
who'd have told you, Colonel,
or perhaps there was no need for anyone to say it,
because you when you were dying,
who knows how, you already knew about this,
in some way,
who knows how,
you already knew everything.

On top of Motastepe hill, on the outskirts of Managua
a huge sign in white letters
ROLTER
could be seen from many streets in Managua
and young Juan asked me as we rode in a car
what those big letters
ROLTER
meant and I told him a make of shoes
and it was so people would buy those shoes.
"But when the Revolution triumphs those signs will disappear
won't they?" the child said to me.
It was a few days before the October offensive
about which he knew nothing,
anxious days for me.
That afternoon he played Sandinistas and *guardias* with other children;

problem was, they said, nobody wanted to be a guardia.
Frequently after the triumph, the big letters
reminded me of Juan's words, as yet unfulfilled.
For a year now we've seen from many streets in Managua
on the hill instead of those letters others:
FSLN
and me also remembering the child's words with joy.
It was midday one gloomy overcast Sunday.
And there are days when you beg for a sign.
Very intimate solitudes. As
when little St. Theresa on her death bed
had doubts about the existence of God.
Then from the car I gazed up at the huge letters on the hill
and God spoke within me:
"Look what I've done for you,
for your people, that is.
Look at those letters, and do not doubt in me, have faith
man of little faith
asshole."

She was the guerrilla's companion
—although the guerrilla was married—
and when he was killed she understood for the first time
what she'd heard before but never understood:
"the earth wherein the beloved remains are laid to rest."
And ever since then she's loved the land so much more,
which she had loved so much already,
the land for which there is guard duty, battles.
It wasn't only the land where she was born, had always lived,
but now it was also her dead man's land.
Last night when they woke her for guard duty
she was dreaming that he was washing in the river,
on his bare chest the most minute of his muscles stood out.
She has a love buried in her heart,
and some bones buried in a corner of this land.
This is one more reason to defend this land
against the Yankee invasion, against

the Contras,
because she was the guerrilla's companion.

When you receive a nomination, a prize, a promotion,
think of those who died.
When you are at a reception, on a delegation, in a commission
think of those who died.
When you've been voted in, and the group congratulates you
think of those who died.
When they applaud you as you mount the leaders' podium,
think of those who died.
When they turn out to greet you at the airport of a great city,
think of those who died.
When microphones are placed before you,
or tv cameras home in on you,
think of those who died.
When you're the one handing out certificates, titles, permits,
think of those who died.
When the little old lady brings her problem to you,
her patch of land,
think of those who died.
Look at those without shirts, dragged along,
bleeding, hooded, broken,
plunged into tanks, suffering the electric prod, an eye torn out,
beheaded, shot to pieces,
dumped by the roadside,
in ditches they themselves dug,
in mass graves,
or simply on the land, fertilizer for wild plants:
You represent them.
You have been delegated,
by those who died.

The huge airplane flies above the flushed dawn
clouds,
over the Atlantic, and later the Caribbean,
still heading sunwards, and still

into the dawn
and now the earth
        the liberated mountains of Nicaragua
                the mountains recently made literate
and still the flushed clouds, still the dawn
and then descending towards the airport
and we're now about to land
                        and as I look closely at the earth
I think, I don't know why, of the dead,
not all of them, just those,
                                our dead,
in the mountains, in common ditches, in lonely graves,
in cemeteries, at the side of the road,
close to this airport, throughout the national territory,
with monuments, anonymous without any monument,
all transformed into this earth, making this earth more sacred,
Sandino, Carlos Fonseca, Julio Buitrago, Oscar Turcios,
Ricardo Morales Avilés, Rugama, Eduardo Contreras,
Carlos Agüero, Claudia Chamorro, Luisa Amanda Espinoza,
Luis Alfonso Velázquez, Arlen Siú, Ernesto Castillo,
Pedro Joaquín, José Benito Escobar, David Tejada,
Pomares, Silvio Mayorga, Rigoberto, Pablo Úbeda, Gaspar,
Chato Medrano, Donald and Elvis, Felipe Peña,
and so many many many many more:
Let them bury me in this earth alongside you Dead Compañeros.
The wheels just a few meters from the earth.
And a voice should announce over the microphone: Ladies and gentlemen
the earth we are about to touch is very sacred.
...The wheels have just touched down, dear passengers,
on a great tomb of martyrs.

CANTIGA 19

Towards the New Man

In the beginning
at the time the Father created the word he had a drum.
The Witoto tell and sing in their anthropaphagous culture.
He summoned his water
        and it rained on the earth from the sky.
The Witoto Word (*Naikino*) different from *Logos.*
Rather that in the beginning was the Myth or the Dream.
I think they identify the Dream with the Word.
Things: created by the Father from an unreal, inexistent substance,
or with an imaginary, dreamed existence.
The Father dreamed, and his dream was vague, was a chimera,
a chaos without reality.
With a thread of dream he gathered in the void.
He fastened it with a new magical dream *iseike*
[literally tobacco smoke or tuft of cotton].
He sat down upon this imaginary earth.

In the beginning:
What was there before the universe began?
It could be answered:
Simply there was no universe.
Or equally it could be answered: We don't know.
Will scientists ever know?
Let's accept that there is no God in the universe.
But in the pre-universe?
Where did you get such well-shaped hands,
your eyes with such very deep light?
Or what makes that person dying of thirst say:
I'd love if only for a moment to kiss that mouth.

And if the orthodox atheist (some contradiction) says
that the spirit is material
you could say to him, it's a thought,
that matter is spiritual,
and then you're an idealist. So what!
What the hell.

The Prime Minister asked Faraday
what use would electricity be.

The evolution of matter has been towards life
and from life to thought,
and from thought?
                    Towards love.
Everything is structure in the universe
that's to say, society.
      The atom is society,
            the molecule is society,
                  the cell is society,
                        the organism is society.
      Man is society.
The loneliness we suffer comes from being only individuals.
        Happiness is others.
Hyenas do better to hunt in packs
than each one selfishly alone.
The amoeba cut off
immediately tries to rejoin to the group.
The same with electrical forces, or tropism or love.
And from thought, to love.
Adam on his own was unhappy,
in Paradise!

"Jesus says: when you make of the two One
you will become Children of Humanity."
            (This is from the Gospel of Thomas.)
And as for St. John's,
may it not have something to do with quantum theory

the fact that God is light.
That the message of Jesus Christ was
that God is light and there is no darkness in him.
And that,
            AND THAT
      the light is to be united with one another.
They say, or used to say around 1909
that in the beginning all men were Choctaws.
They split up. That's why there are so many tribes
in North America.
Or those others:
"The first men emerged from caves.
Men and animals were equal, and they all spoke."

In all species the youngest
are more adventurous than the old,
more curious and enquiring,
      more disposed then to change, to the new,
            and therefore
      more inclined to death,
to die for change, for the new.
            In all animal species.
      To die for the species.
He rose up in Galilee,
our geological contemporary:
                        "Believe this news."
The new casts out the old,
the new springs from the old (Mao).
But in the Vatican, old wine in old wineskins.
They accuse us because of our triumphalist auguries.
But has there ever been a conservative or reactionary
prophet?
                  And I saw the holy society.
The New Jerusalem descended from the future.
Like the bride adorned for her groom.
"Travelled the half of Jacob's ladder"
according to the Apostle (Martí).

Never before have peoples loved each other as now.
    Aggression is anachronistic.
Survivors of four ice ages.
If the thinking planets exchange signals from afar
what would our message be?

To design computers more intelligent than us
so that they design computers more intelligent than them
and so forth?
Could technology advance to such an extent
that human kind could become redundant?
And if the most intelligent beings in the cosmos, there above,
are supercomputers?
And one day will supercomputers be born of us on earth
which will break the electrical cord with us
and fly off?
Men of the Golden Age, or the Stone Age
    (Higher Paleolithic)
"the best stone artifacts of all time."
    Modern techniques have been unable
    to reproduce their "laurel leaf" knives.
The thousands of mammoth bones prove they were well fed.
They'd have had as many hours' leisure as the lion or the chimpanzee
(and more than the North American farmer).
Each one made up his own mind each day
how much he was going to work and on what.
Whether making a bow or hunting rabbits, it was without a chief or overseer.
The woman if she wished gathered wood, or wove a basket.
Wood for bows, firewood and palm, rabbits
everything was there at hand and everything for everyone.
Each one with his own equal slice of nature.
There were no rents, no taxes, no tributes.
Not a case of some of them workers (hunters or gatherers)
and others nothing but.
Bows and arrows were not restricted to certain hands.
There were no kings nor dictators, prime minister, police,

jails, bureaucrats.
Nobody knelt humbly to salute anyone.
    The Golden Age: scientifically true
    according to Hellmich.
    The golden age must really have existed:
    "According to the laws of psychology and of logic..."

In prehistory, thought faced with invisible forces
painted.
    Not yet having words.
Its cosmic anguish painted. The same
as contemporary art's.
The animal conceived as symbol or the symbol turned animal.
Vertebrate, mammiferous, of the sub-class of Placentalia,
not so far removed from rodents...
Man thought an antelope before saying "antelope."
When he said "antelope" he made the others in the dark cave see
    antelopes coupling.
We owe organized cooperation to language.
Whoever speaks like us is one of us!
There's no language without society
nor consciousness without language.
Language which unites each of us to each other
and the living to the dead.

The ancient stars, that blind Borges mentioned.
Their movements noted down on bones by prehistoric man.
    Known (astronomy)
        since ancient and infinite time
    says Philip the Opuntian.
With straight and curved lines in the dust
trying to draw the heavens.
And Frobenius, that from the earliest migrations of peoples
they began to take note of the sky.
    The coming of the kingdom of heaven on earth!
In matter all is movement, change,
"from changes of place to thought."

From the displacement of particles to social changes.
There is no motionless body.
Matter exists only in movement. Or rather:
movement is matter's existence.
And there is no movement except in space and time.
    Night/day
                Capitalism and socialism.
    "I have come down to deliver you from the Egyptians"
Without the victory of matter over anti-matter
the universe would be nothing but radiation.
Let's imagine a planet of human beings
(each one more complex than a star)
all united in a single communion.
There are for example insect societies.
    Society so perfect
      that more than society it's now an individual.
        An island without any life
        recently emerged from the sea
    and little by little approaching
                the desolate island
    a solitary coconut.
                Communion...
            SOUVENIR OF MY FIRST COMMUNION
                Camilo Torres Restrepo
                (in his sailor's suit)
Like we had framed on our Solentiname island.
Where it had arrived like a solitary coconut.
        Your blood wine for all
        your body bread for all.
Childbirth is also violent.
    To plunge our lives into the future.
To transform yourself into something greater than you.
      A biological urgency.
Their country's soil they turned red with their hemoglobin.
        Their ethical machine guns.
A violence that does not act like violence.
And then the whole people a single guerrilla.

If God is angry, why not us?
Kingdom of God
mentioned in the Gospel about 100 times
or more, 90 in Christ's mouth
geologically our contemporary.
May your Kingdom of Heaven come to earth.
"...from slavery
to the brotherhood of sacrifice" (Martí).
"...a war
inspired in the purest abnegation" (Idem).
Columbus had already encountered socialism in Cuba.
(Besides the leaves not falling, and the nightingale singing in November,
and the point you should love your neighbor as yourself, without *meum*
and *tuum*.)
The workers of the world, the "unlearned" workers
—from seed to cotton
to cotton thread
to cotton shirt—
they are building paradise
and re-sowing paradise.
The poet is prophet, seer,
like the Congo monkeys that howl when it's about to rain.
A metamorphosis of man.
We are the men who make up or will make up Mankind.
Parrots in the wild have a highly creative language,
it's said. Only those in captivity
are the ones that mimic.
Or like monkeys that don't reproduce in captivity.
"It has never happened that one society
permanently dominate..."
(Quoted incidentally in *Time* magazine.)
A book has been written entitled *From Africa to the Stars*
(From the descent from trees to the emergence into the cosmos).
1) The descent from the trees
2) The trek across continents
3) The navigation of the seas
4) The venturing forth into the open cosmos

(perhaps with artificial intelligence).

And how surprised I am to find myself reading with such interest
things like
cotton crop up 25.5%
from last year
coffee exports US$124.2 million
up 17.5% from last year
an expected increase of 13.6% in sugar
maize production fell by 5.9%
gold fell by 10% due to
Contra attacks in that region
likewise shellfish...
When did this information ever interest me before?
It's because now our wealth,
however small it may be,
is for being
for everyone.
It is
for the people, then,
love for the people,
this interest. It's
because now these numbers are love.
Gold brought out of the earth, solid sun
cut into blocks, will become electric light,
drinking water
for the poor. Translucent
molluscs, with reminiscences of women, smell of woman,
brought out of the sea, from their underwater caves
and colored coral gardens, to become
pills, desks.
The sanctity of matter.
Mamma, you know the value of a glass of milk.
Cotton, soft shreds of cloud
—we have gone off singing to cut cotton
we have grasped clouds in our fingers—
will become zinc roofing, roads, and

it's because now things economic are poetic,
        or rather, with the Revolution
the economy is love.
From Africa to the heavens.

We can have great love for one person only, or a few.
Love for the whole of humanity is not loving anyone.
The distant starvation we see at home on TV
is distant starvation and not at home.
Turn the other cheek yes. But feel as on one's own
the blow to another cheek. And who loved many
even without knowing them and gave his life for them?
                                                            (Something new.
The new man. If not, he wouldn't be new
the new man.)
We have seen him:
eyes open, black beard and black curls,
stretched out in the washing place like the Mantegna Christ in Milan.
Can it be that the universe will abort the new man?
One day humanity will love itself entirely like a single couple
although that is still a geological time away.

"Selfishness has still not withered away in Cuba"
Carlos Rafael told me in the Central Committee,
just the two of us, everything was white marble empty at that hour,
in the middle of the night. I was catching the plane at 1.
"For the workers it could be a television, for us a car."
And he said: "I don't know whether one day
                religion will wither away in the world
or won't wither away and we'll be defeated."
And me: "With the help of Christians it will wither away."
        Surrounded by white marble gleaming under the light.
Me meaning to say that Christianity is not a religion.
Circa 1972.

In the foetus we still have a tail.
        Still in a very primitive phase of our evolution.

But how do inanimate atoms in living beings
come to be animate? Scarcely
have we awoken from inert matter;
and inert matter takes us to its breast,
when we are sleepy, for example.
"The mind is, to a certain extent, inherent in each electron."
        A vague life there was first
        floating in the water,
and it learned to unite becoming a cell.
Life is association. The ease
of organisms to associate:
            the progress of life.
Our body's cells are communists.
And one day we will be a single cell.
            The thinking planet.
    Consciousness of the stars.
In all higher animal societies
there's an instinct for social discipline.
Wolves, pigeons, etc.
        whence the communism.
And democracy a physical law of the universe.
Or are we a game of draughts
played by blind chromosomes?
From one generation to another the transmission
of individual experience.
First imitation, then language, books,
communication of knowledge, inventions.
    The old to the young.
    And knowledge continued to grow.
Hardly 10,000 years
(there are trees from that age)
agriculture invented.
And until then and not before, violence.
When we function with the lower part of our brain
which is from the alligator.
The problem, how to escape from that part of our brain.
But, for example, there is no spirit of competition amongst Eskimos.

"Ecologists are fully aware that a system with many species
is more stable than one with few."
Impossible to love without hating. "Love your enemies..." but
hate enmity. His purpled Eminence the Cardinal
with his face of national guard who had dogs' faces
hates his enemies and loves enmity.
"Love hatred"
is not the precept.
The feeling of blame, remorse
is also Darwinian.
Selfishness is against nature. Nothing grows except with the others.
A flock of little sparrows is feeding in a meadow
when the falcon arrives,
and there is one who cries out first
laying itself open to be the first to fall to the falcon
but alerting the others.
For it's nothing but a biological law to restore the balance
the Revolution.
Balance because *they enrich* capital.
Work not paid for in the salary.
They enrich capital with surplus value.
An egalitarian distribution of calories.
The temptation of parasitism has always been there.
At every level in the advance of life there are parasites.
Yet parasitism is not an advance but a step backwards
to lower levels of organization.
Dependency is so pleasant that the parasite
feels no need to advance;
he advances
backwards.
And any modification on the part of whoever he depends on
kills him.

I have a niece who complains about the Revolution
because bras are extremely expensive.
I've no experience of having breasts
but I believe I could go around with breasts without needing a bra.

My friend Rafael Córdova lives close to the little town of Esquipulas
and he told me that before, many funerals passed along the road
        with very small coffins,
four, five, six, eight funerals
    every afternoon,
they were children's funerals,
        every afternoon.
The old don't die so much.
And a short while ago the grave-digger of Esquipulas called on him:
"Doctor, I've come to ask for a little something,
    I'm out of work.
    There are no more funerals in Esquipulas."
Before bras were not so expensive.
Now in Esquipulas there are hardly any funerals.
You tell me: Which is best?

Yesterday I went into a supermarket
            and I saw the empty shelves;
most of them empty; and I felt something of
the melancholy of the empty shelves,
    but more than that, joy
at the patent dignity of our people
                in the empty shelves.
These shelves once so well stocked
with every shade of essential or non-essential goods
or as they are in other countries. It's the price
we're paying, a small people fighting
the Colossus, and I see them crammed
with heroism, the empty shelves.
    The price of independence. And why there are
thousands of Sandino's cubs loose on the mountains.
And so just as those rows of colorful goods are missing
the lady on the pavement showing her wound is missing,
the child with eyes white as marble reaching out his hand.
    Children romp around in their barrios;
            the older ones, at ease.
And the police without rubber clubs on the streets

to hit the people,
nor tear gas bombs
nor water hoses nor anti-riot shields,
because of the empty shelves.
They are without goods
essential or otherwise, but full of sacrifice
and pride the empty shelves,
the pride, arrogance if you like, of a people:
the empty shelves.
It's not for sale nor surrender.
And I went away, regretful but cheered by the empty shelves.

An obstacle placed in an ant trail
may momentarily confuse the ants
but eventually they'll manage to find their way.

It so happens that we became man in society.
The mystery that animals that haven't seen themselves in mirrors,
for example fish,
and don't know what they're like,
frogs, iguanas,
recognize members of their species,
without mirrors they come together with their kind
(socialism, communism).
Life is nothing
but the organization of a structure.
And in society we became man.
We recognize human faces
because they are the same and different.
We'd recognize no one if they were only the same
or only different.
Liberty and order
—not "law and order"—.
Liberty with equality.
This is the life we have to nurture. Let's recall
Kandinsky vice-president of the Academy of Beaux Arts
Chagal director of the School of Painting in Vitebsk

futurist cubist constructivist times
Mayakovsky hoarse in the squares
Eisenstein in the cinema.
With Lenin dead it all came to a halt. Political crimes
because of the personal traits of Stalin.
Beria, who was enchanted by opera.
And the suffering of his victims caviar to him.
But looking now as though the October Revolution is returning.
And poets who have already sung
the New Havana descending from the heavens.
"Reconstituted" says St. Paul.
The reconstruction of our bodies you might say.
Biologically human
upon becoming psychologically one.
Ants pat each other with their antennae.
Behold the reign of the transnationals approaches its end.
And wars will be a thing of the past.
From the original gas to the new society.
And beyond.
Beyond the most distant radiogalaxies
with weak radio signals thousands of light years away,
where the universe's last light-waves peter out.
And could the universe have an edge?
It wouldn't be a limit of space but of time.
And beyond the limit there'd be nothing but deep darkness.
"The deep outer darkness."
Depart ye accursed of my Father.
Those eliminated from the consciousness of the universe.

Let's take something round like the earth:
the lines from a single point continue to diverge from each other
until reaching a certain equator after which
they begin to converge towards a single point.
Divergence and convergence.
Such is evolution.
An irreversible unification.

CANTIGA 20

The Music of the Spheres

In the beginning
God shaped the cosmic dust with his fingers.
So why do the galaxies revolve?
What set the universe on its spinning motion?
    "The basic fact of the universe is its expansion."
The most basic of life's realities
this expansion.
That's to say, the density of the universe decreases,
the galaxies draw further and further apart,
and light travels ever onwards.
A static universe is impossible
by the simple fact that the sky is black at night.
The entire night would shine like the surface of a star.
Each point in the sky would be a star and all of it
like the surface of the sun. But night is dark
and the universe neither infinite nor eternal.
Einstein had made an algebraic error,
                    overlooking a division by zero.
With this corrected, the universe ceased to be static
and glided into motion.

    The music of the spheres.
A harmonious universe like a harp.
Rhythm is equal beats repeated.
The beating of the heart.
Day/night.
The coming and going of birds of passage.
Cycle of stars and maize.
Mimosa which unfolds during the day
and at night folds back.

Rhythm of the moon and the tides.
And of crabs who know when the tide is going out
and before it goes out find their burrows.
A single rhythm in the planets, atoms, the sea, apples
that ripen and fall, and Newton's mind.
        Melody, chord, arpeggios.
                        The harp of the universe.
Unity
behind the apparent multiplicity
that's music.
        Difference between music and noise...
The sound of the bell lies in its shape.
Or incidentally, girls' legs.
            Matter is music.
Matter in perpetual motion in space and time.
Rhythmic hearts and stars.
The universe sings and Pythagoras heard it.
        The music of the spheres,
a music closer to jazz than to classical music.
            The disorderly dance of things.
All accomplished through the play of large numbers.
And between the harmony of the stars and that of atoms
        the anatomy of the human body.
With those proportions they must have built the temples
according to Vitruvius. Those of the human body.
            And the social order, like that of the sky.
            Also within us the *dance of the stars.*
            Observing the movement of the stars
            they perceived that there was order in the heavens
            and thus one day there could be order among men.
        The cosmos sings. But for whom?
Why is the blackbird so musical
when the mating season has passed?

Pythagoras discovered amid the pines of his island of Samos,
the harmonious pines,
that if the number is not exact in the string

the sound is discordant.
And the musical intervals in the string
were the same as the orbits in the heavens.
Furthermore salvation in another life.
His movement must have been revolutionary
since his followers were mainly slaves.
        The universe is music.
                The pulsations of the stars.
Even in the IV century Athanasius pursued the simile:
"...taking the universe into His hands as though it were a lyre."
Asteroids respond to the rhythms of the sun and the moon
the same as an oyster. They dance the same dance.
"Our interest in an atom
is because of its relation with the whole universe."
It is maintained that the universe is *isotropic*, that's to say:
the same in any direction
for whatever observer in whichever of the galaxies.
On a vast scale, naturally; in the galaxy, solar system or
Inter-American system we are not isotropic.
The Pima Indians say that they dreamed their songs.
A man withdrew in solitude to dream up a songline.
They also sing the song the Creator sang at the beginning of the world.
Electrons sing in choirs like seraphims, cherubims,
thrones and dominations, says physics professor Dr. Raymo.
Out of some elegant equations of Maxwell's
radio was born.

    Rhythm. All is rhythm.
The rhythm of the sun and the moon are the rhythm of life.
    Owls by night and doves by day.
    Flowers waken and then go to sleep.
    Cocks at dawn and frogs at dusk.
Annual rhythms in the breeding of animals,
the migration of birds and the flowering of plants
according to seasonal changes,
the length of the days and nights.
Lunar day and lunar month in the tides,

and the tide in the life of oysters.
    Lunar rhythm all along the coast.
At high tide mussels open to gorge themselves
and at low tide crabs rake over the beach.
The heron knows when the tide will go out
and abandons its nest to go down to the shore.
Palolos rise in their thousands from the depths
on the nights of the waning fourth quarter
October and November moons
to release upon the sea surface their semen at daybreak.
Women the same: their menstrual cycle is the synodic lunar month.
And oysters and crabs even adjust their lives to the tides
in laboratories thousands of miles from the sea.

In Solentiname I gaze at the moon through the mango's thinnest branches
and I think of the bluish ball of earth in the moon's sky.
        Let the heavens come to earth.
The cosmos as change.
Its structure is change.
    Ever-changing spider web of light.
Meditation as contact with the rhythms of the universe.
    Returning is the motion of the Tao.
    Going far means returning.
Now separated some from the others by spacetime.
        Your kingdom come.
With its 90% of matter that is invisible.
    To this out-of-the-way corner of the universe.
Matter, where you and I are...
        And the fact that all stars are in motion.
    The cosmos as change.
                The heavens.
It applies to us too
for whoever may be watching us in the starry night.
To believe that only we inhabit the galaxy
is to return to pre-Copernican concepts.
In the sky the natural movement is circular.
The curvature, according to Eddington, is not metaphysics,

nor of mathematical fantasy.
        Heat is movement. Merely
the energy of molecules in motion,
merely the movement of individual molecules.
And love, which is heat, is movement.
From the particle to the absolute, movement.
We never abandon the traditions even when we don't dance,
say those Amazonian Indians the Witoto,
because we work only to dance.
        Matter in formation had a music
and its echoes are the songs of the whales in the sea depths
or Beethoven's Quartets.

To Kepler in Upper Austria it was a motet:
Saturn and Jupiter the bass, Mars like the tenor,
the Earth and Venus the contralto, Mercury the baritone,
and on occasions the six could be heard in unison.
The celestial movements an unending song for several voices
(heard by the mind, not the ear)
music which with discordant tensions, with syncopations and cadences,
the same as man uses them imitating those natural discordances,
advances almost at six voices towards a contrived ending
in the immeasurable flow of time.
        The Thirty Years war had already begun.

From water, from invisible hydrogen and oxygen,
invisible life emerged
that created the blue atmosphere
and the greenness of the earth.
Due to life the green of the fields,
green come from the sun.
        Fields are green because they don't absorb green.
Just as the flash of a photographic camera
is sun. A flash of sun.
Beautiful is the earth seen from the air
especially where it meets with the water!
        Animals and plants, all

of us from the same microscopic ancestor.
We are notes from the same music.
A universe harmonious as a harp.
—The wings, the tail and the neck,
all of it moving rhythmically...—
The heart and the aorta have rhythm
the same as that of a musical instrument.
The Navajo cult: verses and songs.
Called *hatal*, "song."
As also they hunt with song.
Motionless in the woods they start to sing
and they are drawn towards them attracted by the rhythm...
To Mrs. Koestler-Ilg they said:
"The non-Araucanians stole our land
but they are not joined to it with their bare feet."
And to Le Roy, the African chief lowering his voice:
"There are more things about us
than those recorded in the white men's books"
(pointing out to Le Roy the firmament).
Symphony of the universe.
Creation is a song.
The creation which has yet to run its course.
In giant lenses the universe's past
is still gloriously present.
And though with brief lives, we live in the days of creation.
In spite of tragic entropy.
The tyranny of the second law of thermodynamics.
Perhaps another explosion will occur and the universe will be reborn.
At the beginning of time there was a "singularity."
A "singularity" is a physically impossible situation,
that is, impossible within our physical laws.
Or let's say that it's a mathematically incorrect function.
Where do we come from and where are we going?
From the Improbable to the Improbable.
The mystery of life is not how individual molecules
operate but how they cooperate.
An irrelevant quality at atomistic level.

You. Your body beats rhythmically, your molecules
undulate, your atoms vibrate,
within your atoms your particles dance.
And deeper within you is empty space
full of oscillating fields of energy.
From the void spring suns, flowers and girls.

In the street, by the gutter, I saw
a crumpled sheet of newspaper with
a photo, the photo of a face.
The hair, the head of hair rather, was
such that, at a glance,
I couldn't tell whether it was a man or a woman,
unisex style as they say nowadays.
But the curvature of that face,
like the curvature of space and of light,
curves of the eyes, arched eyebrows,
the double curling line of the lips,
the undulation of the cheeks and the chin, the
forehead sloping backwards, the nose
upwards, the ears spiralled,
oval of the entire face, his or hers,
around it the round halo of hair,
and the whole body, male or female,
must equally have been a wave of curves.
In his image and likeness. Whose?
The one we've never seen, since he is
beyond space, yet in everything we see
the circles of his fingerprints
(sun planet petal fruit fish snail).
Pure male, or pure female Spirit: also
pure curvature? Pure spiritual curvature?
"Nothing natural is made in a straight line."
The wind swept away that newspaper,
paper made of waste, itself now waste
to be recycled again into new paper.

Atoms are empty.
From the hydrogen atom to man.
But it is not a chance meeting of atoms.
Matter:
form of the spirit.
A non-random ordering of atoms and photons.
Or as if matter were made of spirit.
"Physicists speak of subatomic particles as though they had
an objective reality."
Matter always in motion.
And it never rests.
If atoms were immutable, there would merely be
a dead universe.
Nothing is or is not, all things in the process of being.
And what's real?
Is jealousy real?
Love is real.

The bodies of gaseous spheres that we call *stars*
held together and lit up by their own gravity.
Their light is nakedness says Rubén,
he who brought harmony from the sacred forest.
Suppose reader that we wished to see star HD193182.
The star could not see its beauty
except through us.
We are the star seeing itself; that sees
its own self.
Born in the fire of it
and cooled down so as to be able to think and see.
Protons, neutrons and electrons
are the human body, the planet and the stars.
Consciousness emerged from the unconscious.
So in us the planet loves, dreams.
It is the Earth that sings this *Cosmic Canticle* in me.

The music of the spheres.
"The spheres are not the planets but electrons and atomic nuclei

and the music is not of sound but of light."
$$E=mc^2$$
Photons—particles of light—.
The ether's violins Alfonso mentioned pulsate their clarity.
"If our eyes were more perfect they would see the atoms singing."
They say the proton resembles a Bach fugue.

Now they are on an Oklahoma reservation.
But they came from the stars they say.
Once they were pure and beautiful because they came from the sky.
All were then *Tzi-Sho* (the tribe from the sky).
Why they came down from the sky is not known.
It's never mentioned in their myths.
Did Wahkon-Tah expel them?
They had led an orderly life in the sky, they know,
because they were living among the stars,
and upon the earth they only had *ga-ni-tha* (chaos).
Buffalo, eagle, bear, pelican, beaver
had no names. They gave them names.
It was the first thing they did.
The elders, however, began to find signs of Wahkon-Tah
in them, and in everything that surrounded them.
They began to draw apart for periods from the village noise,
and thus they became wise men. They organized
the form of government according to what they had known in the stars.
Order in the buffalo hunt.
Open out in huge circles on the prairie
and begin at a given signal.
Their songs and dances in accordance with the order of the stars,
and a language for communicating with Wahkon-Tah,
he answering in the flight of the sparrow hawk,
the whistle of the owl, the coyote song,
this they told for the benefit of pale-face writing to Mr. Mathews
by then no longer on the beaming river Osage
but on the reservation,
by then as for the animals, only their names.
At astronomical distances from the stars.

The oak on the hillside full of acorns and bees
and the sheep laden with wool
because of just judgments...
Just as the bad time for Alaskan Eyaks
is for crimes...
"If our heart is good when we dance
then it rains"
        (a Pueblo Indian in the dusty village of San Ildefonso).
Likewise the laws known to the Hopi:
an untroubled heart
and compliance with the rules
maintains the order of the stars, the rains, the crops.
What an individual does affects the whole tribe
and the cosmos.
Pacifists, Gandhians for 2,000 years,
they've never signed a treaty with the United States,
nor declared war on anyone, not even on the United States.
                Political, moral and cosmic harmony:
Yin and *Yang* for the Prime Minister too.
The four seasons pass in order
when the right thing is done in everything.
Confucius awaited the coming of the wise men.
(From the west.)
                        And because of good actions
                                the sun and the moon will keep their times.

CANTIGA 21

Robber Barons

And coming down (or up) to earth again:

Pirates and traders in Negroes were already gathering
on the corner of Wall and Water Street in the XVIII.
In 1790 financiers already displayed, they say,
"a serene indifference in the face of public calamity"
time-honored since then on Wall Street.
In the XIX the destiny of Nicaragua was already being gambled
in a place called Merchant's Exchange
between Wall and William Street.
Days of terror and others of calm,
unpredictable like the sea, Wall Street.
"They didn't drink or gamble or go to brothels,
they spent their nights calculating and poring over ledgers
while others drank, and laughed, and danced..."
(THE ROBBER BARONS)
After the war with Mexico
an orgy of speculations.
Those railroad owners never went to jail.
The divine right of millionaires.
Like birds of prey in the galleries of Congress.
Railroad concessions
meant free chunks of land the size of kingdoms
with timber coal copper iron gold oil silver
and the future cities.
So Huntington stopped selling time-pieces.
Cold distrustful vindictive sarcastic hypocritical ruthless.
"I've paid out a fortune to get these laws passed"
writes Huntington
ordering the letter to be burnt.

They'd turn up at a small town saying: if you pay so much
the train will pass through here, if not
through somewhere else.
If not, they killed off the town.
The train would pass three miles from there.
Worse than it not passing at all
was to be three miles from the train.
The skeletons alongside Huntington's Union Pacific tracks...
"A change akin to that of the religious experience
called conversion."
Carnegie's
when for the first time (in London) he saw steel.
The iron age is over, he bellowed.
Visions of the gleaming metal crisscrossing the United States
and he the absolute king of that metal.
That shy Carnegie, "fearful of progress."
Cautious. He loathed adventure and being a pioneer.
(There's no money in being a pioneer.)
His profits: opposing the historical process.
Resisting progress. Holding it back.
Lowering production. Crushing businesses.
Bankrupting companies.
Rejecting advances proposed by technicians, experts, inventors,
workers.
"He's lost nothing but his honor"
said Gould.
The Mephistopheles of Wall Street. He had agents
and not friends. "Closest thing to a vulture in any man
I've ever known."
He'd scour the country like a vulture
seeking out bankrupt railroads.
Nothing in life interested him
except dividends.
Daniel Drew "the Sphinx of the Exchange,"
"he always thought the worst of men, same as Vanderbilt."
Whenever he wiped someone out he'd find peace
in the divine office.

It was said he wouldn't hesitate to sacrifice a friend
yet that he was "genuinely God-fearing."
A mystery to people, like Vanderbilt,
on account of his sharp and shady speculations.
"Can't I do as I please with my money?"
asked Vanderbilt.
—He owned New York, the Exchange, the highways and the railroads
and the bulk of the ships—
He never lost a day's interest
on the smallest amount of money.
The works of art which Vanderbilt bought:
"money well invested"
because paintings increase in value with time
especially after the artist's death.
Armour, the butcher, naturally became a millionaire
during the Civil War. Peddling pork to armies he became a millionaire.
Cook retired to his Philadelphia castle with its
theaters, fountains, conservatories, Italian gardens.
As for Morgan, (Pierpont Morgan) not the pirate, Providence dealt him
the good fortune to trade arms in a War. Hence
his trip to the church to sing hymns.
The secret of his success was, so they said,
being free of the encumbrance of moral scruples.
He was able to perform that miracle by which
"an upright man can turn paper into gold"
(and gold into paintings, manuscripts, antiques).
And he whose early days were marked by prudence and self-restraint.
In the blue money-box every cent he earned.
Already as a child he began to lend (at 7%)
and would give 10 cents to the Cleveland Baptist Church.
He had no time for relaxation or friends.
Devout,
he began to grow rich with the Civil War.
His chaste accountant's soul
feared none but God
(neither judges, senators, competitors,
nor the press, nor the general public).

"The most reviled man of his day."
The one who dodged every regulation.
Rockefeller's eyes were awesome.
He threw himself into the oil business with evangelical fervor.
He never slept at night, scheming, calculating.
His soft voice. His soft footsteps. But with a ferocious passion
which was money,
but stony-faced as he took it.
Like Carnegie, he detested being a pioneer.
Advising moderation, no gambling, no drinking, saving.
"Silence is golden" he used to say,
and in silence he crushed all his competitors.
Fraud, murder, terror, bankruptcies.
In 1882 his company
was turned into 40 companies:
Standard Oil.
And so his millions grew as did the lines on his face.
By then an old man, he said at a dinner: "I discovered a new world
though at the time I didn't know it."
(The monopoly was the new world)
He created the mother of Trusts, Standard Oil,
an empire as vast as the British.
In its wake came all the other Trusts
(whisky, steel, sugar, meat, iron, coal, copper).
The means of production in "socially concentrated forms."
Or "centralization"
(monopolies).
Forcing the others to draw less from the wells.
Standard Oil machine operators
belonged to Standard Oil
like the machines. As powerless to seek a wage rise
as the machines.
"God gave me *my* money" he would say.
Like a shark's his mouth lipless.
Carnegie's vision was
in that London conversion of his
the thousands of shimmering tons of steel rails

throughout the United States.
Everything came easy to those people.
The interweaving of railway lines.
Bringing railways together,they brought industries and businesses together,
and railway networks, which were networks of industries and businesses,
networks and more networks,
and so one person owner of everything,
and as a result still more owner of everything.
Buying and selling:
capital, industries, men and raw materials.
They went on to become patrons of the arts, benefactors of churches,
owners of newspapers and of politicians.
Their businesses well-structured and smooth-running
but behaving on the Exchange with bacchic frenzy.
Nativities purchased like shares and bonds.
And the Rembrandts going up in price like the railroads.

CANTIGA 22

In An Unexceptional Galaxy

In the beginning
when the expansion that is still with us began...
    First there was Chaos according to Hesiod.
The sudden appearance of matter and space
exploding out of nothing.
        How did things start to emerge from nothing?
If galaxies fill the whole of space, how do they expand?
    Unless it is space that is expanding;
    simply the scale of all distances.
And the start of expansion is the creation of the universe.
        "The closest thing to the act of creation
        that science has discovered."
Nothing physical could occur before the start of expansion
which satisfies the requirements of an act of creation.
    Before the expansion not only was there no matter
    but neither time nor space.
If something happened "before," it was before there was before.
    But a Mechanism separated matter from anti-matter.
"The quantum leap from nothing to time"
Coleman mentions.
Agreed: creation may be explained without the need of a creator.
But maybe
the universe started to be when the creator ceased participating
(the supposedly atheistic hypothesis of Atkins).

        The timeless photon.
Almost all the universe is empty space.
"Possibly the most conspicuous of its characteristics is its emptiness."
    There's also the metaphor that chaos is order.
And the possibility of black holes within black holes within

black holes.
And the arrival at your destination before you've set out.
And the fact that anti-matter is matter oriented backwards in time.
                Newton discarded.
        And the whole of Einstein continues to be supposition.
The "universe" after all, is a hypothesis, says de Sitter.
(And if the "universe" is merely a part of the Universe?)
The question of how many sub-atomic particles there are in the universe
can be answered.
But there are questions that would require a new mathematics
to be answered.
And other questions that would require new theories
for phenomena outside the ambit of existing theories.
New laws of nature that could be waiting to be discovered.
"There's still something missing in physical theory
and physicists don't know what it is."

        Scientists searching now for the *real* reality.
"The laws of quantum theory are not about particles
but about our knowledge of particles."
Nature has a sense of humor and is pulling our leg.
We don't see light, merely its effects on eye molecules.
        And light and matter have become muddled to us,
                particle/wave
or Schrödinger's theory
what do I know about that equation
and the theory that the entire universe is merely one bubble
(never mind if you don't like it)
in an infinite foam of universes.
The so-called Treiman theorem.
                —Sam Treiman of Princeton University—:
"Impossible things usually don't happen."
Einstein was horrified by that balance in modern physics
between genius and madness.

And to gaze at that above which is all emptiness. Emptiness, that's to say all silence.

Where supernovas explode
in total silence.
Meteors fall silently on the moon,
opening huge craters
in silence.
That stormy brilliant river above us
of stars, dust, gas
                    (The Milky Way)
which is silent. And furthermore
    the greater part of its mass is invisible.
The non-brilliant Milky Way:
        like saying in the realm of dreams.
"What's typical of our universe is black empty space."
And if the center of our universe is a black hole...
round one hundred million suns sinking together
into a circle as small as the size of the earth,
or a tennis ball, or a grain of sand, or less.
Is it for you in your practical life an absurd universe?
Is there someone beyond the silent void
who listens to the faint cough in a child's throat in the night?

        We cannot speak of where.
There is no cosmic limit and therefore
there's no cosmic center.
    We're in a world without center or border.
"The world's center is there where the world is thought."
    Here where the earth's crust trapped the light
    and out of it made life, and life that would multiply
    and then think.
We are on a planet which is full of questions.
Such as why the distribution of galaxies on a grand scale
is so uniform.
Such as why there are galaxies more millions of light years away
than the age of the universe, without ever having reached there
moving at a greater speed than the speed of light
to an observer,
        without them even having had to move.

All this on account of the curvature of spacetime.
And that the real world is not of particles and waves
but observation of it.
"The word 'quantum' refers to the aspect of nature
which goes against commonsense."
The same as what Feynman has said, that
you had to discard commonsense to understand the atom.
Where do the stars go which sink into themselves?
Before we never knew we were travelling in a space ship.
Or are we merely a disposable planet?

Quasars billions of light years away from us,
separated by billions of years of time.
Perhaps the size of our solar system
and brighter than a hundred billion suns,
brighter than galaxies.
To the extent that there are astronomers who refuse to accept it,
and it's still not known what they are.
Whether chains of exploding supernovas
or nuclei of runaway galaxies heading towards black holes,
towards unfathomable centers of permanent darkness.

The child swimming in calm waters
as in a state of imponderability.
And suddenly in a totally different medium.
Helpless now in the face of earthly gravitation
he tumbles from one side to another.
And beneath the cascade of noises and colors.
Already in the dark he heard a melody
the beat of the maternal heart.
Could already distinguish between tranquil
and restless rhythm. (Four-month foetus
he was smiling or screwing up his tiny face.)
Now he has entered a vaster rhythm:
time.
He has been born to time. But he was born knowing how to make sounds.
The scream. And to understand sounds made to him in his mother's arms:

"All is well, the world is good."

Let's suppose there are several million civilizations
at this moment in the galaxy.
If we are not alone in the universe we must be the youngest.
        The rest, superior beings.
                Could they be transmitting?
But how to tune in to the right star?
We could be surrounded by extra-terrestrial messages
without the adequate tuner. (Like when we were on the brink
of discovering language.)
Planets with their days in light, from their homely star
and their nights of infinite distant stars,
we among them.
Will our minds understand one another?
Our machines and theirs?
It seems it's inevitable that there be stars and intelligence.
Why shouldn't there be other heavens and other earths? thought Teng Mu.
Perhaps from there they might tell us of the new society.
...It would be to believe that the solar system solely existed
so that they could look at it from other places,
tiny, in their most distant starry nights
and nothing more.
Night and day the stars shine, day and night,
by day we don't see them.
The universe is all night, with stars,
night and day only night.
In the interstellar spaces only light or deep darkness without twilight.

Light lights up nothing without an organ gazing on it.

        "For example, let's consider the universe
        a few million years after..."
Or at the time it was the size of a grapefruit.
            The temperature at the moment of creation.
Hydrogen began to form small clusters...
To be able to gaze on worlds in the present and in the past!

Alfonso's equations:
distance=silence
vision=sound
(Equations in poems by Alfonso Cortés).
The universe is not bound by space
but space by the universe.
There is space as far as there is matter,
a space without matter wouldn't be space.
In a universe expanding like a football
without center of expansion or center of the universe.
Of course the expansion of the universe is that of space itself,
it's not that the galaxies scatter like frightened pigeons.
The flowing on and on of time in the expansion of the universe
is the shift from the state of hotter to colder. However,
the equations of relativity, it's said,
permit a way back in time's journey.
The present depends on the past. And the future on the present.
Did the past equally depend on the future?
Without future there's no time. And without time there's no beginning.
There is no experiment for the physical passage of time.
Late and early are relative.
Just as relativity rendered distance meaningless.
The concept of space and time
is subject to new changes.
For example, possibilities of travelling to other spacetimes.
The principle is maintained
that the universe is a region of spacetime
which dwells in the future.

The Persian sufi Al-Sufi gazed from the turret or minaret
into the pearl-sown sky
like a nebulous shock of camel hair
vaporous, blurred
more than 2 million light years away,
"tenuous like a night candle through a sullied glass"
thus Andromeda appeared in a telescope for the first time in 1611.
100,000 million galaxies can be seen through telescopes now.

Structures that have existed from the dawnings of cosmology.
Through materials of the earth we have gazed at the heavens.
Raising up eyes into the nocturnal sky
to lights which emerged before *Homo sapiens* existed.
And radiations generated when there was no Milky Way.
We see it as it was, and not as it is.
Astrophysicists are archaeologists of most ancient radiations.
From a wheelchair the entire universe.
Hawking, deformed, in a wheelchair because of amyotrophy
able to move merely a few fingers imperceptibly
to speak through a computer with a metallic voice,
the expert on black holes, determined to read, he says,
God's thought, searching for Grand Unification,
until such time as all physics is explained, the origin of the universe,
its workings, its end, and there are no more Physics Nobels.

There are numbers in the universe which cannot be written
except with a universe of zeros.
In spite of everything *you* are important, you, molecular structures
on a middling planet of a common or garden star
in a suburb of an average galaxy.
We are self-conscious spacetime.
We are the explanation of the Cosmos according to Hawking.
We are the mid-point between atoms and the stars
and between the mini-particle and the observed universe.
—The decidedly strange form of the human body—.

Midnight in Solentiname,
and I gaze at the stars from the window by my bed.
Our galaxy 100 light years in diameter
and more than 400 million stars.
They thought that it was wheat scattered by Isis.
And the Bushmen: the embers of campfires.
And our telescopes detect galaxies
thousands of millions of light years away.

Billions and billions of galaxies and baby galaxies.

Lights as old as the universe.
We see galaxies heading away said Eddington
like someone who sees an airplane go by, not knowing where it's bound.
A bit of black has greater intensity than the whole night.
In this patch of night in my window
how many planets are there without life
and how many with life, flying by?
What will our brothers' anatomy be like
their biochemistry, their music?
Sagan calculates around a million technical civilizations
alone in our galaxy.
Reagan was chopping wood on Sky Ranch.
And he had a brainstorm
Recalling the film *Star Wars* directed by George Lucas.
He had been worried by the squabbling between bishops and missiles.
The advances of the peace movement.
He'd already caused quite a scare with the "open window" business:
in the skies of the USA, a gaping hole left by Carter
through which the entire Soviet arsenal could enter.
(It had yet to occur to him to inspire fear with the imminence
of the invasion of the Nicaraguan hordes.)
He had the flash of insight and flew to Washington.
And he gave a speech very beautiful in parts
and it's thought some of them written by him.
"The balance of terror is immoral"
(with which he wrested the crosier from the bishops
and the placards from the pacifists).
"Better to save lives than to avenge them"
Star Wars is for peace said Reagan.
It's just to destroy the missiles before they reach the ground. Thus
to make nuclear weapons obsolete from the sky.
It would fill the children of the XXI century with millenary happiness.
Pax Americana.
Nostalgia for those golden years and happy days
when only they had the Bomb.
(Now the innocent missiles were pathetically
defenceless in their silos.)

Thus the screen-man declaimed on television.
Words with hot-dog simplicity.
American as the corn of apple pie
Pie in the sky!
Pentagon and State Department stammered.
NASA blamed the films of his younger days.
NATO next day leapt alarmed from its bed.
Was MAD over (Mutually Assured Destruction)?
The balance of terror had Biblical authority.
No longer any war on earth but in the uncertain sky?
Wasn't *Star Wars* just a film?
This was riding into space firing into the air
John Wayne (or Reagan) style.
Without thinking how easy it is in space
to blind infra-red sensors and deafen radars.
And the difficulty of ionizing hundreds of kilometers of sky
to conceal a vehicle for 3 minutes.
As well as submarines so huge
the ocean would scarcely be deep enough to hide them.
Without mattering to him that the whole world together could not pay
that astronomical cost
Reagan flew back again to chop wood on his Sky Ranch.

The larger the ball of gas,
or rather the pressure inwards,
the hotter its center.
The stars, and on their fringes the planets.
A universe that exists as though to be observed by us.
The mystery of why a world ideal for life appeared
with Big Bang.
Darwin thought:
The beginning of life had to be part of a general law.
We have measured the universe or at least we have calculated its age.
If the solar system were the size of an olive
our galaxy would be the size of the earth
and Andromeda would be as far away as the moon.
The distances so great because time is so long.

And because the stars separated so much
our existence was possible.
Apparently immutable in the night sky,
they change,
                    some no longer exist.
Astronomically ephemeral like human life.
To ancient supernovas we owe life
since through them we have flesh with heavy elements.
So many stars have died so that we might live!
They are born of gas and dust
and in the end they will sink into the night their gas exhausted.
Ephemeral as flowers and as human life.
In a boat in Solentiname while it was growing dark,
from blue to black, the first stars,
and soon after really full of stars.
Without the shore now. Bobbing up and down,
                    only the galaxy above us.
Did you see that light? No, which?
        Yes, and that other one?
Same as the ones above, but level with the waves:
appearing and disappearing, solitary, scintillating,
Don Patricio's tiny light, lights of the Obandos,
            of Doña Saba, of "Moustache"...
Life and consciousness are properties of the stars.
Macrocosm and microcosm are inseparable units.
The whole sustains the parts which in turn are the whole.
Cosmic and atomic are the same.
A unity exists in the universe which goes beyond its uniformity,
                the unity that without everything nothing can exist.
Matter which is particle and wave.
And particle and wave are you and I.
Waves like those of the ocean, those of sound, those of light,
waves come from where and going where?
How life emerged from inorganic matter.
The boundary between matter and life is confused,
and even life is confused.
We are not life in the cosmos but living self-knowing cosmos.

And if it is to end,
                    what lies behind it?
There must be a boundary. But I ask
what might the boundary of the universe be like?
            And what might not lie beyond the boundary!
Looking further out in telescopes
we gaze further back into the past.
And already we are a most distant past
in telescopes which on most distant galaxies are gazing at us.
"Mathematics may scorn small magnitudes
but not the infinitely large, or the infinite."
            And truly we have an instinct for infinity.
"No mathematically valid means of eliminating infinities exists."
(Although there are theoreticians who eliminate infinities from equations
dividing an infinity by another infinity.
With which you can get any result.)
A hundred thousand million galaxies in the observable universe
with roughly a hundred thousand million stars each.
            Not to mention non-observable universes.
The galaxies rotating, gigantic girandoles.
Unimaginably enormous
on a cosmic scale the galaxies are insignificantly small
and groups of galaxies are the atoms of cosmology.
"How God made it," said Einstein.
"To know his thoughts. The rest is details."
            And human life of middling rank in the universe:
we are to an atom what a star is to us.
"Don't write about something so remote as the Galaxy"
Silvia says to me.
                    And me: "But we're in it."

CANTIGA 23

Room 5600

Returning to earth dwellers:

They had a happy childhood on the banks of the Hudson
on a 3,500 acre property
            with 11 mansions and 8 swimming pools
      and 1,500 servants
            and a huge house of toys
but once grown up they moved in to occupy "Room 5600"
(in fact floors 55 and 56 of the highest skyscraper
in the Rockefeller Center)
where hundreds and hundreds of foundations and businesses
are managed
            —as in reality is the case—
      as single *fortune.*
Dependent on Room 5600—the millionaires in Venezuela
private enterprise in Brazil
      and you and I.
First came the ads in Latin American newspapers and radio
emanating from Room 5600
   ("a formative education for the young Rockefellers
in the vulnerabilities of the press")
every program with the press divided into 2 categories
      "economic warfare" and "psychological warfare"
doing with the news, Nelson explained to the Senate,
the same as is done militarily.
And Room 5600 has undercover "observers"
      (like the first spawning of the present CIA)
informing on the proprietors, editorial line,
personal opinions...down to the lowliest reporter,

from which emerged its "propaganda analysis" dossiers
systematically organized on Latin American public opinion.
Thus in Room 5600
they learnt the rudiments
of news manipulation.
"They soon discovered that *news*
isn't born of facts
but of group interests." And so it was that
Latin American news (edited in Washington)
    with economic incentives and economic pressures
reached Latin America from Room 5600
together with canned editorials, telephotos, flashes, "exclusives,"
cartoon strips
    (and Walt Disney for the cinema)
until 80% of the world news for Latin America
(originating in Washington)
was strictly controlled and monitored in New York
by Room 5600,
and thus all the businesses of Latin America
(and its misery)
        had to do with that Room 5600.
An operation which only required sufficient funds
from Room 5600.
        The mind, the passions.
What the landlady of a rooming-house thinks.
    The stroller along the deserted beach.
A silhouette of lovers kissing beneath the moon
(Room 5600's influence greater than the moon's)
The opinions of Octavio Paz or Pablo Antonio Cuadra.
Whether you say rose or you say Russia
    Room 5600 influences that.
        Perceptions conditioned by Room 5600.
And thousands of Latin American journalists
invited by Room 5600
to Miami Beach where it's all fake, even the sea's fake,
a servile sea out in front of the hotel.
So that

NICARAGUA TOTALITARIAN COUNTRY
SANDINISTAS PERSECUTE THE CHURCH
MISKITOS MASSACRED
TERRORISTS...
That's why, Yankee journalists, "La Prensa" is censored.
Monopoly over what the public reads, hears, sees,
as they saturate the air with carbon monoxide, mercury, lead.
As for the press:
"Silence was imposed on the poor"
This from Nelson. From David, the younger one,
the Chase Manhattan Bank
—"tied in to almost every major business in the world"—
in the same Room 5600
where the whole of the huge dispersed fortune
is only one, in a single Room.
With as many public relations people in Room 5600
as they had servants in their childhood.
Their criminal image thus transformed into one of philanthropists.
About whom it was said they did
everything, as with oil, to Yankee politics,
except refine it.
Corporations growing carcinoma-like.
And thanks to Room 5600
the holy family dumped in trash heaps.
Children playing next to streams of shit
on account of their monopolies.
Their monopolies growing fat on malnutrition.
Monopolies making the planet more expensive,
bread and wine,
happiness, medicine, *The Divine Comedy*.
Manhattan seen from the sea like a holy mountain
and as though celestial the skyscrapers erected by usury
in one of which:
Room 5600, its Luciferian lights.
The gleaming waters of Lake Erie without fish
because of its sewers, those of Room 5600.
Ducks coated in oil.

Toxic wind over deserts and dead rivers.
Contaminating the species with radioactive iodine
                                        Room 5600.
Chocolates or napalm, they manufacture them both.
And manufacture *facts.*
At dusk you look out from the car, over the sulphurous swamps
the tremulous fires of the oil refineries like Purgatory
and above them like a city of Oz
the glass skyscrapers lit up
    Wall Street and Rockefeller Center
with its Room 5600.
Every secretary of state since Dean Acheson
    that means since I was 25
has worked for a Rockefeller organization.
        —Do you remember those new companies
        lusted after on the Exchange like nubile maidens?
Their orgies with voluptuous and smiling surplus-values
in Room 5600.
        —Does Rembrandt pay dividends?
And the dividends from the Vietnam war.
    ESSO profits reaching stratospheric heights.
1 gallon of gasoline which cost the planet to produce it
1 million dollars...
    And Venezuela selling its oil for trinkets.
    12 year-old girls on sale in the North-East.
                The acidic yucca flour.
            Sterilization of women in the Amazon.
Monopoly even on life.
The millions flowing back to them as though through oil-pipes
    owners of land banks industries human beings
as though through oil-pipes from where the fields are enormous
and the leases minimal.
They flooded New York with "moral bonds"
    (that's to say fictitious)
Hence the bankruptcy of New York
on account of the millions in Room 5600's "moral bonds."
Terrorizing entire peoples with ferocious stories.

Its vampiresque shadow over culture, academies.
The whole weight of the printing presses over us.
Subjected to the whims of its limited companies.
That's why, Daniel Berrigan, the Nicaraguan young are fighting.
Be it milk or poison
never mind the product
bread or napalm
never mind the product.
David, for example, lunched with a Mr. Carter on Wall Street
and once lunch was over
chose him as President of the United States.
They continued their happy childhood
in Room 5600.

CANTIGA 24

Latin American Documentary

That the Chaco War was between Esso and Shell (Galeano)
    you should know this.
Or the millions of Paraguayans killed by Rockefeller
    you should know this.
Paraguay: "there's not a child who cannot read and write"
that was in 1845.
            (It's in Galeano.)
The balance of payments with a large surplus
also in 1845.
Later Carleton Beals couldn't find a painter, a poet.
All abroad.
        Nor books.
Like the exile in the VIth century before our era.
Now throughout Europe it's the diaspora.
There economists and sociologists
roam the streets aimlessly.
Once more like the great pilgrimages to the Land without Evil
—through the rainforests, seeking to cross the ocean,
    in the direction of daybreak—
free of death, of mosquitoes, of foreigners;
fertile lands to cultivate freely;
        free of vast estates.
They settled for staying in their huts by the sea...
    In the small square the men with their timbrels,
    the women with their bamboo pipes.

The manuscripts of Fray Bartolomé de las Casas
property of the Creole Company of Caracas
        ("while the Indians last...")
once kept in the convent of St. Philip Neri.

"If Your Majesty were not to remove them from the Spanish
without doubt all shall perish in few days."
The following day the shares of Anaconda rose
(fell by half when Allende took office).
Scientific knowledge of reality is necessary to the prophet.
And barbarism can strike suddenly like a bolt from the blue.
A fat man shouting in the street "We won-on-on-on-on!"
shambling like a fat man, fingers in V
euphoric over the military coup
and the military shoot him from a truck.
ITT was cabling frantically from Santiago
requesting economic chaos in Chile.
Never a more meticulous massacre.
"But though they cut down all the flowers
spring will return" (imprisoned priest).
Or how the Army took the decision to murder the Guatemalans.
The U.S. embassy suggested it be done out of uniform.
"...and that was the last he was heard of..."
(evening paper)

First the big party, and they were laughing,
they looked at themselves in mirrors and laughed,
painted, feathered, with tooth and shell necklaces
and following the drunken orgy on *cachaça,* the massacre.
THE OPEN VEINS OF LATIN AMERICA
Clothes infested with epidemics.
For the children cholera-laced sweets.
And when his Eminence the Cardinal left
his hour-long meeting with the Justice Minister
asked by reporters if he touched on the Mato Grosso genocide
he replied: "We had it in mind to talk of that affair
but we forgot about it."
Flee from the mountains they must
countless hordes in hiding there...
They ceased to be slaves without becoming free.
Now they dance the *Dance of the Conquest,*
monotonous dance, monotonous,

melodies based on Spanish melodic models,
monotonous *Dance of the Conquest*,
and if the sound of the flageolets is so sad
        (the melancholic music of the flageolets)
it's because they are not theirs, they are
defective instruments which were imposed on them.
    Also some time back Perilla wrote to me
    that in Los Llanos he uncovered a terrible secret:
    tiger hunters who at times went hunting
    for non-animals.
(Also right there in Colombia:
        "absolved by the defence argument
        that they didn't know killing Indians was a crime".)
In Brazil in ten years they stole
82 million dollars from the Indians.

"*O Globo*" also in favour of blood exports.
And there in Haiti
the legislative chamber, the Church, the judiciary
sided with terror.
    Jubilant Te Deums for Baby Doc
TE DEUM LAUDAMUS
        "during the present state of siege"
(Guatemala once again)
—that the poor should not mill around the tourist zones—
        "...negative image of the country..."
    But bombs raining down on the Petén.
And the Cardinal Archbishop of Guatemala
with feudal mitre and beneath oligarchic pallium
in most solemn procession trampling over the oppressed.
The oppressed, and a carpet of flowers and colored sawdust.
She who wheels around her two handicapped sons in a small cart.
The TB sufferer living under the rusty remains of a car.
It's enough to ask: Who makes the laws in Guatemala?
    The majority of Latin American bishops
    professing the Monophysitic heresy
        (without wishing to offend the Armenians).

Just as the Cuban Catholic Church had fallen into the old heresy
of Docetism.

And Argentina
    news that in the Argentinian night the press hushes up:
Cacho's in jail, they arrested him the following week at
        I'm telling you what we know from Coca
        at two in the morning they rang the bell.
            Poor neighborhood under moon-silver
            distant sound of *milonga*
And Cardinal Daniélou in the banquet
to the 400 Argentinian officers did not say:
    "Don't harm anybody, nor bring false accusations
    and be content with your pay"
A good priest yet he yielded to the temptation of idealism.
    Led to a red car, the whole neighborhood saw it.
    That was the last time his wife saw him alive.
            My neighborhood, my neighborhood
            how unsettled is your soul
            like a pining sparrow.
Lights of these cities like the firmament braided with stars
        laughing lights: Rio...Mexico City...
And all around a cordon of tears
/shanties chabolas jacales favellas villas miseria cantegriles/
Cod goes off in Sao Paulo and they add creolian
so that the poor won't retrieve it from the refuse
and Carolina María de Jesús in a notebook
which she fished from the refuse, wrote
that her father told her I'll give you 100 *cruceiros* for your cunt
and she gave it to him and he only gave her fifty.
The girl tore up the money.
        —Señor Montero, forgive me but you told me
        that we were going filming.
            Through the rain the letters: MOTEL
        —Señor Montero, I don't want. You told me
Four months later I found out I was expecting.

Obese general like a ball of cheese in limousine with pretty girl
Paraguay again
and the prisons bursting, 300 thousand in exile
and almost half the land
property of 25 people
exactly.
    But the landowners' land-grabbing law
    Allende dusted off to grab back from the big landowners.
    —In a dusty folder kept by an old one-eyed man.
    It was frightening notaries with cut lilies.
That mine in Lota which I visited,
the owners once had a castle in that mine
and Versaillesque parties
and under the castle at 1,000 meters below sea-level,
beneath the parties, in the coal
their miners sweated black sweat.
And the textile factory that at the official exchange rate
imported machinery (looms) from Paris
from one of their own firms
which sent unusable machines, no longer working,
hundreds of looms that would never weave any thread
the dollars remaining in Santiago on the black market,
and I lunched there with the proud workers, now nationalized,
kissed babies in their creche,
and there Pinochet later killed so many workers,
the workers of SUMAC hanging from trees.

    "Trees of such beauty..."
        (Vespucci to Lorenzo de Medicis)
That it felt like being in the Earthly Paradise.
    Oh the chateau tropical amid coffee groves,
the woman on a divan, tired
from doing nothing, the black nanny
whisking the chocolate...
Hunger another of its traditions.
And in Port-au-Prince presidential palace
out of a musical comedy.

Close to which, coconut palms, blue-turquoise smelling of salt,
the picturesque thatched hut, and in the doorway
the child with elephantiasis.
    Exactly like an elephant's leg.

What are you going to tell me, che, it's the System.
They pay their newsmen and their gangsters.
    Propaganda and torture.
The people flattened as though by bulldozer.
    Shining blood on the asphalt.
And that reporter told me
"We have orders to print any news against Allende
and to suppress any news favorable to Allende"
    the boy on Costa Rica's "La Nación"
This is "La Nación." And the nation.
Monseigneur Pimiento, President of the Bishops' Conference
        (which? it's all the same)
gave his backing to the State of Siege.
Children knocked down by firemen's hoses.
The sick student under their cudgels.
                His collar bone.
Boot upon pregnant belly.
        The stench of the Buenos Aires slums
        rising up to the Lord of the Hosts.
Or again in Brazil
            wire on my testicles
revived with ammonia to that horror
for aspiring to a world of love and union.
        Electrodes.
Electrodes for all.
He sold all the islands, banks, rocks, territorial waters.
And so, the Haitians exiled without leaving the country.
        Zombified church.
Interrogations in the National Palace
and thrown into sulfuric acid in the President's presence.
With the result
"at the least whisper of wind in the trees their conversations freeze."

All the shares in the Haiti National Bank
bought up by the National City Bank. So
        (words of the Adviser to the Treasury)
        "Haiti lends money to Wall Street."
So it's also been said:
    If Haitians didn't sell their blood
        what would they sell?
Duvalier junior inspects the troops dressed as a panther.
In a panther or leopard uniform
        yet the beast's face is more human.
Who demonstrated in effect he had no political prisoners
having earlier to that end killed them all.
And the Swiss official from the International Red Cross satisfied.
    "Haiti's offer is substantial"
(starving figures, lining up, to sell
the amber colored plasma in their veins,
their proteins, globulins, mineral salts, antibodies)
    "supply like demand very buoyant"
What they sell, the richest part of their blood.
    The open veins. And off it flies
                to the U ess A
the frozen plasma of the Port-au-Prince poor.
    The daily bled.
Also the export of cadavers.
100 a week to American universities.
Also the Homo Caribbean and The Blood Export Center "estimate
4,000 liters a day of Central American blood..."
    (Somoza the biggest exporter)
        and the dictator swiftly sweeps by in his macabre Cadillac.

On the corners, leaning against shop fronts.
Daisies sprung up from the economic putrefaction.
The young whore in Puerto Rico: My first kiss was in the cinema.
    Don't remember the boy's name.
It was in the Royal. A film with María Antonieta Pons.
And the boy put his arm round me an' all, and went to kiss me
and as he kissed me he stuck his tongue in my mouth,

he was hugging me and squeezing me an' all,
a boy of the very nicest and best,
but you know with a gentleness like with a flower
like when someone goes to take a budding rose
and put it in a glass and doesn't want the bud to fall off.
(The young Puerto Rican whore. That's how the young whore told it all.)
Or again Uruguay blows from the butt of a machine gun
in the police station naked doped with ether blindfolded
jail enclosure heavily fortified military police guard dogs
couldn't see who was doing the interrogation he was North American
in English what were we doing contact names names
addresses, or no che you're in Argentina
Argentinian night
boats that will remain forever on the wharf
shadows that lengthen in the night of pain
in another room another beating more blood
same answers given again and so on—
coal boats that will never set sail.
Ass Wind: evil wind, of punishment,
anthropophagical wind. The hurricane wind.
It brings the devil. When the water spout arrives
sweeping away trees, crops, animals,
man remains motionless,
it also penetrates the body, produces death.
It's capitalism, imperialism in Peru.
Just like the X-Kamnakul wind, when it comes
the Maya take out gourds of ash
to draw crosses on the ground.
And now a poor and sad city, Potosi!
The open veins.
The young Puerto Rican whore: they ask in English.
And you'd say yes. He was saying: *How much?*
You suffer a lot in this fun life.
One night an American wanted
—let's put it crudely
two fucks for five pesos.
You know, he wanted me twice for five pesos!

The jubilant ringing of bells greeted the New Laws.
And some were saddened.
    They cursed Fray Bartolomé de las Casas.
Without man there is no world
the Chilean peasant said to the anthropologist.

"Walin Kili was digging the earth to sow yucca
and he brought out a shining yellow stone Walin Kili.
That's how the gringos came to Wasakín.
That's how the fish began to die, the shrimps
because of the cyanide. Our river before was crystalline."
(And like the shrimps and the fish: the Miskitos and Sumo.)
    And soon none will be left in Brazil. Due to
titanium thorium uranium manganese bauxite zirconium thallium
mercury
    "those that remain hardly know they are Indians."
Equally the monkeys, the toucans, the iguanas.
In brief, the Amazon.
Of the 200,000 Portuguese words
in the shacks of the North-East only an average of 300.
Julião spoke to them in parables:
    Wages are like a lump of sugar...
Casaldáliga seen as diabolical
and St. Monseigneur Romero.
    A conservative Christ
and his Vicar on earth a Utopian Capitalist Pole.
El Tiempo El Mercurio La Prensa La Nación El Comercio O Globo
    EXTRA! CAMILO TORRES DEAD
They toast as though with champagne with the blood of the poor.
God sick and tired of so many high masses in Colombia.
100 children dying daily of hunger
in the delightful Colombian countryside and the Cardinal:
"you should trust in the mercy of My God."
And in Bogotá on Corpus they bring out
the Body of Christ in that huge green monstrance
with so many emeralds that the people call it the Letttuce.
    "I was hungry"

Sick and tired of pontifical masses.
But to the pectoral cross Camilo preferred
the cross of Jesus.
Had he preached in the language of Pastorals and Encyclicals
he'd have died of natural causes.
The Rector had forbidden us to mention his name
in the Seminary of Christ the Priest.
They buried him secretly in the forest saying
"let's hope he never rises."
James the Apostle quite categorical: liturgy
pensions for widows,
nurseries for children,
and not to be contaminated by capitalist mentality.
My society is not of this Establishment
Jesus said to Pilate.
And that red-and-black poster, in so many students' rooms,
like a Sacred Heart,
it's not the President of the Bank of Cuba, nor the Minister for Industry
it's el Che risen again.

Whoever wants a telephone has to buy shares from Trouyet
which Mr. Trouyet himself will later purchase at a lower price
which oscillates between—A vulgar assault.
Who nevertheless donated the chapel in Cuernavaca
work of angelic architect, Brother Gabriel.
Madero told them:
—Fine. Now the Revolution's over. We won.
Villa said:—General, the Revolution's not over.
—It's not? Course it is.
—It's not true—says Zapata—. No, general,
the Revolution's still not over.
Expropriated of their land and their history.
Collective memory now mere tourist exotica.
Schizophrenic socio-economic system.
The commissions having met, the certificates discussed etc
one stood up: "Seize them without paying a peso, nothing,
nothing, because God granted land deeds to no one.

To the Colombian peasant we say: compañero, invade.
Now he's conscious and not like a damn fool.
They're invading and creating a huge fuss, they say.
Go fuck yourselves. Because with our children we've shed blood.
We bathed the roads in blood."
	Their hands are full of the poor's surplus value.
Take from the mouth of every poor person a little sugar
(through a small rise) for holidays on the Côte d'Azur
Because of the cement monopoly
the mother sleeping on the pavement clutching her little ones.
The onset of the plunder of everything, says the Chumayel.
But it will descend, says the Chilam Balam of Chumayel
the justice of God in a fell swoop across the world.
For the time being they go down to the market
in their tattered queenly costumes.
	Called the rubble of the national economy
	thanks to whom the national economy exists.
And the entire Guatemalan legal system
is criminal.
			In Bolivia
"everything exactly as it was in the Colonial period
except for the Coca Cola ads."
		The open veins.
The child news-vendor, the prostitute, the beggar
on Revolution Avenue.
The poor began to plant corn
but the caciques did not want this,
and they spoke amongst themselves, they formed committees:
well, we're not going to let them plant so as to keep our laborers.
So the laborer, poor man, he goes to offer himself so
			they'll give him maize.
Vasconcelos said: "Here in Mexico
there's no literature because the truth is hardly ever spoken."
Administrative corruption, land problems, etc
	short stories ideologically impoverished
		and José Revueltas in jail.

The first night was in the Silver Cup.
It has some letters which flash on and off.
That night, 'cause I was new, me sat in the corner.
Then Luz Celeste brought me a man.
You know how ashamed it makes you,
you know what it is to go day after day and day after day
to that business?

The old Jew had had a jeweller's.
He says: "Rabbi, we had all we wanted to eat.
But there were children starving in Cuba.
We had no ration books
but the poor were hungry.
Tell me Rabbi: what does our religion say? Rabbi
you see those shoes?
They're not as good as the ones I had. But you saw
people barefoot on the streets of Havana. Rabbi, what's
best according to the religion? We shopkeepers made a living
but Rabbi, young girls were selling themselves on the streets.
Rabbi, the peasants couldn't afford a doctor.
Tzelem elohim, Rabbi? Now we don't have some winning while others lose.
We eat or suffer hunger all together. Is that bad, Rabbi?
Tell me, Rabbi: Didn't we do well to remain here? Religion-wise,
Rabbi?"

Like the dreary drizzle of Colombian towns
in misty muddy streets, ever more muddy:
the oligarchy.
The coffee growers rancorous.
Streets of San Salvador:
like dogs run down by a car.
"no completely convincing evidence"
(the massacres) says the State Department.
The President of the World Bank proposes
instead of an increase in per capita income
contraceptives to reduce the capitas.
Argentinian nights.

Taken away in a car with her eyes blindfolded.
Destination unknown.
I guess at the twinkling
of the lights that in the distance
The 110 volt prod, the 210
"time you get out you'll be no use to any man as a woman"
For me the whole of life was
like a spring sun.
Puppet or tyrant governments.
Or puppet and tyrant.
United Fruit and the Yankee army squabbled over
who should control Honduras
until the State Department resolved the dispute.
General Ubico was a sentimental soul who
was never moved or took pity.
—Alone? I'm always alone...
He used to say he had no friends
only domesticated enemies.
His hatred extended to all written thought.
Once having wanted to burn the national archives.
Then came the firing squads.
Thereafter he began beatings in his office.

Continent devastated by National Security.
So many loves shattered by National Security.
The soft steps of the rubber soles.
Next it will be the sitting on slimy excrement.
The soft steps of the rubber soles
day, night, they keep on pursuing you.
Then comes the pit with water and con-
fessions muttered amid shadows and pentotal
it seemed that everything was over, no voices could be heard...
Ay my beloved Buenos Aires
never shall I see you again
Young men's bodies torn apart in the ferns.
And by the way: that expression that so typifies them
(Hitler, Somoza, Reagan)

faces as if smelling a foul smell.
Bodies thrown to the sharks
in Trujillo City.
Blue-turquoise reverberating,
blue lazulite celestial glimmering, glassy gleam,
blue lapiz-lazuli translucent blue
turning to methylene blue—the hills emerald
that moment, pearl-colored clouds,
smell of salt, of seaweed,
reefs teeming with submerged life:
and prisoners
one by one being hurled
from the cliff.

And here I can fit in the Jabali.
Jabali Gold Mine and Trading Company Limited.
A vast cemetery
brimful of crosses.
Only the huge wheels have remained in the hills,
empty tunnels,
and decaying crosses on the hillside.
"Like tunnels made by a colony of large-headed ants"
said the old miner,
like the tunnels in a *zompopo* ant-hill
that's what the graves were like in the cemetery.
The young men were hale and hearty.
And like tunnels the miners' lungs.
Within six months they were in the ground.
It's calculated that in the "good old days"
there'd be 3,000 cases of silicosis.
And on the streets of Santo Domingo, Chontales coughs... Miserable
discoverers of rich veins who remained in misery.
Great bars of gold, weighing 90 and 100 pounds
passed through the hands of the poor
who were always poor.
And not just those crosses:
also many graves lost in the hills.

The Secretary of State had been
deeply disturbed by violations
of the Monroe Doctrine in the Dominican Republic...
Which explains Lilís, the country's most terrible tyrant, alone
surpassed by Trujillo.
Trujillo and God.
He ate simply.
Breakfast was light. Lunch frugal.
His drink just a goblet of cognac.
Punctual to the point that punctuality was an half-hour earlier.
Friends—he had none.
Clemency—unknown to him.
If ever he gave the impression of pardoning,
it was a political manoeuvre.
If dishonesty proved ineffective
he resorted to murder.
Every form of deceit was second nature to him.
Secrecy and unpredictable reactions, an instinct.
His inveterate habit of uncertainty.
His greatest strength was cynicism.
Brutal with everyone, excepting his children and grandchildren.
Beneath his two-cornered, ostrich-feathered hat
the immense rancor.
Pitiless even in his magnanimity.
Ecstatic at human suffering: trem-
bling with pleasure his small goblet of cognac.
The airplane that came in the afternoon from Puerto Rico
would fly low over the ominous island,
in melancholy twilight.
Or boat passengers viewed with fascination and terror
Trujillo's sinister island
slipping away in the blood-colored sunset.
"*Cemetery*—he said—is a Greek word which means
inexorable warning to the living."
He gave orders to kill with his voice sharpening but without emotion.
Imagine the effect if the Somoza delegation was horrified.

The ones he chose, almost always virgins.
Ghostly political parties.
The foreigner who stepped out onto the streets at night
the slightest gust of wind shook him to the bones.
From the Puerto Rican plane
the sugar-cane plantations
seemed sad or ghostly in the dusk.
Something mysterious down below.
The passengers gazed and were silent.
And from the sea there in the distance, pale or powerful
police lights, apparently, on the sea surface:
the infernal promenade and boulevards.
The only thing he didn't admire in Hitler
was not using decorations.
His collection of 2,000 suits and 10,000 ties.
"In the photo, wearing one of his most splendid uniforms.
On his left the Pope..." (Same one who refused
to receive Gandhi in loincloth.)
Those on the afternoon flight leaving behind the sombre hills
suddenly completely eclipsed by tragic black storm clouds.
Or to the boat passengers it was the will-o'-the wisp
glimmer of Trujillo City with its tongue-tied population
and its prisons, sinking into the night and the sea.
Galíndez enrolled for a doctorate at Columbia
was completing his thesis on that period
and he entered the New York subway at 10 p.m.
between 57th and Eighth
and nothing more was ever known of him,
merely that he'd have woken in a cell prior to torture and death
and Trujillo standing there!
Thrown into a cauldron...? Or to the sharks according to others.
Or put into a block of fresh cement
and the block dumped in the sea.
Such total control
that he didn't need to kill so much
(according to Galíndez)
From the plane

you felt you were flying over a satanic country.
Or at night from the boat,
the eerie lights
of Trujillo City.

CONFIDENTIAL MEMORANDUM FROM ITT
...that you tell Mr. Kissinger that Mr. Geneen wishes
to come to Washington to discuss the interests of ITT
being disposed to offer seven figure sums
since all along we've dreaded an Allende victory
and tried to alert other companies in the community
PERSONAL AND CONFIDENTIAL
We've recommended over and above direct help the following:
that we and other businesses in the Chilean community
feed ads into the Mercurio and certain radio and TV outlets
and insist that key European papers reprint
and with the Savings and Loans company faring badly
and the banks failing to renew credit payments or stalling them
it would be a realistic hope that a bankrupt
economy (runs on banks factory closures etc)
might provoke a wave of violence and our hearts
sigh caressing the dream of a military coup...
And Victor Jara sang there.
Without a guitar and without hands sang in the Stadium
When the officer told him "Sing motherfucker"
he sang.
He sang to all those who were in the Chile Stadium
and to God.
God he addressed like a close friend
why did he work so hard for six days
for such a terrible world.
"A dead man, a bruised man I never ever believed in," he shouted.
And silent in that Stadium the Supreme Being
totally impotent in the face of Pinochet.
And the song lingered there, not borne away on the wind
immobile like the cement of the terraces,
it lingered, adhered to every step.

It's still there, even with soccer, in the Chile Stadium.
In the Morgue his eyes remained open
says one who saw him,
        as though looking death in the eye
                or rather: God.

        Governments like public calamities.
Ubico considered hospitals "sissified."
Papa Doc with his "very peculiar cosmovision."
Trujillo awarded the Rubén Darío order.
And why go on?
Bacurí's body was found on the beach without eyes,
the bright-shiny beach the last he saw
        (prussian, cerulean, cobalt)
and his mouth gashed to his ears.

The people who make the railways, the bread, pins,
or high up there finishing off the skyscraper:
'uneducated' because they transform reality.
        And those lights above Caracas,
                        above the skyscrapers
the mountains like a starry sky:
they are the paltry lights of the poor.
Their cordon of misery there in the sky.
In other places they're hidden, not here:
            they can be seen from anywhere, and in the full sky.

If we could see once again Zapata's bonfires!
He'd said:—Well now, no way
now they've all elected me, well now me.
And now no way: they support me.
—Well we're all here—they replied.
He fought for liberty, water, plots of land.
But what went wrong?
            Right now they're selling their little houses to the rich,
            their few springs, dying of thirst,
and the rich: next reservoirs

next this, next that.
Guest Airlines was bankrupt. And what happened?
The National I-don't-know-what covered Mr. Trouyet's losses
with money from the starving Mexican people.
He who donated the chapel in Cuernavaca, Morelos.
Hold as enemies all the rich,
Morelos would say.
Temple of God.
Temple of God.
Temple of God.
Temple of God through donations from the den of thieves.
'The rich who sweep by in their cars that throw up dust'
(Granada still unpaved)
thus that beggar praying in La Merced,
praying at the top of his voice before the altar in La Merced, Granada,
"The rich who sweep by in their cars that throw up dust"

On the elegant avenues of the walking mannequins
scavenging like dogs
trembling not from malaria but from hunger
their beds are crumpled newspaper on the pavement
El Tiempo El Comercio La Nación
Should I make these lines more poetic?
The subreal poet wants these lines to be more poetic.
And the famous cycle of the Recife crab
faeces crabs humans faeces
people eat the crab that eats people's faeces
but since there's ever more hunger and consequently less faeces
the crab's growing scarce on the dunghills.
The prisoner with no light
thinks of the island of birds,
the solitary island of birds, where there are only birds
and from afar its smell comes to us, of bird-shit
(long before it can even be seen from the boat across the waves)
and a screeching of birds above the surf breaking on the rocks.

Then came his mania for washing his hands and changing shirts

told by the servant engaged to the chauffeur in the Presidential House.
        They cut off Báez Bone's penis.
It must have been his blood that stained the shirt.
        You Medrano, tractor driver, to whom they read my *Hora 0*
                        and you understood it.
Nicaragua was a Middle Ages in which Radio Havana could be heard.
          That 'Moorish' palace above Managua.
        He'd watch movies in the intervals
between torture sessions.
Would he side with the good guys or the bad in the films?
        The Pentagon's favorite.
                He learned how to torture in West Point.
"Torture? That's not torture, they're piffling exercises."
        The floor and the walls covered in shit and piss.
Then talking rambling incoherently on the television
                "my philosophy..."
He never knew how to smile. Only laugh.
                I'm talking about Somoza III.
(The Miskito with his tongue cut out and his mouth sewed up with
wire)
"...he gave him a smash with the butt which broke the bone in his face
he handed them rope so they could tie up my husband
and they handed him over to the station that was about 3 in the afternoon
that they put him through you could almost say Christ's passion
like you hang up a mosquito net they had him in the air
his body naked worse than Christ because Christ had a loincloth
they gouged out his eyes cut off a piece of his tongue
and gave him acid when he asked for water and stitched his mouth up with
wire..."
        (When nobody mentioned Miskitos abroad.)
Like when that pirate (Lolonés?) came into the lake
who ate the hearts of prisoners.
        He would chew little pieces.

The girl's name was Melania
and she hired an express launch to Solentiname
to tell me, almost exclusively to tell me:

Those hungry faces,
I keep seeing them even when I switch off the television.
Around the time young Laureano was saying in Solentiname:
—They think we're NOTHING. As though we were worthless.
With his furious emphasis on NOTHING.
Fonseca had spoken to me of the peasants' poetry
quoting one to me who said to him one night:
The moon is the light of the poor.
They paying the bills of someone in Miami, in...
Which means that three out of seven peasants...
Here are the statistics.
The same as happens to Uruguayan wool, etc. (Now commonplace.)
"The peasant is idle"
he says at the Terraza Club between whisky and oyster cocktails
with no other task than that.
Another who'd said: "I give them work": he gave them work true enough
but not the fruit of their work.
By Royal Decree the sale of Indians was authorized
at fair prices.
Medrano the tractor driver:
—My first conscious tears as a child:
my little friend crushed in the sugar mill,
with no help towards the wake, the burial and the mill-owner
on his knees before Monseigneur Simon Pereira y Castellón's ring.

In the telescopic sight. The child is in the sight.
He's playing in the school yard.
In the telescopic sight he and the ball.
The guardia laughed afterwards.
Like someone who's killed a bird.
Cantinflas's logic is Cartesian,
Coronel said,
compared to Mons. Vega.
(Even before the Bishop excused the murder of children.)

Gorillas in white ceremonial costumes under tropical palms.

The lepers raised their hands to the sky
as Che's raft slipped away.
But not long after the little Cuban boy is saying
(to Iglesias): "You see no shoes in the shops here
because there's money to buy them.
If in Mexico all the people could buy shoes,
how many do you think would be left in the shops?"
Simple: there were none in the shops but on the feet.
Can there be a way out?
                    There can be a way out.
Like the insect longing to break out to the sunlight there straight ahead
colliding again and again:
until the window is drawn back for it
and it flies out to freedom.
    The kingdom of heaven in the planets.
In our cells the heroes' chromosomes.
    On his poster there he is
    like a traditional Christ but with a hard face.
He required of others what he required of himself.
"I *was* a doctor" said Che.
As Madero said:
—Now. Now the Revolution's over. We won.
        Villa and Zapata:
—General, the Revolution's not done yet.
        —No, general,
the Revolution's still not done.

CANTIGA 25

Visit to Weimar

In the beginning:
there was no space and there was no time, since it was before time.
        The universe was shapeless and it was empty.
Out of nothing something emerged and time began.
Time which is space.
                Space in which there are atoms and spirit.
Elemental particles formed 92 atoms
and these atoms thousands of types of molecules, molecules
whose properties stem from the elemental particles
and from which cells come.
From the moment molecules learned to create other molecules
it was inevitable that one day there'd be people writing about molecules.

We went through Weimar and naturally
                        stopped off at Goethe's house.
There are his paintings. A Lucas Cranach...
        An Italian primitive...
Also a pencil sketch he made
            of his beautiful wife asleep in the garden.
The piano where the young Mendelsshon played.
The Greek statues, his mineral collection.
        The desk on which he wrote *Faust*.
The humble bed. The armchair he died in.
The drawing rooms very elegant because he was Prime Minister; his
                                                            bedroom
        modest like Lenin's in the Kremlin.
The sofa where he talked the night away with the Prince of Weimar.
"Deep considerations about nature and art."
A time he devoted more to natural sciences than to poetry.
Here he discovered man's intermaxillary bone.
Also the vertebrate theory of the cranium.

In 1790 he began the study of color theory.
(The same year he wrote *The Metamorphosis of Plants.*)
It was a snowy day when Schiller came to live in Weimar.
        Here he chatted with Napoleon.
                In 1815 he was appointed Prime Minister.
        (It was also a kind of Ministry of Culture.)
This was the intellectual capital of Germany.
        Here the young Heine boasted to him
        that he too was writing "his" Faust.
                        And how delicious the plums of Weimar!
        The devastation that Schiller's death brought him.
Palermo's Botanical Gardens led him to the protoplant.
Working on *The Metamorphosis of Animals*
he argued with increasing emphasis
that the poetic art is "a common good of humanity"
and in all times and places it exists in thousands of people.
        Poetry writing could be taught to the masses.
Only culture and barbarism concerned him—he said.
        Gradually he was being left alone.
                In 1827 his Charlotte died.
                        The following year, the Grand Duke.
But he had written: "On high peaks there is always calm."
At the end of Volume II, Faust, now blind, has a vision
of "a free people living on this earth."
He fastened the binding of Volume II with a lock and key
and shut it away in a cupboard so they wouldn't read it.
Later, he no longer left his apartment for the elegant salons.
The day he was in his death throes in the armchair
        he thought he saw a letter from Schiller on the floor.
And 15 minutes from there
                                set in the woods
we enter the "Highway of Blood."
                        The prisoners themselves paved it.
It ends in desolate platforms
        where hundreds and hundreds and hundreds of trains used to arrive.
They open for us the imposing bronze gates
                                        with floral grating

and huge letters in reverse on the grating
which can only be read from inside, when the gates have been closed:
EACH ONE GETS WHAT HE DESERVES
like the entrance to Dante's inferno
Lasciate ogni speranza, o voi che entrate
It's the entrance to Buchenwald.
Barbed wire within barbed wire within more electrified barbed wire.
The horrendous watch-towers.
And we saw the cremation ovens in red brick.
The "special" cells for those who resisted,
where heroes bellowed out to the whole Camp
not to surrender
from the tiny hole with bars, before dying.
It was truly another city.
With as many inhabitants as Weimar.
The bodies walking skeletons
their steps faltering
their terrified gaze empty.
Everything well-ordered.
The name of each one who was going to arrive
sent beforehand to the concentration camp
with a copy to the Central Management of Concentration Camps
cc. to the Gestapo, etc.
"With reference to previous discussions
I attach in duplicate for the appropriate end
the list of those unfit for work"
(*Signed*)
Buchenwald Camp doctor.
In the surroundings, mounds of dead.
The grey multi-storey building where they left their clothes.
Girls with elegant dresses
emerged in the blue-and-white striped uniforms
and the number tattooed on the left arm
many now to perish out of sheer sadness.
Human skin was good for parchment.
For writing poems on, love poems.
For binding books.

For lamp shades.
They shrank Jewish heads (like the Jivaro), as souvenirs.
And doctors experimenting as they pleased on live bodies.
There was 18 hours work in December, amid snow and wind,
in little more than a flimsy jacket,
and due to the cold many flung themselves onto the wires to die electrocuted.
The children herded apart
their barbed wire within more barbed wire within more barbed wire.
Close to them a small wired pen with little bear cubs
(the children loving those bear cubs)
and when the children cried with hunger
the guards poured the bears lashings of milk
right under the children's eyes,
the cute bear cubs
and the children crying, screaming.
Blurred lights in the snow sweeping back and forth
searching for the fugitive
and deep bark of police dogs behind the barbed wire
and its echoes.
You could tell whether they were burning bodies in the ovens
according to whether the smoke was black or white.
And also from the delicious smell of roast meat.
The pastor's voice exhorting them gripped to the bars
in the final cell.
We saw the device "for measuring a prisoner's height"
and at the rear the shutter which opened nd a hand came out with a pistol
for a shot in the neck.
Beforehand a "doctor" examined their teeth
looking for gold.
That's because they later discovered there was money in dead bodies:
Hair, gold teeth, lard, skins for painting.
The capitalist economy gone mad.
"Contents of consignment:
2 kilos of hair in curls and tresses"
At the platforms the death trains kept arriving.
And in Weimar no one knew anything.
They merely saw a forbidden zone and a file of trains.

But they had their suspicions
when a military truck crashed right in the city center
and heaps of dead spilled out onto the street.
These were the woods where Goethe walked.
Close to here the oak beneath which Goethe read.
And which the Nazis took great care of.

...One day a person writing about molecules.
We were once a cloud of gas the size of the solar system.
Later, a ball of lava.
The earth revolved for five thousand million years
and began to talk. Basalt, granite,
found a throat.
The harmonic intervals of the notes of the scale
that Pythagoras discovered:
the same as the planet's, the same
as the intervals of sea waves,
of sand dunes, of pendulums.
A moon so that there'd be tides, and for lovers.
The organ made simply to pump blood
became the seat of suffering, dreams and love.
92 atoms only
everything in existence.
The unity of humanity and the union
with all that surrounds it.
Everything appears to interact with everything.
There is speculation
that before the expansion of the universe there was a contraction
on an infinitely minute scale
of galaxies, stars and cosmologists.
"The present theories of Physics strongly suggest
the indestructibility of the Mind in the face of Time"
Schrödinger has said.

CANTIGA 26

On Earth as in the Heavens

In the beginning
from the moment time began...
And before?
"Presumably the universe began in a chaotic state."
And before?
Before there was any before.
        A proton and a neutron join together
            to form a deutron
    the simplest of nuclear systems
but a new proton arrives and separates them forever.
    That's how everything started.
"Time still without time,"
say the Chol, in their woods where the rains never end,
when the world was shaped in this liquid darkness
before the sun.
            Dissipated the fog of electrons...
        (And it has been transparent ever since then.)

From the beginning there was a union.
Although the proton and neutron are separated forever by a proton.
    "It is not appropriate for man to be alone"
Which is why a man alone is not human.
What's human as community:
        Animals don't laugh,
            fish, herons or chimpanzees.
And alone man does not laugh.
    It is not appropriate for man to be alone.
Einstein began his Relativity analyzing a simple problem:
How can two people some distance apart synchronize their watches.
Yet though the speed of light is a universal constant,
long ago, a long time ago, in Granada

where every night the clock on La Merced struck 8,
your light was not my light, Carmen.

Once in the Pacific, off the coast of Nicaragua,
fishing red snapper with Bosco
in the blue sea with blue sky,
        the sea like blue ink.
And suddenly two turtles, coupled,
one mounted the other
        making love in the sea
as they've been doing since their species began
in order to reproduce and produce more and more species
the same act in the sea for millions of years
out of love
for the human species
and at its culmination
communism.
The act that has been performed since the world began.
And I thought of Matthew 19:12,
there is also the one who does not marry
out of love for the kingdom of heaven, for communism
like a turtle alone in mid-Pacific
    alone under the heavens
        betrothed to the heavens.
Once again a meditation in a DC-3:
I don't know why I recalled that line from Novalis
"To touch a body is like touching the heavens."
The Air Force pilot was unfurling the national map
for the dark-skinned nine year old
    (our land below us)
his hand brushing against her little hand.
Down below Muy-Muy, rivers, Nueva Guinea where Felipe fell.
    "It's like touching the heavens..."
        But if they don't believe in heaven?
Obviously it is not the blue atmospheric canopy
    that's still the earth
and flying in a DC-3 through the sky of our liberated land

is the earth.
But the infinite black night
of the stars, with our earth full of humans loving each other
        and all the other loving Earths
                                        is heaven
                        is the Kingdom of heaven.
And what did Novalis mean?
            To me he's saying:
smothering a baby in kisses,
a couple in deep caresses,
a handshake,
a slap on the shoulder,
the human touching human,
the union of human skin with human skin
is like touching Communism with your fingers my friends.
                "Jesus says: Whoever has found the System
and may have become rich, let him renounce the System"
            (Gospel of Thomas.)
In the case of multicellular organisms
the cells changed from I to us,
and the selfishness of cells, their unbridled regression to I
is cancer, and Mr. Kirsch who began his fortune at the age of 9
lending out to other children at a percentage
until he became the millionaire he is today
says that the perfect dinner consists of just two people:
                        You and the waiter.
The maximum of private profits for,
solely for, more fucking private profits.
Which brings about systematized inequality.
Freedom, the freedom of enterprise,
of trade, not the freedom of people.
Economic doctrines against the grain of the human heart
will bite the dust,
and perhaps this poem will be read in a thousand years
when *Newsweek* will no longer be read...
            In the 43rd year of the Nuclear Age...
And Coronel says to me

that in Nicaragua today a poem without politics
would be an emasculated poem.
"My peace I give you, but it's not the peace the system offers" (Jn 14:27).
As he also said that His kingdom was not of this system.
On earth as it is in heaven.
And because sending algae to Venus to turn
carbon dioxide into healthy oxygen
and lower its temperature with rainfall
or breaking Jupiter up into small habitable planets
"perfectly feasible in the next ten thousand years"
but that man might stop being selfish
or a classless society
never enters their heads.

The rising of the full earth above the moon's horizon
—our sister moon scarcely a light second away—
bluish, amid white veils, behind only blackness
(we've seen the photos).
This earth our cradle of life.
Life which is nothing more than organized electromagnetic energy.
Organized for evolution.
The rapid step from the amoeba to Einstein.
Evolution, not so much competition
as cooperation.
And once again they will grow on the same stalk,
said the *cacique* Coteeakun,
they and the white men.
Still no travellers have arrived from other solar systems.
Will there be selfishness in the other systems too?

Mr. Kirsch's dinner for two.
Money to make from it more money
and for others to do the work.
And so they with their Rouaults and Picassos.
French chateau in pink stone
in Dallas, Tex., with chandeliers, one once owned by Mme. Pompadour,
or the Fairs' residence "not as big

as a football pass but almost"
or the case of Mr. Urschel who cited his mansion
on rock—the planting of ornamental trees a little difficult,
you know, a thousand dollars a hole.
And Mrs Graff tells that she was working in an oil field
and when it hit her
she was travelling through Europe with all her diamonds
refinery owner with not such refined manners perhaps
but now you see 850,000 dollars for a Cezanne
which the artist sold for—
And to them money becomes an arm according to St. Augustine;
        or a leg, or a penis.
And as such it hurts.
Perversions which are irruptions of archaic instincts.
                                    (Report from Tokyo Zoo...)
And those who are honorable in their private life;
at home they're not criminals.

            Yet anyone, standing here, would say it's not moving.
            And time is one-dimensional
            which is why there is only a future ahead.
                    The past will not return.
In whichever direction he gazes the astronomer
sees the same quantity of galaxies.
Since we are at the center of the universe or
in a universe without center.
Whatever the case: "o homem e um animal que ama"
            writes Thiago de Mello
and for this reason he's more beautiful than the morning star.
            That shout of Thiago's: Erneeeeeesto...
On deck, in a remote part of the Amazon,
Barreirinha, who knows in which channel of the innumerable channels,
24 hours away by boat from Manaus: "Look, how clear the stars
and the nebulae, the nebulae, Erneeeeeesto!"
Stars, dust, gas,
everything up above sings the canticle of hydrogen.
The celestial movements a continuous song for several voices,

syncopes, cadenzas, clausuras...
according to Kepler in *Harmonice mundi.*

Maxwell noted in his equations
that electricity and magnetism travelled at the speed of light,
he didn't believe it was coincidence,
and he identified electromagnetism with light.
In his equations he saw light in a new light,
visible light was electromagnetic waves
with wave lengths of...
And with his theory Hertz built the first radio.

Gravity which is nothing but distorted void.
And it's what binds the universe together.
Shapeless and cold and tenuous gas
gradually becomes round, hot and dense (star)
because of gravity.
The "intricate and elegant" universe Sagan says.
Naturally atoms vibrate (like lyres).
Molecules undulate melodically, and crystals the same.
And the harmony of human anatomy. The music of the stars.
Dirac points out the importance of an equation being beautiful.
Or Einstein who rejected ugly equations.
The rhythm of the pendulum, the waves, the heart, the seasons,
of radio and television waves.
All matter is rhythm.
The cosmos music.
Salomón de la Selva's remark to CMR in Mexico,
in a bar in Mexico: "If a sentence lacks rhythm
it's because it's not true."

And the lie is against the species (human species),
the lie is contra natura,
against human nature.
The "secret" bombing of Laos.
Presenting Grenada as a great power.
(Animals don't lie,

just as they are not cruel nor murderers, not even lecherous
nor sexual perverts.)
        Anti the war
                and pro the war
        is the candidate
                (Nixon)
Where they may be against the war, against.
Wherever in favor, in favor.
        Yes and no, said Nixon.
(Because politicians have to be flexible.)
—Shall we or shan't we support this program?
—Let's say yes in the marginal districts,
where we know we're ahead let's say no—
        said Nixon.
"Creating an image," and it's created through language.
For politics is a question of language.
Slippery in ambiguity as a fish in water.
(With a chorus of Madison Avenue bards
the same who sing so lyrically to Coca-Cola
            the ones with the Pindaric ads
        now in political hype
                which acts upon the sympathetic.)
His rhetoric making about as much sense as static.
One of the problems was Nixon's lack of humor.
To a certain extent that could be corrected.
The other a lack of warmth. This was corrected
by getting him to use *fiery* words
without appearing to have been rehearsed.
"To cause the public to make an emotional leap,
or what theologians call a leap of faith."
        The sound of applause is brought down
                camera two homes in
                        Nixon emerges wearing make-up
        raises his arms and smiles.

Carlyle considered the sight of the stars to be sad
for the amount of suffering in them if they were inhabited

or if not, for all the loneliness.
Returning, dear reader, to our reality:
politicians of Hollywoodian unreality
with cosmeticized faces discussing
life and death issues in 10 seconds.
"You could put forward a candidate from a mental institution
provided that in addition to being mad he's rich."
And intelligent people I know who read the paper every day
failing to remind themselves daily how the news is fabricated.
The *sotto-voces* in the noisy editorial offices to make *facts*,
facts which you easily digest like corn-flakes.
    Including the tiny country Nicaraguita.
You're deceived into thinking that Nicaragua kills three million Miskito's,
not that Nicaragua even has three million inhabitants.
    The science of Semantics. Analysis for example
of that catch-all phrase in the CIA's constitution:
"Also *other* functions and services" (my italics)
which has allowed it to do as it pleases
almost never with the consent of Congress
and never of the North American public.
        Their 3 categories of propaganda:
    1) To tell the truth to certain people
            ("white propaganda");
    2) half or distorted truths
            ("grey" propaganda)
    3) and the "black."
Honorable in their private lives. At home they're not criminals
posing with the wife, the dog and the kids.
Like Kennedy saying, we prefer democracy
but faced with a Castro we go for a Trujillo.
"They taught me to do these things in the CIA
            —Hunt declared to the Attorney General—
false press releases, telegrams and such like."
And put epigrammatically by an ex-CIA agent:
    The public cannot know whether it exceeds its powers
    because it cannot know what its powers are either.
I'd add: much less the extent of those powers.

Let's recall Henry Adams' statement that since George Washington
the evolution of the presidents of the United States
contradicts Darwin's theory.
(At present a Neanderthal in the White House...)
"We should Americanize you
—the North American Indian said—
The North American system was
each one respecting his brother's vision."

We stroll along the streets of a New York neighborhood,
small shops, restaurants, Dry-Cleaning,
three-, four-storey apartment blocks,
red brick, cement, grey brick,
we move on to an Alpine village,
cobblestoned streets of a tiny Mexican pueblo,
next to a river with a medieval mill,
the dusty streets of a Wild West town,
with its saloons, a window with shattered glass,
on a hill an XIth century castle,
then back to apartment blocks, a bank, a liquor store
out of any city in the United States,
but if you tap anything, it has a hollow ring,
it's all plaster,
they're only exterior walls, there's nothing behind them.
A policeman up the street, with his badge
and notebook for taking down violations,
could be for real or a famous actor.
And the producer (Ed Lewis) who's showing me round, tells me:
"neither the director, nor the producer, nor anyone else
calls the shots on a film
but the bank that finances it".
And as I came away and saw the banks, restaurants, Dry-Cleaning,
it seemed to me that whatever I tapped would sound hollow,
Hollywood, the whole of Los Angeles, everything
was just walls
with nothing behind them.

The pain if they were inhabited
and if not, so much emptiness.
In a windowless basement in the west wing of the White House
bristling with signs: Top Secret *Top Secret* TOP SECRET
each night the experts are there
starless basement
piecing together a picture of the terraqueous globe in the last 24 hours
with snippets of information from all its sources
satellites that kept an eye on China
spies in Poland
diplomats in Red Square
Contra advisers on the Honduran border
gathering it all together in a black folder for the president who'll
find it on his desk after breakfast next day
the destinies of the globe each day dependent on
what is cobbled together in the windowless basement night after night
and nightly placed on Reagan's desk
in the black folder.

The curved void.
Spaces so immense they slow up the light.
The truth is that light is slow!
100,000 light years for example, to cross a galaxy.
Our own with 200,000 million stars
tenuous like the void or harder than diamond.
And how many galaxies are there? Which accounts for
"In my father's house there are many mansions."
As though comparing it to New York with its illuminated apartments.
And as Chesterton commented: a homely image of heaven.
Milk spilt into the sink
repeats the pattern of the Milky Way.
Matter on the outer reaches of the universe within telescope range
is the same homespun matter as our own.
In a glass prism bought in a village fair
he saw that white light comprises all the colors of the rainbow;
and when an apple fell he deduced the Law of Universal Gravitation
and in order to demonstrate it he created Infinitesimal Calculus.

From bacteria to doves to astronauts
the ingredients are no more than two dozen molecules
of moderate complexity.
          But chemical combinations
     created beings who quibble over the mysteries
          of chemical combinations.
Minuscule planet of an insignificant star in a small galaxy
determined to understand the totality of the cosmos.
A round rock going around a star
with a life composed of the most common atoms
what else are we but something very ordinary in the universe?
—Or astrophysical and biochemical accidents unlikely ever to be repeated?
It's outmoded to regard him as a Swiss watchmaker.
          But who made
          the Swiss watchmaker?
The uniquely terrestrial concept "world"
in a few thousand years went on to be intergalactic,
celestial.
     The discovery that we are in the heavens.
What according to Sir Fred Hoyle religion is,
leaving aside masks, dances, altars:
an imprint we carry within us:
     "I come from something situated in the heavens."

CANTIGA 27

Dance of the Millions

Its windows a copy of the Pitti palace
and the arcades, from the Strozzi palace
(façades more Florentine than any in Florence)
and in its vaults the gold, the gold in bricks
        gleaming yellow bricks
from those banks and other banks. It's opening time
        for the Wall Street banks
eight-thirty a.m., time known as "lunch-time"
on Wall Street, with London in mind.
                                        They make calls to Tokyo
to bankers already in their beds and to gnomes
                in Zurich tucking into truffles and wines
and now all agreed
and cigar smoke wafts from the Florentine windows
along with words like
                                "a hundred million"
                                        "three hundred"
                They phone round again from Wall Street
                        5 in the evening Frankfurt time.
The cocoa won't be fumigated. The farmers are fleeing.
Besides the crop was already poor,
                        "we're not panicking"
by now the papers have splashed across 8 columns
                                                REVOLUTION IN GHANA
            You know, 3 cents on cocoa and your money doubles.
            It rises 6 and it doubles again. And Nestlé
            has to buy cocoa.
"Hello... Don't worry" (mellifluous over the telephone)
"Don't worry. A drop of rain now
and we'll have black blight. Just imagine that cocoa
all its pods turning black. Should see how ugly."

And Nestlé will have to buy at 50 cents.
They've never seen a cocoa tree—
to them it's just a piece of paper on Wall Street.
Violence disgusts them. Disasters. But the truth they love.
And the truth this morning is that
despite what they say in London
there's no cocoa.
And Nestlé will have to buy at 70 cents.
It's night once more on Wall Street.
Dark the Florentine façades.
Down below the gleam of the yellow bricks.

And the shares of yester-year, what became of them
the beloved shares
that quintupled your money the same day?
Motorola. Do you remember? Ay, Motorola mine,
they'd buy you at 2 and sell you at 11 the same day.
Company of mine, your breasts are jars of honey.
"I had few shares that morning (he told me)
and 25 million dollars in cash,
a disaster! (and me surprised
that 25 million dollars in cash
could be a disaster)"
The most scientific form of swindle this century.
For this reason:
"We propose to abolish it entirely"
said Fidel in the year 1962 of our age.
The old provincial money-lender, Don Salvador Noguera,
now nothing but old skin, was the saint's treasurer
and he had placed on interest, the alms of St. Joseph,
patron saint of Solentiname, there where it would earn lots of money.
In a box the jewels (I didn't like to touch them)
trinkets, children's rings, love-tokens, pawned-items,
"the widow, the orphan..."
at 48% interest, more than that on his own money,
I mean higher than the interest on his money
a figure I don't recall, a bit less,

it being St. Joseph's money.
In all innocence.
Trinkets trembling in his hands.
The old man died soon after and I don't know who got the pawned items
and St. Joseph's money at interest.
"Abolish it entirely."

The undeniable fact that destruction brings profits.
And increased production losses.
Farmer who'd come from the San Juan River, or rather
deeper in, Río Indio, purer jungle,
an honest man certainly, told me in Solentiname
that he had just started up his lumber business.
Should have seen the most gigantic cedars!—he tells me—
when un-for-tun-ate-ly
the world war ended.

Natural selection's no longer valid with nuclear weapons.
It can't control them, nuclear weapons, natural selection.
Missiles with their own intelligence.
Murderous satellites in orbit above us.
And the order for all-out destruction is already there in the computers.
Neanderthal man with nuclear weapons.
The problem is:
We lack biological mechanisms for not killing ourselves.
Because our bare bodies were incapable of killing each other
(neither horns, nor claws, etc)
Until a man picked up from the ground a donkey's jawbone
or maybe it was a giraffe's thigh-bone.
Killing one's brothers has no connection,
no connection, with the DNA of our animal past.
Armaments aren't part of our biological inheritance.
Nor torture chambers
part of natural selection.
Biologically we're harmless monkeys.
Hitler, Reagan... (Naked). So then the problem is:
There's no biological inhibition for oppression or war.

Generals bald as the Capitol cupola
or with angular features like the Pentagon.
Others with projectile-shaped skulls
and brains the size of a golf-ball.
—It's the greatest thing since the nuclear bomb.
      Another rambles on vaguely about a militaristic peace.
—A lethal zone of 300 hectares– another enthuses...
      Fat and with their cigars and their caricature faces.
—And tell me
how could there be order in the world
if everyone were simply
to follow his conscience?
Aping intelligence, in front of the barbecue, apron on
and Manhattan on the rocks,
innocently contemplating his celestial pool.
      Far removed from there:—My God
            if only we had more 20-mm
            if only we had more 20-mm in the Phantoms
prays the young man.
"Military objective is any person, thing or idea..."
the manual says. You fall asleep on the 3rd page of the manual
but for the thought of the bombed kindergartens.
Military objective
any thing an army man decides to attack.
      ...or idea...
To him it was instinctive, the Colonel says.
An instinct. While young people hesitate a split-second
before releasing their bombs.
—Bombing raids have now become a bit awkward
due to lack of bridges left to bomb.
—But if the wind blows from the north you can tell
from the stench whether the B-52s scored a hit.
The war which the Cardenal of New York called
a camouflaged love.

Fact is, fresh conflicts, fresh dividends.

The finger always on the button.
The bombers always over our heads.
Their horror of peace... Darío
was the first to call them enemies of humanity.
More and more wars (after the world one)
and a Mr. D. K. Ludwing with bigger and bigger
tankers. Or whether a Mr. Thornton (nuclear submarines)
could have a special interest in peace. Or
whether Howard Hughes etc...
(Manufacturer of guided missiles.)
Thermal bombs for human life,
only for human life nothing else.
The benefits only for the monopolies,
the manufacturers of death without competition.
So we get
France against Laos and Cambodia, Holland
against Indonesia, France against Vietnam, the U.S.A.
against Korea, England against Kenya, France against Algeria,
the U.S.A. against Laos, England against Cyprus, France
against Tunisia, the U.S.A. against Vietnam, Israel against the Arabs,
England against Anguilla...
And so we get
what the generals most fear,
fear most,
is peace.
So
life and death destinies of distant lands in attaché cases
which pass through the revolving doors of the Carlyle Hotel.

And an infantile President in the map room,
in the room with huge maps,
every night poring over his map, picking out
this pagoda, this little cement house,
this irrigation system. The following day's objectives.
Suspension bridge linking two villages. Whence:
as though 60,000 garbage bins were to fall crashing to the ground,
or rather the missiles, which are not merely phallic symbols.

Capitalism was a regime which forbade us to love.
Or at least a phenomenon marginal to love.
Capitalism causes us to revert to crystals instead of cells.
        Selfishness ontological.
The death instinct found in man
is not inherited. It's not an animal instinct.
                It's acquired.
"Thatcher's and Reagan's concepts of biology
aren't so inaccurate as far as non-human animals are concerned."
        Inequality as a moral imperative.
Which is why the revolution's *contra natura.*
Closer to the shark than to the bees.
It's certain life devours itself.
That it lives off death.
But photosynthesis, inexhaustible source of energy
—the sun—was a fundamental factor in evolution.
Life a mere devourer of life wouldn't have lasted.
Let's denounce therefore their phenomenon marginal to love,
their money-mania,
their laboratories for destroying life
with potentially dirt-cheap biological weapons,
        their celluloid Celestial Jerusalem
        with cash register chorus,
he who had, so they said, 1,000 virgins in Hollywood
and not a single child,
wheat brokers in May and Chevrolets in October,
the God of Rockefeller, Carnegie, Morgan,
Henry Ford who said "history's bunk,"
AP and the rest of the myth agencies,
the cowboy on a white horse setting the world to rights,
the Phantom Strangler.

The owner of *Playboy* and a plane with a ballroom,
the owner of millions as well as women,
the millions bring him the women he wants,
and the naked women bring him millions.

Heffner lives with the curtains always drawn,
with his day secretary and his night secretary,
in a life without sun nor seasons, where the outside
only penetrates through newspapers, magazines and television.
And he has no need for the plane with its ballroom.

The vulva, the phallus, breasts,
weren't pornography
but sacred symbols in the caves.
Cannibalism dates not from that age.
It's from more advanced cultures. More recent.
        Miss America is descended from Isis, Ceres, Aphrodite,
as Cox saw it.
But it is also that of the singing of a Magnificat on television
for the one who exalts the powerful, heaps riches upon the wealthy
and sends the poor away empty-handed.
"The marriage of religion and economics" Fuentes mentions.

Production, the sacred work of man
for what will yield bigger profits. A casino? A Casino.
Who in Cuba owned the hotels, the railways,
the baseball players?
                things, things, things
production of things for men things
but the bad thing's not things
but the things that are abstractions.
        Bank notes bonds shares are abstractions.
"The pale-faces have ideas, the Indians visions."
Monopolies, trusts, banks, limited companies.
                Their greed is figures on the Exchange.
        The abstract
versus the concrete, the illusory
above the real.
Like the one who during the Second World War,
Nicaraguan Minister of Health, adulterated all the quinine,
a doctor incidentally, mixing it with talcum powder.
Calculate then all the fevers. Or real deaths.

And the Dance goes on.
For them only what's theirs is real,
only what they own exists
and they own it to destroy it.
Preferring production to love.
The mechanical to the living.
With no eye for admiring landscapes
but yes the mythical hoardings.
—Where do you live?
—Palm Beach.
—Yes, but where do you live?
—Palm Beach.
—But where do you live in your real life?
Their reality is like a convention of Jaycees
(who officially believe in God and free enterprise)
those from Nebraska dressed like sailors in the convention
those from Georgia with a symbolic peach on their backs
those from Kansas in green tunics with a yellow sunflower
and Nevada with wide sombreros and leather trousers.
This is the dance.
The buffalo was reduced to the nickel coin and the zoo
and the Indian to the other side of the nickel and to the reservation.
Not long ago, one spring morning,
a group saddled up the horses
"as in the days of old but silent and sorrowful."
—Where to?—they asked them.—To the buffalo.
—But there are no buffalo.
—We know that.—Why are you going then?
—We always go at this time of the year, maybe we'll find one.
Instead of fertilizing rain
acid rain.
Trees withering beneath acid rain.
Poisonous snow.
Lakes without a fish.
Phytoplankton dying.
Sulphur falling from the sky over the fruit.
Pines bleached by sulfuric acid.

Beauty posing, before pornographic cameras,
celestial flesh of woman, unlife-like luster, unreal
on the cover.

Amortizations	Interests
50-48	670.59

The bread of life, of the wheat trust.
My customers are nothing but respectable people
said that brothel owner in Rivas
to Father García Laviana.
Meaning rich people and/or Somocistas.
That's why the Spaniard García Laviana cast aside his cassock
and joined the Frente, and died in combat.
In a place called "Hell", for fuck's sake!
because of the respectable customers.
So women might feel discontented with what they have
the president of Allied Stores Corporation explains.
"We're not selling lipstick, rather we're buying customers."
In fact they do sell lipstick but a lipstick of illusions.
To the cheery chant of cash registers.
...they were decent customers...
This is also the dance of the Greek millionaire
Onassis, collector of fleets of oil-tankers
and Greek amphoras and famous women
(who recently bought Jacqueline Kennedy asking for a discount)
owner of a gold bath-tub in which Churchill once bathed,
collector also of Errol Flynn, Churchill, etc,
whose age no journalist could ever pin down
much less what he was worth,
condemned to wander through the wine-dark sea
on his $5,000,000 raft, he put in to the Bahamas
and amid the pink-fingered aurora posed for photographers

with his newly acquired wife.

Rose Mary, the model was very beautiful in the flesh,
        to me too,
and he loved her a lot, Joaquín, in the flesh, *really* loved her,
his model. When she left him he suffered so much
because he kept spotting her everywhere, on the subway,
Times Square, bars. (Not the beloved you never see again.)
He was in a bar with me for example, and behind the counter
on the wall: she on metal, almost life-size,
displaying an iced beer and her candescent beauty.

Nobody even knew whether he was alive.
        One of the world's richest men.
Hidden away in the penthouses of luxury hotels
all over the world. *Desert Inn.*
                                        Paradise Island.
        Managua Intercontinental Hotel.
He took over the whole upper floor of the hotels.
        The windows covered with black drapes.
Adhesive tape around the edges to keep viruses out.
Once a Hollywood beau, the sight of him
provoked horror.
Tangled beard down to his navel.
Dishevelled hair halfway down his back.
His fingernails two inches long,
those on his feet yellow and curled like corkscrews.
Walking very hunched, when he walked. Naked.
Holed up in hotels he spun a web which ensnared an entire state,
reached the highest levels of the United States' government,
intertwined with tentacles of the Central Intelligence Agency.
It's said he bought and sold a hundred Richard Nixons
including Richard Nixon.
                        A myriad of companies.
                His fortune was 2.5 billion.
                        A million people working for him.
A very select mafia protected him from the outside world

but not from himself.
          A sun-less, pleasure-less life.
A hermit billionaire.
          His food for years, day or night:
          cans of Campbell's chicken soup.
Didn't smoke. Didn't drink. Just injected a clear liquid.
Told Somoza he was the first hippy.
From 1970 on he watched no television, so he didn't know
what day it was, nor even what month or season.
But he did watch films, yes. Many times the same one.
One he saw 150 times.
The outside world teeming with bacteria terrified him.
Contamination from other human beings terrified him.
Those who typed for him had to wear white gloves.
When they touched him to lift him up it had to be with a Kleenex
—"insulation" he called it—
     In school he'd said that he was different from other people
     because people didn't interest him
     only minerals.
When they gave him a spoon it was wrapped in Kleenex, with the wrapping
bound with another Kleenex so as not to contaminate the first.
His enormous nails seemed heaven-bound in prayer
asking for a perfect germ-proof sterility.
For years he lived lying down watching films,
immersed in a two-dimensional world he could select and control.
From his room in the *Desert Inn* he phoned out:
          "Bob, I'm feeling lonesome."
He who set new flying records
and was seen with so many beautiful women in the 40's.
Archetype of the American hero.
It was said he was the epitome of what every North American wanted to be.
They compared him to Narcissus, the beautiful youth.
                                        And like Narcissus
self-destructive.
Who had 1,000 virgins in Hollywood and not a single child.
He'd pick starlets as concubines
he paid their rent and never saw them again.

Never slept twice with the same woman.
In the Dance he had two roles, the Prince and the Pauper.
Said to Somoza he'd whittled his friends down from 15 to five
and from five to one
and then none.
He welcomed him in the anteroom of his private plane (in Managua)
and beforehand they cut his hair and nails.
He told him he was the first he'd received in 23 years.
("He asked me how it was I spoke such beautiful English
and I said it was because I'm a Latin from Manhattan.")
Later he took over the top floor of the Managua Intercontinental.
With Somoza he was planning a chain of casinos in Nicaragua
—Land of lakes and volcanoes—
like his chain in Las Vegas.
Tourists would swamp us right down to Solentiname. God spared us from him.
The midnight earthquake.
"He asked me what was happening and I told him, earthquake,
and that the whole of Managua was tumbling down. As he didn't seem to hear me or understand,
he showed not the slightest concern. Spoke of wanting to see a film."
Ushered down and out of his hotel, he was indifferent to the ruins
all about him. But half-naked, defenceless in the immense dust cloud
of germs which rose above the devastated city,
he who always kept everything around him sterilized,
a kind of deity of Sterility,
flew off that very dawn in a private plane
and didn't stop until he reached London.
He never asked about the death toll.
He died naked in the penthouse of an Acapulco hotel
like one of the *New York Times*' Most Needy Cases.
A poor soul despite a billion and a half dollars.
In a darkened room, silent and timeless,
at the foot of the bed as always the screen
and at the head as always the projector.
He left no child, no will to anyone.
In his Las Vegas casino chain, a minute's silence.

The cards, the roulette, the dice, the ladies by
their slot-machines with coins in paper cups paused.
"Okay, minute's over, play on."
            And in the ballrooms the dance resumed.

CANTIGA 28

Epithalamium

The Great Mystery, SACRAMENTUM,
the separation of life in the two sexes.
        That polar separation.
"Even now the true significance of sexuality is hidden from us."

                Without sexuality
there'd be no diversity in unity,
merely identical beings like blue algae,
a world of twins alone.
Sexuality is not only two in one
but the union of two for a different one.
In effect it is the source of diversity, of difference,
life's asymmetry and its beauty.
To unite to be no longer only the same,
                                        and to die.

It began with the infinitesimal, humble courtship of two algae cells
in the romantic watery medium.
Their amorous flagellae draw close to each other and caress
and then the cellular contents fuse.
Sex created death.
Sexual multiplication (not reproduction at all)
                brought about the need to die.
Sexual multiplication is not reproduction but variation
and being born is that.
        The amoeba never changes because it doesn't die.
Love and death were evolution's means of acceleration.
        And so in order to love one had to die.
                The amoeba reproduces without changing or dying.
So that death then is a condition of evolution too.

Death not by accident but
a necessity prescribed by the genetic program.
Sexual multiplication demands disappearance.
Sex is variety, and variety evolution.
Sex is one of evolution's two inventions, and death
the other.
Sex also evolution's principal instrument
because natural selection is sexual selection. And death.
Which is what Darío said, I don't know why, when into the mouth
of that Centaur he put:
        "Death is the victory of human progeny."

The green Chlamydomonas in the sea, single-celled creatures,
reproduce by dividing asexually
but sometimes after dividing and dividing
the solitary Chlamydomonas produce sexual cells
which pair and make a single cell
which produces a new individual Chlamydomonas
creating the variability of the new generation
in other words—sex a contribution to change
the invention of sex so as to accelerate
        —through more and more deaths of new separate individuals—
                evolution's
                        modifications,
                                transformations.
Beyond the roadside ditch the plant-life
(the road was in Cuba)
is one green amorphous mass
but if you look more
closely
each specimen is a being in its own right, individual, a-
symmetrical
product of a seed, its own,
itself a product of two individual creatures,
and further along the young mulatto girl in yellow
by the asphalt waiting for a bus:
a product also of two and individual.

But the pain of being an individual, of being alone,
        of not being two,
painful not to be two.
        Loneliness of being one.
Yet I am more myself
the more I unite.
            TO PREVENT OUR EXTINCTION.
                To love is to be eternal.
Not two separate but one union.
An atom's nothing but empty space and fields of energy
yet it seeks out another atom.

Like for example love in the hydrogen atom:
union of positive proton with negative electron.
The cosmos may have begun with only two particles
of opposite electrical charges.
And it is the same as saying that the universe is made of light.
Father Ángel that Ash Wednesday in Managua
    (me an acolyte)
Planting the ash cross with a flourish on people's foreheads:
        "Light you are and unto light you must be transformed."
He himself already light now. Angel of light.

    ...of opposite electrical charges.
He hugs her,
hugs her from above with his front fins;
for hours the couple drift united,
            without waves or currents parting them.
Or when the torrid rains come
    in the torrid zone
and the vegetation grows green again, all of it deep green,
and the animals come into heat
                        (and love truly does
            come out of the sky).
Our caresses are not because we're human, says Gourmont,
but because we're animals.

The pleasure in the caress is
because it's useful to the species.
A thirst vaster than the ocean.
Or hunger: "The species' hunger" said St. Augustine
who suffered it so keenly.
Skin merged with skin,
Caress against caress.
Souls bound in the binding of bodies.
And one whose soul is moon-desolate.
Ah, my people for whom I sing.
Girl thinking of boy
or boy of a girl.
Difference in their likeness.
Likeness in their difference.
It's all there.
Wanting always to be with the other being
wanting to enter the other being
be the other being
take a hand
hand not one's own hand
mouth thirsting for thirsty mouth
wanting to enter.

The woman opening herself and the man entering
is the natural symbolism
of a more mysterious communication:
two in one
and
one in two
(becoming more themselves the more they are united).
And in this light the sexual act makes sense.

Life is duplication of the gift received.
Life has one function alone:
new life.
From life to life.
Life transmitting life to itself.

What lizards do is turn out more lizards.
Isn't procreation the reason for our existence?
Given we're all children. Children of one and the same father.
The deaths a condition of evolution.
We die so that more may be born. For the others.
Stars die
to bring about the birth of other stars.
    Stars are born of stars
and we owe our bodily existence
to events which took place billions of years ago
in stars that lived and died
long before the solar system began.
And we will return to being stellar gas again.
                    Hydrogen I will be but hydrogen in love.

CANTIGA 29

Quantum Canticle

Approach this rock by the sea, and look:
it's almost entirely empty space
(look at it electronically)
it's evanescent foam, all of it,
like sea foam that's born from the rocks and on the rocks is undone.
Ephemeral particles that are neither here nor there,
coming and going at the whim of the waves of an empty sea.
Particles which spring from nothing and return to oblivion.
From emptiness to emptiness they travel.
"The word reality cannot be employed for particles."
In principle there is no absolute emptiness.
Or an absolute emptiness in every sense.
The electron may have emerged from nowhere
but it left something in the nothingness whence it emerged,
a kind of hollow in the emptiness, or invisible bubble of nothing.
"The position of a particle in space
is dependent on its position in time."
Gravity is spacetime curved, turned in on itself.
And at the same time spacetime has the structure of foam
and it evaporates like foam on the sand.
Chaotic sea where even the common notion of place disappears!
And where space itself can change and move
(and become foam).
We live on an earth of indeterminate electrons,
interchanging photons of confused position, photons
lost in the fog of quantum uncertainty.
That are like the almost invisible tennis ball
which capriciously makes the players run

with indeterminate movements but also with well-determined movements.
A world which is nothing but a structured nothingness.
The phantasmal semiforms of the void
in the agitated sea of virtual quanta which are the whole of space.
Elemental particles that seem not to possess internal structure
and together constitute all known forms of matter.
Ghostly particles coming and going, appearing
and disappearing.
Particles which dance wild rock in a hall of adorned nothing.
They are not
exactly phantom electrons those of quantum equations
but phantom realities, phantom worlds
which only exist when they are observed.
Einstein could never accept it his whole life long.
Uncertainty as an inherent property of matter.
This intangible quality of quantum particles...
"Nobody understands quantum physics"
said Feynman.
Thus the quanta:
just as there is no order in these cantos.
Shiva is none other than quantum mechanics.
Matter has no substance, only rhythm.
The wild dance of particles to the sound of quantum music.
Gravitational waves have no real substance; they are
simply undulations of nothingness.
Particle and wave.
Particles undulate like waves in the sea
and simultaneously are the grains of sand in the sea.
They are the concentric circles of a stone in a pond
and simultaneously the stone that falls into the pond.
A ball A that travels to a place B
will always travel along the same path in identical conditions.
But particles travel in a thousand ways, however they want.
As though mathematics doesn't exist at that level in matter,
merely sub-atomic anarchy.
The discipline of the macroscopic world breaks down in that world.
The reality underlying the unreal quantum world.

The impalpable palpable world!
Can nature possibly be so absurd?
Heisenberg asked himself in the park at dawn, in the wavering
Danish light, following his lengthy discussions with Bohr.
Bohr who rejected theories for being insufficiently mad.
(But note, the Dane also rejected the theory of nuclear terror
and Churchill wanted him thrown in jail.)
And not only is the particle blurred in space,
worst of all is that space itself is blurred.
Not only is it not known where a particle is,
but it's not known where places themselves are.
Virtual protons can spring from nowhere for an instant.
What appears to be empty space is full of virtual particles.
An electron swims in a sea of phantom particles.
Even at rest an electron is not at rest
but among the particle waves of the void.
Solid matter largely made up of empty space.
Something solid, this book say, is almost entirely empty space.
As though it were a grain of sand in an empty theater.
These things were discovered
at the same time as abstract painting was being discovered.
Einstein believed that it was false.
And the photon which is timeless,
Big Bang and present time the same instant as far as it's concerned.
The photon which seems to be the frontier between nothingness and matter:
particles which are not genuinely matter
but certainly the binder of matter.
Without which there'd be no structures nor activities nor consequences.
According to quantum physics
in regard to quanta
the sequence of time is meaningless.
Sub-atomic particles in their erotic dance
move about in any direction
also towards the past.
According to quantum physics
time, potentially, is reversible.
We are matter certainly, but what is matter?

Made up of uncertain electrons
in a sea of probability waves.
The diverse components of the universe
are not diverse.
According to Bell's theorem
all things are united in the base.
What base?
Might it not be chaos
the root of matter, merely chaos,
random changes subject to the laws of probability
alone?
The insubstantial particles of matter.
Or could it be like saying: the spiritual matter of the cosmos?
Asimov has spoken of a "semi-mysticism among scientists".
Nagarjuna's *sunyata* ("emptiness").
And given that an atom for the most part is empty space.
Atoms are full of emptiness!
Transparent like the spirit
matter is nothing more
than empty space
and fields of energy.
What energy is we don't know.
(Not the faintest idea.)
Each atom sings its song, as the Lama said,
and the sound makes the dance.
The electron's position is never the same
nor different.
It is not motionless
nor in motion.
"The object in motion does not exist
merely its movement."
Only the dance
without dancers.
Particles which are and are not,
or cease to be in the instant they are,
in a confusion of creation, annihilation and transformation.
Creation and destruction is the dance.

Empty atoms and so full of appetites and desires.
Creation and destruction is the great cosmic dance.
        Nothing is born of itself, nothing perishes.
It's the dance of Shiva.
                Permanent, only the change.
The vast empty heavens within atoms.
Because the fact is that objective physical reality
is composed of emptiness.
Great dreamer who in the long night dreams the great dream of the universe
said the emperor Kien-Wenn.
        Is the universe a dream with neither space nor time?
According to Heisenberg's principle
at sub-atomic level there is no exact science.
"God does not play dice" said Einstein.
                        But could he be playing billiards?
Billiard players know:
the slightest touch alters everything for the three balls.
Even atoms obeyed determined rules
it was once believed.
But rebellious aspects were discovered in nature.
Instead of the rigid clockwork mechanism
the unpredictable zigzag of the electron.
Instead of the object considered solid
vibrating phantasmagoric energy.
The electron with nothing internal, not "constituted" of anything.
The electron surrounded by a cloud of virtual particles.
The electron without orbit or trajectory.
Impossible to ascertain how it travelled from A to B.
"In fact electrons behave in certain aspects
as though they could be found in many different places at the same time."
Extravagance of this creation
        exploited in commercial microelectronic devices.
The sub-atomic particle goes where it will.
It prefers the shortest route, like you crossing a park,
but like you it can wander off to read a newspaper on a bench,
or take a detour to the ice-cream seller, to the water fountain,
or cut in further to where a couple are copulating.

Particles vague entities
no longer the tangible, palpable billiard balls.
As to whether energy is substance...
Particles so insubstantial
that they are almost the speed of light.
A particle travelling tentatively from A to B, stumbling.
Every path is an improbability to an uncertain destination.
Not one case of not being able to know at the same time the position and movement
of an electron,
like in which country a person is now and travelling on which airline,
rather that an electron *cannot have* simulataneously position
and movement.
"Anyone who is not shocked by quantum theory has not understood it,"
said Bohr.
What's considered real, made up of non-real elements,
or which cannot be considered as real.
And Schrödinger, he of the dead-alive cat: "I don't like it
and I regret ever having got involved with it."
Quantum emptiness teeming with virtual particles.
And according to Sitter, the only thing expanding is empty space!
Are we anything other than an order in the chaos?
How is it that a collection of disorganized particles
and even of disorganized molecules
can become a fish, or a lily, or Aristotle?
The music of the spheres present in atoms too.
The study of the heavens like a branch of the study of particles.
And what is almost mystical:
physics laboratories, the scientists
who study particles, are made of particles,
particles studying particles.
Pauli maintained that there had to be a neutral particle
as yet undetected.
And there was: "neutrite," neutrino in Italian.
The ghostly neutrino
manifest merely in the so-called weak force,
and which almost doesn't exist.

(The so-called weak force which exerts no attraction
except in cases like the explosion of a supernova.)
So insubstantial neutrinos
that they almost completely dispense with solid matter,
very close to being a pure nothingness.
They pass through matter as though there were no matter.
Elusive to the point of being spectral,
yet despite their intangibility they are what most abounds in the universe,
the universe being in effect a sea of neutrinos
and their total weight is greater than that of the stars.
Matter seems ever increasingly less materialist.
"The strong mystical aroma of the new physics" (P. Davies)
Or at least quantum materialism is increasingly more phantasmagoric.
Sub-atomic quantum particles so illogical!
Also particles so small that actually they don't have parts.
Quarks, without spatial extension,
substances with nothing in their interior,
but which are fundamental constituents of matter.
Just as protons and neutrons make up the atomic nucleus
protons and neutrons are composed of quarks
which we observe in ordinary matter
(a woman, an apple, a Newton)
while others make up sub-atomic particles so fleeting
that they play no role in ordinary matter.
Without apparent structure,
that is, incapable of being reduced to something smaller,
quarks always occur with other quarks, never alone.
In particle accelerators
they've never been seen in a free state.
With an electrical charge lower than that of an electron.
Three types of quark are postulated, with "tastes" and "colors."
Color and tastes are quantum properties particular to quarks.
Quark is a word taken
from a nonsense word in Joyce's *Finnegans Wake.*
Three quarks for Muster Mark!
They are existence without extension.
They are points without dimension.

And without them there'd be no sunlight
nor atomic nuclei nor you nor I.

But my questions concern the world beyond the quanta.

CANTIGA 30

Dance of the Stars

In the beginning, naturally, not even physical laws existed.
We emerged, it would appear, from an amalgam of chaos.
From electrons and nuclei atoms were born,
and then galaxies, stars, diamonds,
DNA, and ladies with diamonds.
        As nuclear physics discovered
                the elements are transmutable.
Hiroshima! Was that the alchemists' dream?

But it takes place within stars too and
that is the light they radiate.
The isotopes in nuclear reactors behave
as those in the center of stars.
Protons give rise to antiprotons
and the antiprotons swiftly annihilate themselves
                                        (or they wed?)
with other protons, in a huge explosion
of energy.
And neutrons and antineutrons are born in pairs
which cling to each other
                                    and kill each other:
        Marriage of matter and antimatter!
(Such is the nomenclature.)

In an Art School classroom in Vienna:
Exquisite the face
        and more so the naked body
        on a carpeted dais,
                                reclining,
before the male and female painters

with easels, brushes and palette.
The great mystery
that it's possible in experiments to observe an electron
without knowing what that electron is like when not being observed
    (something which verges on the mystical I think)
because we've no idea what it is when it's not observed
and this is the essential characteristic of the quantic world,
our incapacity to state whether it exists when unobserved,
nobody has ever seen an atomic nucleus, says Eddington,
but merely the experiments, which is
like drawing out from within a block of marble the face one wants,
the quantic world is what's observed and where nothing's real
at most a clutch of coherent illusions
like saying there are several varieties of neutrinos
with their respective anti-varieties,
the equations give no indication of the particle's behavior
when it's not observed, and the interpretation of particle is
in our mind, and it may be nothing more than a coherent illusion.
        Reclining in front of the easels.
Polished and motionless marble-like whiteness
        hair like sunlight
                pupils Alpine blue
    the breasts perfect but distinct
on the one side round like an apple
        from that angle
on the other side arced slightly upwards
        with volcano-sharp silhouette
            or here rather, white peak of Alps
lower center the navel
        like the center of the world
knot of the cord of life that has linked us all together
and lower still
        above the closed legs
            the soft hair
                like a tender grass
around the rim of the fountain of life.
We move on to another room in the School

leaving behind the Secret Garden.
Nobody knows what the quantic world is like
we only know that that's how it is.
A ghostly world of probabilities...
The human body exactly midway between microcosm and cosmos.
Dependent on the minutest of chemical affinities
and on the thrust of the most immense masses.
The nuclei of your atoms born in the nuclei of stars.
Through the thin gassy layer
which like a cellular membrane envelops the earth,
—a single cell, the entire biosphere—we gaze at
the sky full of stars and they full of life.
But we're still alone in the cosmos
awaiting extra-terrestrial forms of life
and awaiting more conscious forms of life.
In the wake of the chemical evolution, the biological one
and there's another to come.
It was a lightning ministerial tour
through that studio in the Vienna School of Art.
Again in Paris:
while
on the Quai d'Orsay
Monsieur le Ministre
was delivering his speech
naturally bored
in the elegant salon
I saw behind him
the marble Venus
(copy of copies) as though
with 2 apple halves
very prominent breasts natural-
ly
mount of Venus
very prominent
and quite suddenly I was cheered
because I remembered that
outside it was spring

I felt in that salon the emotion
of the whole of creation and I remembered
the roundness that emerged from chaos
dancing around the sun
        with mountains
                apples
couples making love.

All elemental corpuscles are composed
of the same matter, which we may call energy
                                        or universal matter.
Merely diverse forms, under which
matter may appear.
        The cosmos is spiritual matter. (Chardin)
                And it's not accidental
the universe. It's perfection
like the clock in Strasbourg cathedral.
                The vibrations of electrons.
A positron is an anti-electron, that's to say
a positive rather than negative electron.
        (The world's not an illusion
        rather our vision of the world is the illusion
        or the confusion of the world with the vision.)
The photons of anti-atoms are identical to those of atoms.
        Love among atoms is called magnetism.
                —The atoms' nuptials—.
But the greatest force known to nature
a hundred times greater than the electromagnetic one
binds the nucleus.
        As toads sing all night.
                They sing to the females,
                        they sing for copulation.

        That moves the sun and the other stars.
Man flower and woman flower come together
and male flower spurts out its white pollen.
MYSTERION. *Sacramentum*: "sensible sign"

of the weddings of the universe.
"The visible world is the invisible organization of energy."
—To unite the diverse.
Did I say that the entire universe is sex?
Let's say too: the solidarity of the universe.
Our I will be part of a universal I.
One day the solar system will be ash
not so love.
Electrons and positrons are always born in pairs.
A being that opens itself up and another that penetrates.
Dialectical sex.
Differentiation of the union.
Invariably children of a duality.
The direction of evolution now is
concentration
or centration.
The greater the differentiation
the greater the union.
Fusion and not fission.
The impulse towards union was already there in our protoplasm.
Love, in our genes.
Irreversible love.

Newton saw what united
the apple, the earth and the moon.
The dance of energy.
Electricity, coal, food, are energy.
Energy is rotation which is why we have day and night.
It creates high tide and low tide.
Winter and summer:
The lengthening of the nights that causes the buds to contract
and the lengthening of the days that swells the harvests.
The continual dance of energy.
Movement and rhythm are essential properties of matter.
The music of the spheres.
The melody of the waves of the universe.
All is waves.

Movement and rhythm:
the existential form of matter.
The music of the spheres
and the music of atoms and molecules.
And the heartbeat.
The coming and going of migratory birds
that travel half the globe to make love
(and whales entire oceans).
And the rhythm of the heart:
the harmony of the harp of the universe.

The dance of energy.
The song of atoms.
The calculations of interatomic forces
that unite atoms in molecules...
That's where Alfonso Cortés's line came from,
when we still believed in the existence of ether,
light the vibration of ether:
"The violins of the ether pulsate their clarity."
Alfonso the Mad, in Managua madhouse.
(The end of his poem "Dance of the Stars")
Pythagoras found that if a string gave Do
when cut in two it also gave Do,
cut in three it gave Sol, and in five it was Mi,
and thus discovered that harmony was number.
Musical notes share the same laws of thermodynamics.
Einstein couldn't abide ugly equations
and Dirac criticized Einstein
for dismissing Schrödinger's wave equation
it being so beautiful.
Earthly matter and heavenly matter with Newton
became the same.
The movements of the moon and the planets:
those of apples.
Apparently free atoms
obey a law of universal harmony.
Subatomic particles

are not solid yet neither unreal.
They are not minute matter but organizations of behavior.
    All solid matter is empty.
        There is no matter,
            only energy interacting
with energy.
        Only dance.

    Proton and electron are not objects, they're ideas.
The reality of the unreal. But
    aren't the images in the mirror real?
There's a theory
that the universe may be merely a fragment (for the time being)
of the universe.
Like saying: a bath-tub (for the time being) with lukewarm water.
"The limits of the observable universe are not necessarily
those of the imaginable universe."
And can we really understand the observable universe?
And if the solar system is an atom of a larger universe,
and an atom a minute solar system whose atoms in turn...etc
    and so on ad infinitum
which was inspired by a tin of Quaker oats
which has a Quaker with a tin of Quaker oats
which has a Quaker with a tin of Quaker oats
which has a Quaker...
And if the infra-subatomic lies beneath subatomic particles?
"The Lord's quantum mechanics," says Schrödinger.

Ourselves with the riddle of the universe, and the riddle
of ourselves.
    A self-conscious universe.
All things in rotation, from proton to galaxy,
and the question:
whether the entire universe isn't rotating too...
Yet it seems that time itself may last no more than
a hundred thousand million years.
You may doubt the sense and purpose of the universe

but not its beauty.
                Golden moon above the latrine.
                        Dark cricket singing in its hole.
Long croaking of frogs like the sound of a train
and other frogs further off like another train.
        The blind bat that gives chase with its echo
        and knows which echo is tastier, and ever closer
        until it swallows its echo.
                Black the islands of the archipelago, the lake
                nickel-plated by the moon.
Spectra of thousands of millions of stars
seen in the unique spectrum of a galaxy: like a choir
in which we hear not the individual singers but merely the choir.
About to land in Panama, from the plane, for a split-second
I saw mirrors gleaming, blinding, with sunlight. They were puddles
and a split-second later simply earth-colored water
those puddles.
Green valleys of my childhood with tiny cows
and chalets amid sharp snowy peaks, on the luminous plates
of my childhood, in which I would lose myself
sprawled on the floor of the hallway in León.

Humanity's question identical to the child's: Why?
        Why is the night black?
                                Why whys?
Who put matter or energy into the universe?
Was it taken from nothing
or formed from pre-existent matter?
Who put matter or energy into the universe,
for I want to embrace him, to kiss him?

CANTIGA 31

The Empty Grave

We rebel against this. Not the dying
but because when all's said death triumphs over life.
What's worse, that death should triumph over love.
That
"so much love and to be powerless against death."
They buried Angelica today.
Children's voices rise up behind the walls,
amid the recent-rained freshness of their school day dusk.
It's my infancy over again on this Monday.
Old age and death herald new infancies.
One childhood after another. After, the children will be others.
Their cries are like protests, lashing out against death.
It's no use. The present like a clock running fast
always finishes ahead of their games.
So me a schoolboy in León
some old Monday or Tuesday, a rain-soaked evening,
saying to the old servant Concha
stupid old fool, and she, the bitch:
you'll be old too if you don't die before
and me not knowing which was worse... (Perhaps better
to die before, than be old like Concha).
Is a life not based on carbon not possible?
Isn't it possible, Angelica, to live even within a star,
with a body yes, but not this "body of death" Rom. 7:24
this carbon-based body of death?
Life had always found a way on earth,
from one genetic error to another, trial and error,
changes in amino acids due to environmental changes,
groping its way through the mutations, seeking out, finding the truth
as though evolution had a guide. And might that not be the case,

under different conditions, beyond the earth?
The discovery of another way towards the truth of a new life.
            The Way, the Truth, and the Life.

Life as a cosmological phenomenon,
not only on this earth.

Life emerged from the sea like Venus in the Paleozoic.
The betrothal of the first two cells was in the Pre-Cambrian.
In the Mesozoic it was the turn of flowers with colors and smells.
Reptiles dominated all terrestrial life.
Then they became dragons
            spreading terror through earth, sea and air
      deinos (frightening) and *sauros* (alligator)
and still they parade through myths and in our dreams.
Tupana breathed into the moulded clay and he spoke.
He spoke thus: "How beautiful it all is to me!"
Tupana, the tale goes, was by his side but he didn't see him.
Night came and the moon rose on the edge of the sky.
He said: "What fire is that? Its flame gives no heat,
it is as cold as water."
He could see the water, the earth, the sky, the sun, the moon, the night
but he could not see Tupana who was still beside him.
"What is that whose hairs dance in the sky's breath?"
The tree answered: "I am the earth's flowing hair."
"What's that you have there above yellow as the moon?"
"They are my fruits, from which others like me will be born."
But, the tale goes, he still didn't know how people feed.
"Put the fruit in your mouth, swallow the soft part
and bury the seed in the earth."
The Edenic garden with broad leaves where dinosaurs grazed
are now beds of coal.
Rousseaunian ferns have been preserved in carbon.
The cell came out of the water, was able to hear music and gaze at the stars.
But is there a long term objective in the universe?

Galactic dust we are and galactic dust we shall again be.

But isn't there something which will endure
between galactic dust and galactic dust?
Cloud of dust,
from the condensation of a spinning dust-cloud
the sun was born.
The universe as product of law, not chance.
But which law if not the law of love?
How can blind chance create an eye?
If the sum of proton and electron masses were to add up
to something more than the mass of the neutron
the hydrogen atom would fall apart, the sun would go out,
there'd be no world.
The coincidence of the balance between carbon and oxygen...
The coincidences are infinite
and cry out to be explained.
Or it's a planned work, as Fred Hoyle said.
We are dust.
But the universe holds within itself the seeds of life.
Universe which is grave and resurrection. And death
a liberation of wave energy which is released into space.

Driving along the Mediterranean coast road,
or driving along the coastal road in the Yucatan
each little town its own little cemetery.
And they're sad. Even the one on the exquisite *Isla Mujeres*, Yucatan,
where we saw the Pirate's Grave (he not buried there:
the grave was a gesture of affection since he died God knows where).
Martí also came here, "tiny white houses" he said
and he found it cheerful.
There have always been cemeteries on earth
ever since *Homo sapiens.*
The truth is that the entire earth is a cemetery.
The extra-terrestrials up above
do they too bury their dead?

When fox cubs and tadpoles are born,
and the male butterfly dances before the female,

and the kingfishers cross beaks together,
and the days grow longer and ovaries swell,
the swallows will return from the south...
Will they return from the south?
"The darke swallows"
the ones that flew in September to North Africa
covering the telegraph wires,
casting shadows over the afternoons,
filling the sky with their chatter,
those won't be back.
And the eels that swam down the rivers of Africa
until they reached the Sargasso Sea,
to celebrate their nuptials in bridal gowns of silver plate
like the fine ladies at the court of King Don Juan:
What e're became of them?
The *palolos* of the South Seas
that come up to the surface for their feast of fecundation
in the November full moon
and on those nights cover the entire sea with a phosphorescent foam
and sink back down into the sea never to return?
And the golden *Catopsilias* attired like Queen Thi
that migrate in autumn to the N.N.W.
leaving behind the nectar, the flowers and copulation,
while ahead of them lie only waves, salt, the solitude of the sea
and death (the north-north-west)
N.N.W.
but their direction is always N.N.W?

As leaves in autumn detach themselves to protect the tree
conserving its sap. (It's not that they dry up.)
They strangle their own petioles
so that the lightest breeze might carry them off.
With chlorophyll gone
their pigments become visible, the splendid autumn colors!
And so they die. To enable the birth of others the following year.
And the tiny ear of corn plucked tender in Nicaragua
—chilote—

so that a larger one may thrive?
Figure of the beautiful princess Xilonem (*Xilotl*)
who in a year of drought gave herself up in sacrifice for her tribe
so that it might rain. (According to the interpretation
of Dr Dávila Bolaños who in the last year of the Somozas
gave his life for his people.)
"Like ears of corn we shed our grain"... Pre-Colombian
or present-day maize is the same, the same
Nahuatl poet or present-day man.

What was believed in long before Christ.
　　"Number your organs and they are complete and healthy"
(On a tomb). Inscribed on an Egyptian tomb.
　　Or the (female) epitaph:
　　　　'I am earth, the earth is goddess
　　　　consequently I am not dead'
　　in Latin long dead.
Likewise the Hottentots: that the dead aren't dead.
The Oglalas: that as smoke ascends...
Or in ancient ceremonies of the new moon in California:
　　"like the moon..."
As though ripped from the womb of matter
to go forth into the Great Matter of without
screaming in the full light.
In another placenta which is the globality of the universe.
And the purest freedom begins
in communion with the total reality of matter,
　　in the palpitating unity of the cosmos,
　　　　or heart of All.
　(Extinguished the damp opaque fire of life.)
Dear girl, you are now in another place and in another now.
Why did Martí call death "necessary"
and in the same sentence "triumph of life"?
The Santi Pietri e Marcelino catacomb features a banquet,
a subterranean banquet where, reclining, they order wine.
Irene and Agape serve wine.
　On the plates, fish.

mo-nee-ry, Guarani, ("to make the word flow")
means to rise from the dead
and *mbo-e-te-ry* ("to make truth-telling flow")
means to rise from the dead.
That's to say the Word
which is the part of the soul that doesn't die
(with emphasis on that truth-telling).

Dying is cells breaking down into complex molecules
and complex molecules into simple molecules
until they re-emerge (perhaps in an ear of wheat).
Everywhere my molecules will travel, my electrons.
In this context the Theban sarcophagus is saying
"...transfiguration instead of sexuality..."
We know that your mass of energy will not be lost;
but: to preserve as yours *something* more.
Since each of us is a transitory evolutive phase.
To other dimensions of the universe
different from spacetime.
A waking up.
As when one dreams
that he is falling in a pit and he awakes
on the point of falling.
Condemned to return to the pre-life?
(Chardin asks) Or to the sub-life?
No, Mejía, no Gutiérrez.
What happened with the body of Jesus.
That event in history:
an empty sepulchre.
Hades has been defeated.
Death no longer makes any sense.
Life makes sense.
The iron in your blood will return to the earth's core.
Yet beyond that the surprise awaits.
Not a dream-like world, but so real
that previous reality and dream will seem the same.

The second principle:
decadence augments, or cannot decrease.
The shift from light to the dark depths,
from love to oblivion.
The distance between two distant objects
continually increasing!
The second law of thermodynamics
which is death.
(Life runs against the current.)
Our bodies built of fragile molecules
which can only bear moderate temperatures.
Chayules.
We are like the minute air-colored chayules
which fly for a mere twenty-four hours
and to them their life is of inestimable value
as though it were long.
The ephemeral biochemistry of life.
While the universe tends towards the simple
there is an isolated evolution towards complexity.
Against the current.
Most important of all:
the empty sepulchre.
That there should have been one in History who came back from death.
"Life never dies"
(Augusto César Sandino)
The absence of the corpse.
Free from the second law of thermodynamics.

Together on this same planet through black space.
One's failing is a failing of the whole thing.
One's advance belongs to all that exists.
The astonishing interconnection of all things.
Stones also feel the tides of the moon.
The solidarity among objects, said Teilhard.
Each of us part of a huge symbiosis. All
bound up in dances within dances within dances.
A consciousness even in sub-atomic particles.

"In other words, the mind is inherent to each electron."
And in all a propensity or tendency towards life
or towards more life.
Like the smell of the first rain, of
wet earth, of
wet leaves
after the dry months.
Smell of my first love which was in May precisely
with the first rains.
"In an infinite quantic future
all that is possible will eventually come to pass."
Life doesn't die.
Seeing on that bus trip through the Yucatan
—the little houses, the Indian woman by the well, the flame-trees...—
that the world is beautiful and fertile, fertile,
I felt better about my death
and about everyone's.
Frederick Engels didn't believe in the ultimate victory of the
Second Law:
The universe would by some means reconstitute itself.
By some means, the burnt-out suns.

To be human perishable as the Sun.
The hieroglyphs worn by time's sand
and disfigured by scratches from time's claw
but where it's still possible to read
NOBODY HAS MANAGED TO REMAIN IN EGYPT FOREVER
and lower down, fainter, almost dream-like, they can just decipher:
...and no life which is not like a dream...
Like a famous face on television
and in its wake merely a pulsating white nothing on the screen.
Like cattle—as sung by
the disappeared Simonides.
Generations of leaves which tumble and swirl Homer saw it
for new leaves in turn to tumble and swirl in the wood.
And so what! Our bodies
are particles of sub-atomic radiation

which on the day they are set free
will revert again to the speed of light.
And then there's no longer sex since nothing dies.
Day and night expound it to us (words of Clement of Rome).
Resurrection, day and night expound it to us.
Hence those Dionysian figures standing there, egg in hand.
And in the Babylonian girl's grave
flowers, perfume, lipstick.
Another Egypt happy and decked in flowers
the boats reflected in another ideal Nile.
pir-m-us (pyramid) "Raised out of the earth". Resurrection.
Like the soldiers' return to their homes.
On the pyramid wall: the Nile without a ripple.
Naked girls serving sandwiches and beer.
A lady vomits into a hand basin.
A dancer cavorts while they encircle her with applause.
In shallow Nile flood lands they hunt colorful ducks with nets.
None of this is here but in the beyond.
The same desire through panes of museum glass;
Brancusian sculptures of fertility and phalluses.
Or that paleolithic spiral on female idols.
The island of flowers and fruit of all colors
to the north-west of Tonga, where the dead are
but where canoes can never take you.
The Island of Fruit, of the beyond, in Malaya.
In New Zealand they hear them whistle. Greenlanders:
that they're in their tents beside a lake of ducks and fish.
Or, I don't recall whom, according to the ethnologist, they listen to
the voice of their dead in the cries of certain night birds.
In Madagascar they disinter them to take them for taxi rides and play them
the latest hits. And they tell them the latest news.
The prayer *To be reborn as you are born again!*
to the new moon in a corner of the Congo.
The Bushmen wished to have the moon's face
(only 7,500 of that tribe left)
because it dies and is reborn again.

Giraffes sniffing around in the grove,
in the tiger's pupil a trembling zebra,
howls of an opaque hyena under the moon.
        Beyond the stockade, with drums and song:
                "Death is like the moon,
                who has seen its other side?"
For the Greeks it was never the same, after Socrates's.

CANTIGA 32

In the Heavens There Are Dens of Thieves

In the beginning
"what I learnt from my father who knew it from his father
and he from his father, since way, way back,
from the beginning: he made the stars, the moon,
the animals. He said:
Do not steal from within your tribe.
Do not devour each other in the night."

Atoms from distant stars reach us.
            Stars bearers of life.
The carbon in your body
was once in the incandescent atmosphere of a star.
And it wasn't always there from the beginning,
                        the carbon in your body,
it was synthesized in stars that died
                                        and exploded
and disseminated it like pollen throughout interstellar space
and it reached the earth.
      Life derives from the death of stars.
The iron in your blood, millions of years ago,
was in a huge star.
            Or jewellers' gold:
                        from the explosion of supernovas.
Lakes, iguanas, telescopes, everything
from the fire of the stars.
When stars explode
they scatter the elements of life like spores.
            Death and birth.
                        Or: from death you are reborn.
They are atomic energy—we gaze at them up above—

energy that unravels the roses on earth.
What kinship there is between the stars
the flowers and your face
sweet girl, are you aware?
Even interstellar gas
has the same composition as a bacteria
and a girl.
There calcium dominates, in the interstellar spaces,
which dominates also in organic matter
and is the ash of the universe.
Returning to the stars: stellar species
derive one from the other like animal species.
Birth and death.
Transmitting life with death.
They are born from that tenuous matter
and when they die they return their substance to it.
The sun and the earth emerged
from the ashes of dead stars.
We are made of stars.
Come from the heart of the stars. We are them!
From the heavens, we hail from the heavens,
sweet girl to whom I was saying...
From the sky of suns and planets and moons.
Talking of the heavens
("To the poor alone the Kingdom of Heaven")
do not forget the grain of sand called earth
brilliant like Sirius.

Sparse bird song accentuated the solitude.
Occasionally in the stillness a sudden cry shook us:
some defenseless creature eating fruit
that a tiger or boa constrictor might have caught.
Dawn and dusk the howl of such lugubrious monkeys;
and suddenly, when least expected, the thunder of a huge branch
or entire tree falling, or a sound
like an iron bar against a hollow trunk;
the sound was not repeated, and the ensuing silence

filled with greater sadness.
Olive-colored water
where submerged stems could be seen way down down,
and when the rowers left off rowing
there was a sombre almost painful stillness.
Our voice with an opaque echo
in a damp and viscous air, smelling of leaves,
and from a dark corner high in the branches of a genip-tree
there came a succession of syllables,
always the same succession of syllables
mu ru cu tu tu
calling out to the female
mu ru cu
(or perhaps it was to the male)
tu tu
Until Mr. Charles Goodyear discovered vulcanization.
The Cocama with their spirit called *Mama* (Mother)
dweller of rivers and large trees.
The Witoto all born from a single cave
from where the animals also emerged.
Gentle and affectionate the Secoyas
with geometric drawings on their bodies.
Mr. Charles Goodyear discovered vulcanization
and each rubber tree marked as private property.
It was rifles against arrows.
Along the banks of the Amazon tributaries
without the colorful plumages,
their clothes of *aguaje* bark...
Oh merely a handful, sad,
hustling passing boats for kerosene.

Cartels trusts consortia corporations limited companies
—pillage of the planet—
buccaneers never saw
nor dreamed of coffers of such wealth
"Perhaps you mistake it for a cave where thieves get together?"
(Earth.) (The house of Yahweh.)

Whence
"They have turned my house into..." etc.
Half the planet
for 6% of planet-dwellers.
In Anaktuvuk: their food caribous
that feed on lichens that
feed on rainwater
which is radioactive.
And so the Eskimos poisoning themselves.
One edition of the New York Times a wood,
850 acres the Sunday edition.
1,000 years for an inch of top-soil to be formed.
Standard Oil, monopoly over the Carboniferous forests.
Smooth-tongued voice:
'The bad habit of owning only one car'
In the Gospel according to Thomas that intriguing parable:
"...it's like a woman who was carrying a jar of flour—
on her way the jar was cracked and the flour slowly spilled out,
upon reaching her house she found the jar to be empty."
Destruction on such a grand scale on the planet not seen
since the extinction of dinosaurs in the Cretaceous.
The consumer society
"the supreme pathology of history."
That if a tiny part breaks down
the whole appliance is junked.
Corrosions deliberately in-built.
Alloys so that the metal will last less.
"Progress has been made in torchlights so as"
—General Electric engineer to the directors—
"to reduce their life." Goes without saying there'll be no publicity.
Or the discovery by psychologists that
women are more attracted by red packaging...
Design is not in order to improve the product
but so that it will last less.
The brand on their products is DISSATISFACTION.
Shall we industrialize the comets?
Perhaps placed in orbit around another species' planet

a sign a thousand miles long
DRINK COCA-COLA
There's the economic problem: in the chosen asteroid
what shall we live on? What shall we import and export?
When the aim of production is not to satisfy
all human energy, intelligence, initiative,
raw materials, but is for the production and sale
of the unnecessary.

Those mystical car or airline
ads
get away get away get away
you'll enjoy yourself *elsewhere*
Buy our car and you'll make it to happy land.
In reality you'll make it to the city of meaningless lives,
where souls are mere computer diskettes
and attaché cases cruise along pavements with nobody carrying them,
the future's an escalator you travel up without moving,
love unreal like the lobby of the Fontainebleau Hotel in Miami Beach
or like those whiter than whiteness detergents
which merely exist in the announcers' imagination
or like when she says:
—I like your neck (*caressing his neck*)
And he: It's an Arrow Collar.
And hence the peasant combatant in the Frente Sandinista who believed
that those naked women in the magazines, on posters,
were not real, that's to say they weren't photos of real women,
they'd never been flesh and blood, but the fantasy of painters.

Jesus made a double quotation
when he stormed the temple, that commando raid.
From Isaiah: His house of prayer for *all the peoples of the world.*
And Jeremiah: His house become a den of thieves.
Not the temple, where he never went to pray,
the whole earth was what was profaned.
In meadows aluminium cans that never rust,
almost eternal inorganic plastic,

oil indefinitely in the azure sea.
Commercial Credit unconcerned
about the highly delicate balance,
the fauna, insects, climate, the waters,
much less the beauty.
Color of sunbeam hummingbird sucking cedar flowers
and in flight its luminous belly camouflaged as sky;
or dusk and suddenly the grass a splutter of fireflies.
Company sales rise to 1 and a half billion...

The Pemons told Brother Cesareo that when they first sighted
the buzzard-canoe, the vulture-canoe (plane)
the old men said: "We know no incantations against those things."
Like to Franz, the Swiss, on seeing the first plane above the Mato Grosso
they asked if it was fierce, what it ate, if it drank *chicha*.
And did the white man cut mirrors from the water's surface?
Switzerland was a recently discovered tribe.
The tribe of Brazilian soldiers was of ferocious men.
Radio fascinated them, to hear so many tribes in the world at night.
Having known only the rubber companies
they considered the white man backward in matters of religion.
Ignorant of all that is important, the mysteries that they know.

Tired of his long life in the office
Mr. Hiroki Mamamoto retired to the country
        he loves the country so much!
at the foot of Fuji naturally
and the following dawn he picked up the phone:
could they turn off that bird song cassette, because he wanted to sleep.

The ecological law of everything related to everything,
from fish to bacteria to the inorganic to seaweed to fish,
    an excess of seaweed increases the fish
    and the fish reduce the seaweed
    and we're back to the beautiful balance.
    Many rabbits more lynxes
    and more lynxes less rabbits.

And the ecological law that everything has its use,
there's no waste in the natural world, nothing thrown away,
all life the food of other life,
the iguana with its Churchillian jaw is in communion
with the lilac oak blossom.
The Food Chain, communion,
that's what animals are. Free of individual death.
Free of the fruit of knowledge, language, ethics, freewill,
religion.
They're merely life.
Happy expression of God's eccentricity.
"All things speak.
The skin of the wild cat speaks too.
The wild cat is cautious, silent, sensitive.
It teaches us to approach people gently."
The sacred reality of animals is merely natural resources.
Soft animal skins for the fur coat of Christina Onassis.
Until the Revolution changes it all you're thinking.
But Newton's law is
that an object at rest will remain at rest
and one in motion will continue in motion.
—Peruvian food?—Mario Vargas Llosa exclaimed astonished in Lima.
He was inviting me to dinner and asked what I wanted to eat.
—Peruvian.
—Peruvian???
...Well. Okay. We haven't had Peruvian food for a long time.
The painter Sylzo, Blanca Varela, others were there.
The typical restaurant he took me to, mirrors everywhere,
was super-exclusive Gigi Varese told me after.

"The fault dear Brutus is not in our star"
Their shares polluting the Biosphere.
Shares of a God of dead and not living people.
Shares in Death Inc.
"The Spirit of the earth hates them.
All that the Pale Face has touched is diseased."
Titanium, Thorium. Uranium. Bauxite. Circonium. Thalium.

He hates them although the millionaire Sagona (Lancôme Perfumes) prays each morning in his office
and Texan millionaires on good terms with their God
the God of Texan millionaires
and it was Rockefeller, John D., who said
that the power to make money is a gift from God.
For which reason the poor man is poor.
Because the poor man is poor
because of Rockefeller and Du Pont and Morgan. Even after the age when dinosaurs owned the planet.
"All of them with the most striking qualities
of delinquents."

The memos are optimistic.
Economic recovery continues upward
and there seems no end to the expansion,
contracts bigger than last year's
and growth ever increasing.
The memos are optimistic.
Sales have beaten all records
and consumer demand continues to rise
economists are predicting there'll be no recession
and the economic cycles have been suppressed.
The memos are optimistic.
Money has never been in such good supply
and government and capital are getting along fine
and trade union leaders have got the message
that extravagant claims are not economic.
The memos are optimistic.
General Dynamics has finished its first prototype
of which $8 billion's worth have been ordered
and it was rewarded with the contract to go to Venus
also with the construction of naval submarines
and guided missiles and nuclear reactors.
The Corporation president on weekends chops wood and he too is optimistic.

Mr. Lapham said: "Those who amass new fortunes
in the United States
it's hard for them not to be criminals."
And as for old fortunes, ask St. Hieronymus.

Cyprus was stripped of its copper
so that Mudd could be sainted as a philanthropist
it was left without copper in saecula saeculorum
because Mr. Mudd the philanthropist took it
and the Corporation went elsewhere.
And through the misery of the masses in Kuwait
it is that Kuwait Oil earns thousands of millions
and for that reason English troops in Kuwait.
Roosevelt in bed with his golden boiled eggs
each morning fixed the gold price for that day.
        Gold, odorless and dehydrated excrement.
Gold like Trujillo's who had a toilet of gold.

Only the sun, the air, rainfall, and a few other things
are not commodities.
        Christ also a commodity.
                Children of five, 2 dollars.
                Girls of ten, 10 dollars.
                65 and over, a dollar e/o.
                                Those were prices in Zanzibar.
They can be art collectors without the slightest culture.
Just need an expert. And it's not even important
to like what you buy. It's not essential.
        "To make money, naturally,
        no film is made for any other purpose."
And Ford, being interviewed: the greatest problem
for the Ford
Motor Company? Making more money.
Galbraith defines money very simply:
What is given or received buying or selling.
Plato paid his way in Egypt selling oil.
First it was many things, then metal, and then paper.

The history of money, says Galbraith, leads up to the dollar.
According to Herodotus, currency was invented by a Lydian king
on account of the prostitution of Lydian girls.
        The disciples had brought coins.
        And Francis ordered them to be thrown into the latrine.
It was Bloy who called it the devil's excrement.
        That ass shitting coins in Bosch.
"Render unto Tiberius what belongs to Tiberius" Jesus said.
"Whose is the face engraved on the coin?"
Because the effigy was nothing less than of the tyrant Tiberius.
After him another effigy, Caligula's.
When Caligula died the coins were melted down
so that the people would forget his effigy.
        Leads up to the dollar.
                And the Dance goes on.
"It wasn't exploited to the full" said Paul Getty.
                        (The Depression.)
And of Mr. Ahmanson it was said he was as delighted with it
as the owner of a funeral parlour during a plague.
        A millionaire in the electric chair?
"The law?" said the gangster to the reporter
on a Chicago street corner.
        "The last time you saw
a millionaire in the electric chair?"
They're seated
around the huge mirror-like table
their characteristic faces reflected in the varnish.
            Always huddled together
like robbers huddle together after the raid.
Everyone here? All here.
Doing what
Marx following painstaking research discovered.
        For the weaver weaving, but not the loom.
        The work produces more than it costs.
        The product is worth more than is paid for it.
    For this his reader's ticket in the British Museum.
(the same as in the "Jelepata," before, in Managua:

even girls of 13 fresh from the valley
and José Somoza killed or almost killed one of them with a hemorrhage).
The private appropriation
of what is socially produced.
No sea-gull fighting for its property is as fierce.
But the crime pages are not for the crimes
of the corporations.
Illusory bill of exchange...
They conceal the details...
And every kind of fraud.
The voluptuous Stock Market dancing to the rhythm of the war in Katanga.
Their ledgers the great arcanum.
Typically they're not given to reading books
says *Fortune*
except about management and crime stories.

"Do you know what that means—he says
a million dollars? A million dollars.
A million dollars can change a life. That's
five thousand shares in Xerox at two-hundred dollars apiece."
The biography of each one of them
and the story behind the growth of their capital
are littered with common crimes.
"General Motors could buy Delaware
if Du Pont would sell it."
The pillaging of the multimillionaire hordes.
In the background the song to a soap.
Mellifluous dithyramb to a toothpaste.
A choir of fifty voices singing Buy Buy Buy
(in Detroit)
But the Delaware Indians say:
"The Delaware feast, the Delaware creation feast
serves the entire people of the world.
A Delaware prays for good things for all.
And he prays for future times."
Certainly not for that happy kingdom
where capitalist and worker will graze together.

Mickey Mouse, Donald Duck, Archetypes.
Eisenhower's books Westerns and crime stories.
And Reagan no books.
Archetypes.
Why wouldn't the Nazis talk of
"merchandise" and "share transfers," "bottle necks"
when referring to—
(It was bucolic the railway station at the entrance
to the concentration camp.)
450 million dollars net profit
the First War brought Rockefeller
and 2,127 million the Second.
Wars are the Garden of Eden.

Invasion is "liberation"
after all the effort it took man to learn to speak.
Every word they use should be in inverted commas.
Lieutenant Arnheiter for example in
Group for the Analysis of Progress (meaning-
less words
which conceal a Navy workshop in the Pentagon
to fabricate literally *Artificial History*).
Even though there are clear, precise words, with more than enough
meaning,
such as "5 dollars against population growth
are more effective than 100 for economic growth."
To Vietnamize Vietnam was
to set Asiatics against Asiatics.
Until there's no language with which to communicate
except to say merely an hello how are you.
And thus the words of the director of the CIA:
"Covert action
is what on other occasions is called intervention,
but by secret or covert means."
And the G.B.I. can be described, said the Pentagon Colonel,
as revolutionary and counter-revolutionary war,
the Pentagon Lieutenant Colonel adding, that

similarly terrorism and anti-terrorism,
guerrilla and counter-insurgency and pro-insurgency.
"I'm a bucolic reactionary," he said
leaving us clueless at to what that animal meant
opposed to atheistic and anti-American anti-segregationism.
My entrepreneurial friend was able to put it properly
—50% reactionary, 20% bucolic perhaps—
when he said, must be twenty years ago he said it:
"Twenty years I worked in the family business
believing I was working for the family business
and it turned out that I was working for United Fruit."
See he had to sell Corona Oils to United Fruit.
And not that he was opposed to the system, my entrepreneur. No way.
Don Tomás Argüello, dayworker from Solentiname, used to say in his dialect:
"They should let us sell their seeds each one
according to how much he's sown."
And Don Tomás could follow the tracks of a jaguar
and those of the Bank.

It's said that chess will soon disappear
because machines can play it better than human beings.
"With qualities akin to those we call intelligence."
The growth rate for robots in the U.S. is 30%
and for people 2%.
Also in the infancy of some different beings.
No longer with juicy carbon bodies
but dry silica,
their insect-like brains instinctual and devoid of reasoning
and as successful as insects,
picking up on sophisticated antennae a whisper of dictated orders
at a distance of millions or hundreds of millions of miles
and with their bulging electronic eyes gazing at
faraway, hostile planets.
The conditions are here again, you see
hypocrisy / organization / indifference /
these are the three conditions for concentration camps.

Garden of Eden
where in the afternoon breeze strolls
the God of Rockefeller, of Carnegie, of Morgan.

The country has changed totally for Otter.
Once a man discovered that another was slandering him.
He adorned his horse and painted the covered wagon.
He put on his feathers.
"Do you see this horse and the wagon?"
(The slanderer was frightened.)
"Well, I'm giving them to you."
Naturally, he was never slandered again.
"He was a brave man," said Otter.
"that was his only horse, his only wagon."
The Delawares' creation feast
serves all the peoples of the world. Of the Earth
which gleams like Sirius.

"They made me piss blood. Imagine the sort of beating
but didn't get a word out of me."
That Moorish castle above Managua.
Somoza had a library of deeds
bound in leather, of his stolen properties.
He would caress them as though he were caressing
the valleys, meadows, rivers of his stolen lands.
Christ present in the prison cells
and not in the episcopal palaces.
And just as the bishop of the Canaries, under Franco
issued an indignant protest about,
but really indignant, about
female legs on the beaches,
Mons. Chávez under Somoza III inaugurated
his episcopacy with a crucial pastoral about
that most serious evil:
the miniskirt.
The International Monetary Fund Mafia
still retained an aura of mystery and mysticism.

The hovels next to the Stadium at the time of the Olympiad
they hid behind walls with pretend windows and doors
and cute little red tiles. And the people invented the word façadism.
Dictatorships which seem as unshifting as the natural order
and end in a flash like a bad dream
and the people are on the streets dancing.
    The beautiful news of a new revolution
    through the shit.
    Literally in the case of prisoners in Uruguay:
    in the latrine,
    on used pieces of newspaper
    they read, through the filth,
about the triumph of the Nicaraguan revolution.

CANTIGA 33

The Deep Outer Darkness

"In the beginning there was nothing, neither deep darkness.
And some time later, although a time without time,
he created the light and the deep darkness."

It's not dark matter that deep darkness,
dark and cold matter that deep darkness,
dark matter the nature of which still is unknown to us is not that deep darkness.

The deep outer darkness must be outside matter.
Pygmies sense them in the forest, those spirits.
Hanging in slippery caves like bats.
And up by the polar circle, to Rasmussen, the Dane:
"We don't believe. We only fear.
We fear everything that surrounds us
and which we don't know well. Why snow storms?
And a whole day's hunting to return empty-handed?
We are afraid as we struggle for food on the earth and at sea.
We are afraid of the cold and hunger in our snow houses.
We are afraid of the souls of the dead, men and animals.
We know so little we are afraid of everything."

And just so the Devil may not be missing from this poem.

A handful in a small room in the White House,
not the Situation Room, so as not to be noticed.
Someone would recall that it was an emotional evening.
—Success hangs on the right timing,
first-rate intelligence,
and speed of action.
—It's a high-risk operation with much to be gained.

—Very negative repercussions for the United States
should we fail.
—We've put nothing in writing. All tracks
beautifully swept clean—said Oliver North.
—Not even the official Pentagon order says what it is.
—We now have the aerial photos we needed.
—I'll buy lunch for everyone in the "Exchange," not the White House
Cafeteria, if we pull it off.
—How will we respond if they attack?
—Proportionally.
—No, disproportionately.
—A cancer that's got to be rooted out—said Casey, Director of the CIA.
Nobody mentioned the word murder, Oliver North
would later confide. It was said simply:
—in a military context what's normally a crime's not a crime.

> Jesus Santa Marta, flower of flowers,
> Jesus Santa Marta, flower of wonders,
> Jesus Santa Marta, flower of man.
> If there are guards outside
> sound asleep I am sure to find them,
> should in shackles I find myself bound
> cast asunder I am sure to see them
> Oh powerful Red Enchanter
> just as you vanquished King Lucifer.

And why some called it "the Auschwitz business"
> A wagon load of women's hair...
> 40 boxes of wedding rings...

"Far away, somewhere in Poland, who knows where.
We saw nothing. We
did as they told us."
A rebuke from the house of Knorr (Munich) to the SS in Dachau
for their slowness in the dispatch of human lard...
> "There was a high chimney and I could see flames.
> I heard screams inside. My hut was
> next to the gas chamber."

O golden purple violet grey blue light
"a beauty that defies description"
    above Alamogordo
cloud in the shape of a cauliflower
or like a poisoned ice-cream cone.
"Doctor, is it true that you
are the one that most influenced atomic energy?"
Oppenheimer didn't smile. They were accusing him of treason.
"I believe Lawrence had more influence," he replied.
(Lawrence wanted a superbomb. Oppen was opposed.)
A feeling of frustration and entropy
Oppenheimer's feeling, perhaps.
Strontium 90 in the children's vanilla cone.
    The children who wanted a vanilla cone
    and they gave them napalm.
Behind the transparent curtain
the full moon, now in full daylight,
it appears equally transparent,
everything like a Japanese landscape
or a terse Japanese landscape poem
And suddenly the brilliance of the first A Bomb test
in the New Mexico desert, which was reflected in the moon
    (perhaps no astronomer noticed it)
and it fell back to earth, through the curtain, like placid moonshine.
After my visit to Merton and the Pueblo Indians, in New Mexico
Mr. Gutiérrez showed me round a run-of-the-mill North American city,
gas stations, shops, pizza houses, flowers, children,
    but sinister.
Los Alamos. The little green house, quite old now, where they made
the first A Bomb. With a tranquil pond out front.
Its water used for the A Bomb.
  A gram of matter converted into energy.
In Hiroshima no reminder of the bomb remains, except
the huge memorial park in the epicenter.
After my talk about Nicaragua in Hiroshima (1988)
the conversation with *hibakusha* (victims): Suzuko Numata:
"I saw a very beautiful color, like a rainbow," they translate for me.

Hiroto Kiboura, one eye missing. He was 19 at the time.
"It was a very intense blue light," he says.
Michito Yamaoka, 800 meters from the epicenter:
like the flash from a photographic camera in your eyes.
"So many bodies with intestines hanging out, like sausages.
I've never been able to touch sausages since."
Truman got the news over lunch. At once he proposed a toast.
Liquefied eyes streaming.
Skin hanging off like black algae.
Bodies alive with worms like a heap of rice.
Without houses Hiroshima seemed tiny,
very close the mountains that surrounded it.
Shozo Muneto, hibakusha, says:
"Now the whole of humanity is hibakusha."

Demons are to be found in the celestial regions
says St. Paul in Ephesians,
"that's to say, those who have power, authority and dominion
in this dark world".
The Philosopher's Stone.
This is the creative process which takes place in the stars.
But the alchemists' dream
became our destructive invention.
A planet with five tons of TNT per capita.
And each regular nuclear bomb like the core of the sun.
To launch it you wouldn't need to aim.
The whole earth a gigantic bomb in orbit.
Atomic energy liberated by man
but not man by atomic energy.
A country lacking the capacity to destroy
is scorned.
We've been on the brink of nuclear war because of
reflections of the moon on radar, or a fleet of guided missiles
which was a flock of wild geese.
Even the most unreal horror would be made real.
And all the Titians radioactive ash.
The neutron one leaves things intact, it destroys only life.

Some are at work on a weapon with sheafs of antimatter. Others
with clouds of nuclei and electrons at almost the speed of light.

The reason the pessimistic Izedi tribe adore the Devil
seeing that evil triumphs over good.
        ("Will he not reward the poor Izedis
        the only ones who do not speak ill of him?")
Or some tribes in the depths of Brazil for whom
the Evil Spirit is more powerful than the Good.

Grey or golden sundown,
                    every sundown
from Langley, Virginia (amid bucolic woods
without road-signs—it's the CIA headquarters)
a black limo leaves with a secret report
for his vine-like hands.
His cowboy-film politics, the good and the bad,
and you gotta kill the bad.
        His smile, like that of someone biting a lemon.
"Attack Nic-a-wha-wha" said the director of the CIA
unable to pronounce Nicaragua like you or I.
Reagan had said: "I want a win."

> O beautiful Macuá Bird
> that leaps from branch to branch,
> in mountains most mighty.
> May whoever be foe to me
> be flung into sovereign dungeons.
> O powerful invincible Iguana
> at ease in times of rain and drought.
> If knives they have may they buckle.

"An elegant weapon" Teller told the president.
        The X-ray laser was elegant.
An anthropologist has said that a Neanderthal
in top and tails would not be out of
place at the opera.

Looking for Hiroshima
he saw nothing.
The cloud was rising up from a plain.
Thought the precious bomb had fallen in the wrong place.

They were right to be afraid when they spoke to Rasmussen
but more so now.
When Merton wished to be a hermit in the desolate wastes of Alaska
(shortly before the Bangkok trip)
he found them littered with military bases.
Alaska, to him the most beautiful of the United States.

Suddenly
on the high-speed train
Tokio-Nagoya
framed to measure
as though with measuring tape
in the window opposite
Fujiyama.
Shortly after we passed the Toyota plant, the one that renamed
a region of Japan, calling it Toyota.
Where Toyota also nominates all public authorities.
No candidate elected if he's not from Toyota.
And I discovered that in Tokyo there are 5,000 and in Osaka 25,000
not in cardboard houses but no home at all.
And many young Japanese don't know who bombed Hiroshima
but know every last detail of every North American singer.

There I confirmed what I'd once heard or read:
the characteristic smell of India
is of shit.
Always in the air that whiff of shit.
Perhaps sometimes mixed in with sandalwood.
Seems sandalwood perfume close up's not so different
—handicrafts for tourists—
from the remote smell of shit.

Streets where our small car couldn't get through
narrower than the car.
The throng crammed together
bumping into thin buffalos and bicycles.
Goats perched on mounds of garbage
chewing cardboard, bricks.
On the flat roofs of dirty eating houses
you saw
frayed mattresses, ramshackle camp-beds
of the privileged who don't sleep on the sidewalks.
Down below the dishes are rinsed by youths
in the gutter itself
and served to new customers.
The sacred cows strolling like beggars,
among beggars.
The snake-charmer in rags
with the cobra, its head flat as a leaf
transfixed by the music.
Men crouching in the streets urinating.
Every morning they shit in rows in the parks
wiping themselves with their hands
which they rinse in a little bowl of water.
On the steps the multitude of beggars impassable
—tourists take pictures of them—
perpetually starving like fakirs.
Loads of people who have only what they wear on them.
Their tunics and turbans of tattered princes.
Ten lepers surround the car.
At daybreak the street dead are cleared away in trucks
along with the garbage.
But worst of all the meeting with the Union Carbide victims
in Bhopal, the hibakusha of Bhopal,
four years after the gas escaped they're still dying.
How can I forget the woman with the sunken eyes, coughing,
now her whole life is coughing. The 12 year-old,
skinny as an insect, a tiny black insect.
Their houses are like dog kennels, others smaller than kennels,

of material (rags), broken mats, sheets of plastic,
stones on the roof so the wind won't carry them off.
In the middle of the night a yellow gas leaked from the Carbide plant
and they began to die slowly, in their sleep,
they panted, they fainted, foaming at the mouth,
in spasms, dribbling, drowned in their vomit
and Union Carbide refusing to pay any damages
and it refused to reveal the antidote to the gas
(it being an industrial secret) which was to throw water on your face
and it's said, therefore, that the gas wasn't intended for pesticides
but chemical weapons. Bhopal where they gave me a small bronze tree
with couples like fruit making love in the branches.

St. George of the green hills
rid me of all vermin
whether land or air-borne,
eyes may they have and not see.
As with your magical powers alone
you ensnared Lucifer, Prince of Darkness,
no rocks no thunderbolts, no things
of perdition will rain down,
nor animals of fright will die
nor men in the fields.—Amen.

With Comandante Daniel Ortega in a museum.
We enter a museum which was once a school
but from school it became under Pol Pot
Cambodia's largest prison.
The classrooms divided into tiny cells.
Here you came only to die.
More than 20,000 prisoners passed through here
only 17 of whom survived
that had yet to be killed when the liberating troops entered.
This was Pol Pot's "Democratic Kampuchea".
Here are the photos they took as they entered.
They took photos of everyone.
Some with their hands tied, others with chains and rings around the neck.

The worst thing to see was the horror on the faces.
You could see they were seeing not the camera but death
and the torture before death.
But more shocking still was a smiling face:
a girl, or a kid, someone innocent, unaware
evidently of what was going to happen.
And photos of mothers with babies.
A crude apparatus for pulling out nails.
Pincers for ripping off nipples.
A huge variety of tools...
The tank where they held them under.
The posts where they strung them up.
The cell where Pol Pot's Minister of Information was held
before they killed him.
More than 100 mass graves have been discovered where they buried them.
The children buried with their milk bottles and comforters.
And skulls, great piles of skulls
you can't bear to look at.
Of the 8 million inhabitants they killed 3.million.
They destroyed the factories, the schools, the medicines.
You were arrested for wearing glasses.
The cities were left deserted.
Finally we went out.
There were flowers outside.
In a clean puddle a white duck flapped its wings
bathing itself in water and sun.
The girls who went by on the street
were like pagodas.
And the U.S. now supports Pol Pot.

The U.S. Congress approving aid to the contras:
The senator intones his speech with a baritone voice.
Beautifully modulated. Running up and down the scale
like someone playing an arpeggio on the trumpet, with frequent
fugues,
now it's clarinet;
the long flow of tangled words,

every syllable exquisitely articulated, skillfully
sy-lla-bi-cating
the difficult passages of his appalling prose
with the diction of a virtuoso.
The next orator,
sonorous language,
magniloquent and grandiloquent
quoting from memory long passages from James Monroe
as though reciting
without glancing at his text,
raising his voice (and face)
and suddenly dropping
to a deep bass.
He sat down
acknowledging sweatily the rather tepid applause.
Bertilda bathes her son's wounds
and says "Bright and early I's going to put on the coffee
and I saw that they were beating a kid in the street
and I shouted out: "The contras!"
Los muchachos began to fire,
there were only two of them, and about 100 of the contras.
Los muchachos were her son and her nephew.
"As to how did I feel? I didn't feel nothing, I just thought:
If they kill them they'll have to kill me.
I filled three magazines for my nephew
because now my boy was wounded.
I tied up my two-year old so she wouldn't run around."
Another:
vibrant mixture of modulations of timbre and tone,
with anastrophes,
prosopopoeias here and there, and ingenious paranomasias
and sonorous anaphoras.
His tropes resounding in the ornate chamber,
the ornamentation rebounding the bombastic echo;
few present at the time in the chamber,
but perorating as though before an enormous crowd
(hence the applause).

"Surrender, you sons-of-bitches!" the guardia called out.
"Surrender your mother!" Oscar Leonel replied
as though he were that other Leonel brought back to life.
The shack destroyed
under the barrage of mortars and grenades.
The little town laid waste.
The contras as they withdrew
left behind a scattering of Christian literature.
"Thirty million in humanitarian aid for the contras."
"No sir, thirty-eight!"
High-pitched laughter from one of the humanitarians.
Another thumping the table, as though about to break it;
powerful gestures with both hands as though brandishing a bat;
"There's no problem more urgent (hit)
it shakes me to the core to say it (hit)
that the danger (hit)
from communism in Central America (hit)."
"They killed my uncle,
also Ramón his son, they died fighting.
Ramón's son, aged six,
they murdered him in his bed.
He was asleep and they shot him.
He was wounded and asked to see his dead father.
He ran his hand over his face, and said: See, they made a hole in him here.
There and then the child died too."
Thirty-eight million in humanitarian aid for the contras.
In trousers, jacket and waist-coat the color of night,
sharpened incisors,
bloodsucking lip movements,
Vampyrum spectrum
he emits through the mouth and nasal orifices
similes, prolepsis, apostrophes,
melodious alliterations,
reiterations, deprecations, preteritions, digression,
squeals from his cystic snout,
antitheses, synopses, synonyms and antonyms.
And down he sits. As though he'd been hung upside-down.

Twisted zinc, planks and trees burnt.
What had been the cooperative.
Two days later still smoking.
On the hill
the Catholic chapel set ablaze.
And the little school. The health center.
Antibiotics in the ashes.
And buzzards gliding, round and round.
Juan Antonio aged 15 was fighting alongside Estreberto aged 19.
A bullet in the chest
and he fell stone dead onto Estreberto's knees.
Mario was caught by around 30 contras
and slowly, slowly they cut off his head,
the blood dripping onto the Christian literature.
Texan senator in dramatic pose,
right foot forward,
arms open like a bronze statue,
when they bring him a glass of mineral water.
Still the dramatic pose
now the left foot forward;
he's reading the speech they wrote for him.
In the burnt chapel, where the altar stood,
Estreberto stops: "Christ! My dad's blood's still here."
No tears in his eyes. They just shrank.
Estreberto saw around 30 ambush Leonardo.
They stabbed him.
Juana said you could only see the balls of fire.
She went to fetch little Enrique, three years old, and saw him asleep.
He was dead.
How to bring him along with the other tiny ones.
"No way over this rough land."
She left him on the hillside, next to a creek. For shroud she covered him with a *bijagua* leaf.
With the faintly wavering tone of deeply controlled
emotions,
slowly, not reading, reciting his speech:
"There is convincing evidence (pause)

of the international communist conspiracy (pause)
for the exporting of the revolution (pause)
of Nicaragua (pause)
up to our borders (pause)
and one of the... (pause)... in aid to the contras (pause)."
Arms trembling as though touching piano keys.
    The usher brings him a glass of iced water.
A claw raised asking to speak.
    Point of order.
The Honorable.................. With just a small *bijagua* leaf
there I had to leave him.
        They heard the *guardias* laughing.
Lucía so pretty got a bullet in the face.
Lidia, her they raped and carried off.
The coffee beans, their yard animals, their homes, everything.
    "The children's blood all down my dress."

There's a place on the outskirts of Nuremberg no one visits.
I climbed onto the small, towering platform
                above the huge empty space,
gone the hysterical regimented sea of people,
platform for a single person,
above the void
            —and vertigo of the void—
from where Hitler spoke.
            No tourists or visitors
but for a couple with their camera
down below, far off, minute
amid that entire immense stony repugnant area,
alone
like sole survivors from a concentration camp.
From here he spoke over the heads of the mesmerized masses,
shouted, stamped his feet,
histrionic melodramatic frenetic fanatical maniacal
Reaganesque
    brandishing rhetorical revolvers
            invisible rifles

the peroration of "powerful slogans" as he called them,
terrifying democrats with the Communist bogey,
mouth reverberating
gushing out of it in verbosity the dumbness of the multitudes
a delirious torrent of clichés with demented eloquence,
epileptically,
without transition from the frenetic to the hieratic
with his absolute self-sufficiency and consciousness of genius
based on nothing,
entranced by his own voice
gigantically amplified by the microphone
"One of the greatest orators of history—says Fest—
but without a single memorable phrase."

Nürmberg was the Führer's beloved city.
Site of the annual party (*Parteitag*) convention.
The great *Parteitag.*
The Nuremberg operatic spectacles were by night.
Torchlight procession, emblems, flags, cries of *Heil,*
monstrous stadium replete with monstrous fanaticism,
they were mystical nights,
the endless parade,
wave after wave before him with the Nazi salute
and he, ice-still, with his arm horizontal.
The whole year he dreamed of those Nuremberg nights.
Inhuman uniformity and goose step in ferocious uniforms.
He swept down the broad expanse of "Führer Street" between 100,000 SS
and SA and black uniforms.
150 searchlights converged in the night sky,
all the columns of light brought together in the center of the sky,
and before huge bonfires gigantic swastikas, glistening in gold.
He stepped onto the towering platform and 30,000 flags emerged
and he went into a trance.
And the searchlights swooped down from the sky and fell across the people,
flags and uniforms and shining military bands.
It was no longer over an ale-house table in Munich.
Grand opera setting for

an oratory of fury and social euphoria and mass hysteria
(whose first speech had been to a crowd of 111)
monumental scenario now like the most super-colossal Wagner
for the triumphal finale of infernal *Parsifal* with
the proclamation of the most bestial anti-semitic laws.
"The beloved city" was also to become
the scenario for the trial of war criminals.

Me gazing from the platform at the silenced solitude,
desert of inert stone, worn down, like a dead city,
landscape all empty,
the minute couple now gone,
no one in that place of recent archaism, of
modern architecture already archaeological.
It doesn't figure, and for good reason, in the Nuremberg tourist guides
(but the Castle, Dürer's House, Toy Museum...)
A journalist asked me
why I wanted to visit that barren place.

Me leaning on that iron railing of the platform
where proudly stood that man who was a devil's anointed,
who did so much to increase the death rate,
disguised terror with the idyllic,
incarnation of the frustrations and phobias and hatreds of everyone,
who brought about the revolt on behalf of order
through the hunger and thirst for authority in those times,
gave birth to that monster Totalitarian-Democracy,
Fascist-Socialism, racism imitating communism,
which held force to be an end and ideas a means,
for whom reality was only theatrical effects,
fascinated by all that was false, abominating the truth,
the propaganda maestro behind Goebbels the novelist,
manipulator of himself
as well as of the masses,
a genius at portraying feelings
as well as at concealing them,
when he laughed he held his hand before his mouth,

multitudinous on the outside, with a bunker inside,
never mentioning, not even in private conversations,
nor in the bunker, the gas chamber business,
of whom Mrs. Goebbels had said much earlier:
"he's simply not human,"
the loneliest man in Germany,
who heard *Tristan* 100 times always in an artificial ecstasy,
who was calculatedly spontaneous,
controlled even in his paroxysms,
(only the eyes disobeyed him
roaming restlessly even in moments of statue-like rigidity)
who even in his anger was an actor,
even in his gesticulations, stiff,
who called himself "Europe's finest actor,"
who turned each sharp movement into statues of bronze,
who could never wear a swimming costume,
inhibited, even with a doorman
but masking it,
who laid out his weakness in fastidious water-colors,
whose every action demonstrated that evil is banal,
who could never love, not even his small dog,
who terrorized the earth from this raised platform,
who was loved by many even outside Germany,
and was no one.

CANTIGA 34

Ancient Sobbing Light

In the beginning absolutely nothing existed,
the earth was still in darkness and shadow.
And in the temple of Heliopolis creation began.
(Also it is said in the temple of Thebes, and of Memphis.)
    "It happened that the first light was born,
    where there was neither sun nor moon. The earth was born
    where previously there was nothing for us"
    according to the Maya's CHUMAYEL.

In truth we can see *outwards* in the universe
going back in time (time of light's journey)
almost until creation.
Beyond the first 300,000 years
even with the most powerful telescope we could see nothing
because the universe was opaque.
In the wake of Big Bang background cosmic
    radiation has remained in microwaves.
We've mentioned that before.
Why Being and not Nothingness, Heidegger's question.
Everything of importance occurred in the first minutes of the universe
    —said Weinberg at a Harvard symposium—
and all subsequent events are details.

...Until it transformed itself into our present universe.
"The elegant simplicity of Big Bang cosmology."
Was it born in spacetime to collapse into chaos without any objective plan?
My question's aimed not at cosmologists
but the man in the street.
Could matter travel back in time
and become antimatter?

"Scientific materialism," writes Bernard d'Espagnat,
    philosopher of quantum mechanics,
has become a meaningless association of words.
Bunge says that to say that matter exists makes no sense.
    The fact for example that the atom
        "is full of emptiness."
According to Heisenberg the universe is composed of music, not of matter.
And the fact that the universe is as full of X-rays
as visible light.
Had we glasses for X-rays, what heavens would we see?
According to the Creed of the Nicaea Council (still in use)
we believe in the creation of all that is seen and unseen
although the poor Conciliar Fathers of Nicaea were
scientifically as backward as John Paul II.
A twenty-two year old cardinal lobbied the Pope
in Galileo's favour. Thus his theory of tides was not heretical
    Discourse Upon Things That Float in Water
which adopts Archimedes' instead of Aristotle's point of view
and incidentally it was wrong since it maintained that there is only one tide
a day whereas everyone knows there are two.
Galileo was sentenced to "formal imprisonment" by the Holy Office
although his imprisonment was house arrest and the house was
the villa of the Grand Duke in Trinità del Monte, plus
the recital of the seven penitential psalms once a week
which he legally delegated to his daughter who was a nun.
And this because according to the papal secretary, in the Vatican
"they sighed more for Galileo than for any damsel."
The famous *eppur si muove* he never said
rather that was his friends' epitaph for his grave.
All this to show the difficulties the Vatican got into
meddling with the heavens. Who *was* placed on the Index was
the long dead canon Koppernigk (Copernicus)
for an unreadable book, an antiquarian's curiosity, out-dated.
Now we not only believe in the seen and unseen
but in invisible matter. *Dark matter*. And furthermore *si mouve*.
But if from order our order stems, and that's law,
how did the original disorder produce all our order?

"The distinction between what is living and not living is conventional."
    The Amazulu say they're sad
    because they, the blacks, have yet to learn,
    the true meaning of dreams.
And the fact that it has been said, and is said,
that the substance of particles
"is more subtle than the cloth with which we weave our dreams."
        Under heat and pressure in an instant
        carbon becomes diamond.
And also:
"They're not physical objects in the ordinary sense of the word."
        In an instant, carbon diamond.

As the diamond-cutter
studies his diamond very closely beforehand,
so I too with this difficult cosmic canticle
(although lacking the difficulty of the Austrian physicist Schrödinger
with his mathematical equation for the movement of
enigmatic probabilistic waves and
practical calculations of molecular movement
together with energy levels of atoms that...)
merely trying to say, let's get it straight,
that we are embedded in an entirely distorted reality.
Not only because we see the sun sink on the horizon
8 minutes after the sun has sunk
    but because the sun has not sunk!
Since the universe is round
the furthest we can see with a telescope
is ourselves gazing at a telescope
in which there is the image of ourselves gazing at a telescope,
and the most distant star is our sun!
    More and more the cosmos is expanding
    but where to?
The antiplanets and antistars of antimatter...
      Now under threat from the nuclear arsenal.
        If at least the libraries were to remain.
Matter and form Aristotle said,

meaning matter and energy.
The Hiroshima bomb:
a gram of matter converted into energy.

Enrico Fermi asked at the dinner: "Where are they?"
Our galaxy is so similar to so many others
that there can be nothing special about our Earth.
Life, highly improbable, in large numbers is highly probable.
Those inhabited spheres unable to speak to us! Brothers
light years away. They can't be aggressive or they'd have destroyed each other.
Who can prove to us that we aren't sending messages into the past?
    (There are equations in which electromagnetic waves
    can travel backwards in time.)
Or receiving messages from the future, which is the same?
The theory's speculative.

There we are then, awaiting proof that we're not alone.
Like someone casting a bottle into the sea, we have launched
our messages beyond the solar system.
If they don't have radio, we can't detect them with radio.
Perhaps the civilization perished millions of years ago
but their mechanical descendants have remained,
    a world of robots.
Perhaps we're alone in the whole galaxy
but there are thousands of millions of galaxies.
What we've seen of the works of God is scarcely a spark
says Ecclesiasticus, and there are many larger mysteries
"for we have seen but few of his works."
Perhaps they are so advanced
that they'll show us how to cure all illnesses,
or at least how not to blow the planet to pieces.
Perhaps they've seen our television programs
and are acquainted with our horrors.
An inter-stellar trip? It's very expensive now
says Thomas R. McDonough,
but maybe a thousand years from now it won't be.

Of the (short wave) pulsation of pulsars Frank Drake says:
"If they are intelligent signals they're from a stupid civilization."
An aerial picked up a mysterious message from the depths of the universe,
in Newark, but it turned out to be a truck in the street.

The fact that the 29.5 days of the lunar month
are the same as the month of women.
And human gestation exactly nine lunar months.
There are pulsars as slow as the rhythm of the human heart.
Others fast like an African drum beat.
The stars sing,
their matter is a huge loudspeaker,
the sun sings, and the sound waves from its core
take an hour to reach the surface.
Our artificial satellites rocking in the solar wind
relay to us the moans, the screams and the roaring of the sun.
How to carry on praying that you believe in God the Father Almighty
(in the words of the Nicene Council) creator—
of *heaven* and *earth*?
The universe was not created in space and time
but space and time are part of the universe.
    Infinite in all directions, says Dyson.
That means above and below, micro and macrocosmos.
The sign of the Father in us says Jesus (Thomas's Gospel)
is Action in Repose.
The greater the mass the greater the curvature,
that is, gravity is the curvature of space.
—Those Indians with their round (earth) huts that are
symbols of the cosmos and they speak to them of God like the prairies—.
        We were born 3,500 million years ago
        on the edge of the sea, in a warm swamp.
            We are evolved microcosmos.
I'm no scientist, obviously, but I can see
that present-day science is the same as Empedocles's of Acragas
which stated that the universe is nothing but earth, water, air and fire.
A hurricane consists of nothing more than air and water.
When we die we change into water and carbon dioxide.

Joaquín's: "Water is the blood's eternity."
    We change into H_2O and CO_2.
Without decomposition of the universe there'd be no sun.
Without the depletion of the sun we'd have no light.

The dusty galaxies,
more full of dust and ash than of stars.
    Whistle of melancholy train pulling off into the distance.
Birth, growth and death, are also the universe.
Einstein thought the expansion of the universe so strange
he believed his equations were incomplete.
The problem for this poem is that like the universe
    it must expand indefinitely
    or cave in on itself.
Dragged along by the expansion of spacetime
the galaxies. With a time which is an arrow in a single direction:
death.
        The ultimate entropy which is death.
The second law, the most fundamental in the universe.
Life cannot be understood without the second law.
And immortality does not lie in reproduction.
        Entropy always wins out over energy.
Entropy obeys the fatal laws of thermodynamics.
The fresh, smiling proteins turn fetid.
You hand back to the planet what was borrowed.
And the equations that lead to black holes...
That strange black and empty region of spacetime.
Where any matter drawing close vanishes
and is never to be seen again.
To fall and fall without ever touching bottom?
What happens is that there space is so curved
that space and time are interchangeable.
The graves of dead stars, black holes.
Though a sculptor may bring forth a Venus from the confused stone
that order is not permanent.
    Condemned by entropy to the ultimate chaos.
        The rolling ball comes to a stop.

Hot things cool down.
Lambs are formed of grass, that is, from sun,
from the sun which day by day grows colder, and so they're part
of the collapse of the universe, of the cooling of the sun
and the other stars.
Death is disorder.
As soon as the energy-absorbing function ends
disorder sets in.

In *The Selfish Gene* it says:
if extra-terrestrials came the first thing they'd ask is
have they discovered evolution yet?
Nothing more improbable than living organisms.
Also the miracle of flying animals.
Neanderthal bones in the deepest reaches of a cave
with much flower pollen: 60,000 years ago
those flowers lovingly placed there.
Glynn Isaac's theory is
that it was the sharing of food that made us human.
Bunn corroborates it with the evidence
of so many bones being found together in certain sites...
Hunting in common, and therefore
eating in common.
"The primary act of human culture is sharing food."
The evolution from Big Bang to space voyages.
Perhaps close to another star like the sun
for a long time they've been awaiting intelligent signals
from the solar system.
"Sea monsters are to be seen on all sides
and they swim around the sluggish ships."
The sea, it was the Bay of Biscay, which became like a swimming pool;
and the heroic Phoenician mariners
seem to us like children petrified of the dark.
My thinking is not my neurons
although my neurons think of my neurons
(the most complex piece of matter in the universe).
My dreams are nonsense

but all controlled by my own I.
Reason proved to be not only reason, but also
myth, dream, imagination.
Initially the Theory of Relativity
was understood by a single person: Einstein.
Soon several hundred people understood it.
World which has created a mind which understands the world.
Like the Carthusians with 8 hours for sleep,
8 for work and 8 for prayer,
the Yamanes of Tierra del Fuego (now extinct)
had 8 hours for sleep, 8 for work and 8
to recount their myths.

With the theory of superstrings, matter
simply like different vibrations of a string.
Like notes.
        The music of the string is matter.
And the theory of Princeton professor, Wheeler,
that the universe is in its entirety a single electron.
The reason why all electrons are the same
(none fatter or longer than another)
is because they are a single electron.
The electrons in my body and the electrons in your body
could all be the same electron then!
The innumerable tones of a single string on Pythagoras's lyre.
As with endless songs the Navajos spend
the whole night singing, singing to the wind, to the rainbow,
to the lightning, animals, maize, singing the whole night,
singing that everything is beautiful, and all things are twofold,
everything is beautiful, and every thing made to join with another,
the sky and the earth united by the rain, etc...
so it has also been said:
"At the atomic level everything is an indissoluble whole."
Those lovers who don't merely feel identical,
says Schrödinger, but *numerically* one,
although without any intellectual clarity, like the mystics.

Messages have been transmitted from the earth.
There could be millions of inhabited planets
but the closest neighbour, a million light years away.
We could be receiving messages
but the atmosphere cuts them out.
Or could they be receiving ours and believe them to be
physical phenomena and the music of the spheres?

What did Alfonso Cortés mean when he said
that distance is silence and vision is sound?
And when he spoke of the fluid distance that we do not see?
And of distance without relation and time without measure?
And of an ancient light which in sobs sets the Abyss a-tremble?
My surprise when his sisters opened the old boxes for me
and I saw the manuscripts: the tiniest of scraps of paper,
the size of a cigarette pack or smaller,
with microscopic writing which could only be read with a lens
    (they also brought me the lens)
but ornate, adorned with strange tails,
with the pencil certainly very well sharpened,
tiny sheets of newsprint, yellow and stained.
My shock at seeing the poems in that demented handwriting.
    (Before going mad his handwriting was normal.)
The Song of Space, his first poem after madness set in,
on the final page of a book about Marinetti's futurism.
He told me later in the asylum gripping the bars
that in that poem he'd sought to develop two concepts:
    "As though he wanted to reach eternity
    half an hour before time."
And
    "the origin of things is not prior but permanent."
María Luisa, the sister, read to me another of his thoughts
taken down by her on a scrap of paper:
"Time is the relation between man and all fact."
What could he have known of Relativity when he lost his mind?
    Who also spoke of
        "the motionless movement of the sky."

Raffiniert ist der Herr Gott, aber boshaft ist er nicht
said Einstein: "God is subtle, but without malice."
While the stars move without differential equations.
    Not a creator who created in the beginning
    but continually creates and not directly
    but through physical laws in such a way
    that scientists see no creator.
        And an improvising creator.
Who was called the only alternative to the absurd.
I am a process, he said in the burning bush.
Not eternity without time but time eternal, that is, change,
but change that does not pass, duration without past,
life without dying.
    For him the future has already been and the past never passed.
In the beginning was Love.
What does it mean that love consists
in that God loved us first (I Jn. 4:10)?
The male normally takes the initiative among the species.
St. John also says:
            God=Love
That is, his essence, HIS ESSENCE, is to take the initiative.
The naked soul in the night finally says, Take me!

Finding you I found myself. Finding myself I found you.
My I where God is two.
Reclined on my chest this night,
dark night, are you not attentive to the rhythm of my love?
Present within me
since I was nothing but a fertilized egg,
a series of instructions floating in the cavity of my mother's womb.
    Child of woman, and much earlier
    of a single-celled creature. Like Mauriac
there was no anguish in my adolescence that I did not prefer to You.
Cataract compressed within an electric cable.

    Skybala said St. Paul.

After feeling what he felt
all the rest he saw as dross.
The traditional translation is dross,
in reality he said in Greek *skybala* ("shit").

Confucius sensing it as inundation.
All my life I have searched for a supreme Someone,
to love him not only with all my heart but with the whole universe,
the prayer of spacetime,
        Chardin wrote in Peking.

Jalâl al-Dîn Rûmî (XIII century) said—to non-Moslems—:
There are many roads to Mecca.
For some it is the south if they're in Persia.
For others the north if they're in the Yemen.
For others the west if they're in China.
This is what happens with religions, or non-religion.
A man never sees a camel on the top of a minaret.
How could he then see a thread of hair in the camel's mouth?

His center is in all parts and his circumference in none
according to Nicholas of Cusa. To the Areopagite
"God is small." And scientists discovered
the study of the smallest and of the biggest
are the same.
In India Merton heard the story of the Sufi who said:
"For me to say that I am God is not pride, it's modesty."
I understand him: I am God, but *what* a God, my God!
        I am God, oh biologists.
All the mystics of the world have depicted themselves
says Schrödinger "as particles of an ideal gas."

In my final days in the world
when I was about to become a Trappist monk
I met at a coastal resort a beautiful girl
who was going to be a nun.
                What's more she was a cousin of mine.

I remember those legs.
    Her curves like the curve of the coast.
Her skin was dark like the sand on the beach.
Naked, but for what the bathing suit covered.
    She was about to betroth herself to God.
        The marriage to God!
And I thought of God's good taste.
Mother Ana is still a nun
but at the height of the Nicaraguan revolution
she's a reactionary nun.

Skybala said St. Paul.
But in all things we see opaquely the invisible.
Including socio-economically, opaquely, the invisible.
Amid huge boulders, giant mosses,
the blind ant well knows its way.

A reporter from *La Nación* went to interview Alfonso
who asked him: "Did you come by car?" "Yes," he answered.
He seemed to lose control of his mind. Later he said:
"On the face of it how simple the world is.
But if you begin to study the world it's hard to understand it.
There's no other way than to keep searching after God,
which means, hanging onto the vestments of priests."
And again he lost control of his mind.
Working on the present Cantiga, I visited Coronel
(the poet José Coronel Urtecho) in Los Chiles,
the tiny Costa Rican town close to the Nicaraguan border where he lives,
and he gave me a crumpled letter from Merton, lost
and recently found inside a book, dated April 1964,
in which he said of Alfonso strangely: "He is a wonderful
and symbolic man, perhaps one of the most significant people
of our age in the entire world. To have such significance
one must of course be hidden as he is."

Christianity is madness St. Paul recognized.
Christianity is madness or it's not Christianity.

Not the only, but perhaps it's the greatest madness.
Our thinking, they say, is fragmentary,
and hence we believe reality to be fragmented.

That starry night, ancient light in sobs.
One night there was what I called the apparition in Hamburg.
1,000 people listening to my poetry
and 300 in the street for lack of room in the place
        —you know: the publicity
                fame...and the Nicaraguan cause—
all the faces in darkness (to me)
        the whole auditorium behind the spotlights,
                deafening, applauding shadow,
but now in the light, very close to me,
almost on the stage, sharing with me the powerful lighting,
I saw you
                short hair, a little untidy,
the girl with eyes color of muscatel grape
        or sometimes the mid-ocean color of sea
        or maybe mid-way between green and tender blue
                (and it was as though heaven were watching me),
        that same mouth,
                mouth which in my mouth I drank,
18 year old girl again,
same age as 30 years before,
but German, I presume, this time,
able only to steal glances at her,
she near me in my orbit of light,
        in front of the blinding spotlights,
on a bench; beyond her
maybe three other female companions before the darkness;
and so out of 1,000 faces
I saw hers only.
Well yes, who'd have told me you'd be here again,
the one whom He, with a capital, snatched from my arms,
the one I let go in order to embrace the Invisible,
my ex-cherub whom I kissed so much but not enough,

mouth that I drank from
here again now, 30 years later,
lips lightly curled
with a smile
pupils suddenly troubled by angelic
lust,
like that lubricious angel,
lubricious more from the flesh than from being an angel,
my beautiful urchin girl, whom I embraced
at "Las Piedrecitas" under the stars, do you remember?
whom I embraced in a man's jacket,
my own, I'd lent it to you because of the cold,
whom I let go for God,
cashed in for God, did I lose out?
I traded you for sadness.
Applause for my poetry
with slogans in Spanish
NO PASARÁN
and me able only to steal glances at you.
Pale apple skin, like
an apple just plucked from the tree
that I'd later eat, that night, in my room in the PREM hotel
acidic, sweet, greenish, juicy, fleshy
but it was fruit, and not something else.
NO PASARÁN
It was as if I were losing her again
as if again she'd offered herself to me and again I let her go.
A denial that was hard
and hard still, it was for a whole life,
and now once again the denial,
so fleeting this time,
but even so, hard, painful,
amid the applause from the shadows,
the pain that you were her again
and at the same time, maybe worse, the pain that you weren't.
German girl, I presume, unaware of all this
known to the other who was as you are,

my girl then 18 years old
(she knows these lines are for her)
on that gloomy Somoza night,
lights from the dictator's palace
reflected in the Tiscapa lagoon.
The one who admired my black hair, remember?
and once you called it "incredibly black"
in that restaurant.
The darkness applauded
my poems:
"a love song was their battle hymn
If Adelita..."
and I meanwhile like our war-maimed
paraplegics
serenely seated in their wheelchairs.
But there was no bomb.
There'd been an anonymous bomb threat
which the police didn't believe.
We'd have died together, my love,
me, brief newspaper copy,
like that brief blossom of the *cortes* tree
"when the golden *cortes* blossomed"
and you
simply a German girl (I presume)
with any name.
But the girl who made me again relinquish the one from before
young and fresh this time just as before
while a collection was being taken up among the public,
jute bags with weighty coins and notes;
and 15,000 marks were made that night for the Nicaraguan people.

CANTIGA 35

Like the Waves

The waves of radio, heat, light of different colors,
ultraviolet rays, X rays, gamma rays, are the same
and are distinguishable only by their wavelength.
Waves are a movement in space and time.
They run in towards the shore but not the water, they don't carry the water
nor the boat and the ducks that float in the water and merely move up and
down.

At night, from León to Managua, on the road I saw
that the humble little rural lights and the stars
were the same.
Alfonso Cortés heard them sobbing
"ancient light in sobs"
and with a capital Abyss:
"which sets the Abyss a-tremble."
What's far in space is far in time.
And the stars generators of entropy...
Heat always moves towards cold
but cold never towards heat.
And the amount of chaos in the world increases with time.
"Time is hunger and space is cold."
Cold interstellar space...
How *cold* interstellar space is
is a meaningless question.
The greatest cold is merely zero heat.
Time is hunger and space is cold
said Alfonso Cortés, adding afterwards not just for the rhyme
that prayer alone can soothe the anxieties of the void.
Time's an arrow in a single direction,
from the past to the future, from heat to cold,

from the warm past to the cold future.

The stone fell into the water.
The shore was far.
Imperceptibly the waves reached the shore
but they reached it.

The irreversibility of time. That's entropy.
The irreversibility of time. But Einstein believed
the distinction between past, present and future
was illusory.
"We ask for life,"
this ejaculation on the Marshall Islands.
Life, that order arisen from disorder.
The automobile's motion is the same as the energy that...
Same as saying that entropy increases more and more toward total rest.
To that state of equilibrium which is synonymous with death.
The thermodynamics of non-equilibrium is the one we want!
Life as such is an impulse towards immortality.

It's not non-time
but Recall,
eternal Recall, Eternity.
When in death
you remain totally alone with yourself
and with the Other.
And it's the return to cosmic life.
Hence Martí's: "To die is to journey on."
Mangoes falling is a creative act
and not a disaster.
Curiously
it was in a guerrilla war that resurrection was spoken of
for the first time. MACCABEES.
The dead are alive.
Those who fell clandestinely, the hills;
in each child who plays in the children's playgrounds,
each student with his books under his arm

(Fidel's speech which we heard from afar, in Solentiname).
    If there's nothing after
    those who gave everything
    have lost everything forever.
It's something else that dies, not life.
Life doesn't die, my friends.
                    To journey on.

There are also waves of sand,
waves, too, of wheatfields,
the rocks—slow waves we see curled in strata,
vibrations of the violin string are waves in the air,
and waves the rhythms of the aorta and the heart
and the lines of a woman's body are waves.
Sea-waves are not of sea-water
they are waves that run in sea-water.
The water seems to run but it's only the wave without the water.
The wave is something moving in the water
but it's not a movement of the water.
The wave continues to rise and fall without bearing the water with it,
and without being a line of convex and concave curves
but merely concavities and angles.
The wave gives the water momentary form
but it's impalpable, abstract,
the wave is fleeting, and the water is constant.
The wave is fleeting but is always the same,
and the water is different where the wave passes,
the wave leaves a trail of different molecules of H_2O
and different foam.
The faces that are smiling here in this yellow photo
against a background of blurred waves and a blurred rock,
where will they be smiling now—if they are still smiling?
Some will be far away. The girls are old.
Mauricio is dead. Only this sea is the same.
Only the waves haven't changed:
                it's "Lovers' Bluff"
with the same fresh waves still breaking here.

The atmosphere is full of their molecules
and in the air we breathe the dead.
But mysterious life:
        born merely by chance
        or from inevitable chemical reactions?
The explanation that it came from another planet,
a micro-organism from out of etc...
causing Chesterton to remark
that it was as though a dead person were to emerge from a cemetery
and they explain it saying
it must be a dead person from another cemetery.
A mollusc's cells aren't mad nor unpredictable.
        And an embryo: who can explain it?
                The seed
which continues a process after the death of the plant.

In the calmest lake there are invisible waves.
The water seems motionless like a mirror
but it's not.
The reflection of the red castle on the other bank
has clear vertical contours
but the horizontal ones, blurred, we see in motion...

When the Motumotu saw themselves in a mirror
they believed they were seeing their souls.
        But aren't they surely their souls?
The molecule of carbon I-don't-know-what
which gets into a green leaf, is it now alive?
And before, what? The oxygen molecule in a sigh,
once exhaled is it no longer alive? Let's say there's an "implicit" life
in the wind that bore off your sigh.
Organic molecules have been detected in the skies
by radio-astronomy
waiting merely to receive the breath of life.
Chardin saying that all matter is spirit,
and Dyson that for him as a physicist

"matter's an imprecise and old-fashioned concept."
We have images of matter but matter itself
we do not know
("Our frustration at wanting to measure things without disturbing them")
just as we don't know the spirit.
We're still romping from here to there between things
like a young puppy exploring an apartment.
"General principles which await discovery
radically different from traditional science."
New things could exist with new properties
which previous things never prepared us for.
The essence of novelty is not to be determined.
Not to have to be necessarily and nevertheless
unable to have been in any other form.
But if your existence doesn't coincide with your essence, do you exist?
A silent leaf fell upon the water
and from the leaf there emerged silent circular waves.
A fish poked its mouth through the glass
and in the glass there opened up a corolla of waves.
Across the pond aquatic insects slide
from which some minuscule waves irradiate
although the pond is static.

A ball at rest
does not begin to bounce of its own accord
and bounce higher and higher.
What happens is the opposite.
(It could bounce, they say, in a very big fraction of eternity.)
Every construction,
marble, brick, cement,
is made of destruction.
Every construction, pyramid, cathedral, skyscraper.
On account of the Second Law.
Ay, Second Law
the equation for which is engraved by way of epitaph
in a Vienna cemetery,
on white marble:

S=k.log W
on the tomb of Ludwig Boltzmann (1844-1906).

Entropy:
The perfect distribution of heat. When nothing reversible
could be managed. No body hotter than yours
will heat you. Nor will you be able to give heat to anyone.
Like those pairs of marble monarchs
laid out. Cold king beside his cold queen.
United by one and the same law, the famous Second Law:
That everything reversible is forbidden.
The day will come
when nothing more will happen on the planet.
When there'll be no more wind in the trees, nor trees either.
When there'll be no more waves in the sea, and not even sea.
Down to the last bacteria spore.
Though the sun still continue to shine.
Universe in which each day entropy increases
and death. And black space expands ever more
between the stars.
One day not even the sun will exist
although its light may continue to reach other very distant lights.
The universe will fill up more and more with dead stars
in their black hole graves.
Time's clock will wind down.
Then merely an expanding empty space will remain.
It's the supreme law of Nature,
says Eddington.
If your theory contradicts the Second Law
there's no hope for your theory, he says.
Darwin believed in a perfect humanity in a distant future
but he found the thermic death of the universe to be intolerable.
And Teilhard: there must consequently be another way out.
"Something in the cosmos escapes entropy."
Not merely an exit from the solar system.
If biology transcends physics and chemistry,
can't there be something else which transcends biology?

Will salvation be brought to us by the Computer?
From the evolution of non-natural life?
Or will the day come when the Computer speaks to us and says:
"In all life prior to me I already existed.
The essence of man was not his body but the program?"
No. On account of the famous law we proceed from order to disorder
but it's also that we proceed from the simple to the complex.
How do they explain that from disorder structure should emerge?
Because there's also the law of the increase in complexity.
And it's a complexity which grows with time.
And a life which goes towards more life.
            A life which violates the laws of physics.

Around the castle
all the leaves are yellow and red
like the old yellow and red gold of the castle's coffered ceilings,
the silent fountain, with nothing but dry leaves,
the naked Venus drenched by the autumnal rain,
            vague autumnal rain...
The marchioness no longer treads the path of dead leaves
in search of her lover.
            These are not new pigments.
They were always there. The leaves
simply gave back to the structure of the tree its chlorophyll
(the complex molecule involved in photosynthesis)
and the dead cells separated the pedicle from the plant
so that the slightest of breezes could pull off the leaves
and new leaves be born another spring.
            The woods aren't dead.
Confiscated from the marchioness under the socialist republic.
On the front steps tourists take photos
of live golden, red, orange, scarlet
tonalities. Live? Dead tonalities.
            But the woods aren't dead.

Crash of water against water
one crest against another colliding

undulating back and forth
    and they rise and fall
        from there to here and here to there
            and there against there
    they come and go
high surge against high surge surging higher
or trough against trough sinking lower
or crest against trough and they level out
and again a rush of water rises up and another rises
    and one against the other
            crest against crest
                again they collide
and others fall and trough against trough also collide
and crest and trough again collide
        and one surge mounts another
        or another slips beneath the other
or a surge of water rears and hurtles forward
            and curls forwards
                    all foam
    and further forward rears again
            and again falls forward
all foam.

The Eskimos travelled in kayaks to the highest peaks
and those in the Arctic tell of a huge raft they built.
The Klallman in canoes from giant cedars
which they cut with sharpened stones and elk antlers,
and then ran aground in what's now Seattle.
In the long winter nights around the fire
they tell it, while outside the rain and snow fall.
"The flood was a change. There's another to come.
The world will have another change. When it will be, we don't know."
Only Garagabi and his family were saved, say the Catio,
on a high rock. The Muscoki of Florida:
as a reminder of the flood, the lakes and swamps have remained.
A very long time ago, so much so
that the elders know it through having heard their grandparents

who heard it from their grandparents, the sky turned black
and the waters fell and fell for days and days
and the people no longer knew whether it was day or night.
There was a wise man, Tamanduaré, the only one who spoke with Tupá.
Only he and his wife were saved, in a palm tree.
An autumn came with very cloudy days, the Choctaw tell;
then there was complete darkness, and in it the Choctaw
sang the songs of death. They only ventured out with torches.
Great peals of thunder were heard, and the waters began to arrive...
A long time ago, the Yagua say, the river began to swell.
A couple were saved on a raft
piled with smoked flesh of every kind of animal
and with mandioca.
Until a heron arrived bearing mud on its legs.
Paul Fejos who gathered the tale:
"There is no Christian influence in their traditions."
Only a few were saved on a raft, say the Choco.
The water receded; the iguana barely pushed its little head through.
The Tzotzil: there'll be a new one, a *flood of light*.
God will then create a third class of men
who won't be like the present ones. What they'll be like we don't know.
In Nicaragua an Indian interviewed by Fray Bobadilla:
"Before there was this generation that there is now,
the world was lost with water and it became sea."
The pools and lagoons are the remains of it (Mataco from the Great Chaco).
Only a man and woman Jivaro were saved
on a very high mountain with a cave
where they confined themselves with all the animals.
It rained and rained for many days, say the Kato,
and the heavens fell down. All the bears died,
all the elk drowned, all the deer drowned,
all the animals drowned.
To the Cuna a cyclone. Trees and houses went flying
and the children could only stick their little fingers out of the water.
To the Araucanians the flood swamped the land of Arauco.
The people were saved on one hill, the animals on another.
"Because they did not remember their founder" (*Popol Vuh*).

According to the Macusi, Mucanaima ("He who works by night")
sent great waters. A man was saved in a dug-out.
The Paraguayan Guayaki: A few in a few palm trees.
The Nahuas: The sign of the first sun is 4-water. Called water-sun.
Period when everything was flooded under water,
everything changed into dragonfly grubs.

To the Fathers it represented baptism
("...torrential waters of the flood..."
"...the birth of a new humanity...")
The immersion in water was into the preformal,
a return to the undefined state of pre-existence,
to the indistinct, dissolution of forms;
and the re-emergence was to the formal, a new creation,
a new life, a new man.
Death and birth.
"When we submerge the head in water it is like in a grave,
when we come out, we are the new man,"
Lustrations, ritual baths...
Truly, truly I say unto you.
Whoever is not born of water...
Ernesto Mejía Sánchez baptizing his son Ernesto
with Angelito, Fr. Ángel, and me godfather.
Your painful birth, Ernesto, like that of wheat, which
—truly truly I say unto you in order to be born has to die.
And you screamed. Feeling your birth like a death.
From the blind cosmos where you were warm and comfortable
you emerged to fall into another cosmos. And you didn't want to.
Free foetus, happy as a fish, in the amniotic liquid,
you floated without shorelines, unbound by limits,
but as you grow you find yourself to be hemmed in,
the vast ocean now a cramped cave
where you brush against walls that rebuff you,
the body tucks itself in best it can, curls up, makes itself cozy,
in the waves that rock it to and fro, more and more,
no longer swimming in calm waters,
the last month the month of strongest tides, the waves tempestuous

now, drowning you, thrusting you deeper down,
terrified you curl up tighter, the water tosses you
    —where to?—into the mouth of death,
where there's no more water, no more cave, only emptiness,
chaos, nothing, the cold of the outside,
    you have emerged into the light.
You are free. But no longer like a fish. Still coiled,
curled up, eyes closed, longing to return
to the blind depths whence you came.
But these will not be your last tears nor your last death
because there are more births. All growth
is painful, because growth is birth
and therefore death, and therefore tears.
You will learn also that all death is birth,
and that man has to be born over and over
    until he is complete man.
And you will leave this cosmos to be born into another.
The whole of creation is in labor through us. That's why
it cries out. But the first-born has been born. The first
among many brothers. Take heart then, Ernesto,
keep on being born. Unless the grain dies...
    Also waves those of the wheatfields.

Aboard the "Solentiname," in a storm, heading for Solentiname:
Black lake. Black sky.
In the darkness only the gleam of the huge white breakers.
Ometepe's way behind us and we don't know just where we are.
A tiny light hovering over the waves, firefly
it can't be. Tiny light
over the waves.
Could it be another launch in the squall lost like us
or could it be a port?

    Donald and Elvis:
Boys,
this is an interesting question:
    So you, why are you sacred?

How we should view the pail you used, Donald,
every morning for milking?
You could milk
and write a poem about your milking, too.
The calf attaches its ugly snout
frantically caressing the teats...
By the way—coincidence—there where you used to milk
the "Donald Guevara School" is being constructed
for the training of peasant leaders.
And your guitar, Elvis, is in the "Elvis Chavarría Library"
in Managua, opposite a market,
where the market-children read
(I remember that streak in you, your love of children
and mainly for them you joined the Frente,
malnutrition, infant mortality,
and you died mainly for them).
Now there are two white boats which ply the lake,
the "Donald Guevara" and the "Elvis Chavarría."
Just as now in Solentiname we also have
Donald Guevara Island and Elvis Chavarría Island.
We kept the green nylon cords for a museum,
seeing them made my flesh creep,
cords used to tie your hands behind your back, and like that you were buried
murdered by the Guardia on a Somoza estate
close to Río Frío.
You can tell the cords apart
because one loop is tighter and the other looser
and Elvis had a broader pair of hands.
When I saw the disinterred bones of both of you
I remembered you Donald saying in mass in Solentiname
that the resurrection was not bones coming out of graves
but the survival of consciousness in others.
You'd earlier read one of the Frente's leaflets
for those aspiring to be militant
which spelled out all that could happen to a militant:
imprisoned, hooded, beaten, castrated, eyes gouged out,
buried alive, burned alive.

But you shouldn't talk.
    And the more you talked the more they tortured you.
Donald, we'd like to have your boat which you so loved
not to set it sailing but so that no one would touch it.
I remember Elvis the night you came back drunk unknown to us
and you went up to lie down in the hut loft
and a liquid was dripping onto the desk where I was writing my poetry:
now to us that vomit has become sacred.
St. Theresa of Lisieux at the age of thirteen
    (she wasn't called that then)
kissed the sands of the Coliseum in Rome.
—Though it appears they died not in the Coliseum but in the Maximus Circus.
There are convents where, since they must live off something,
    the nuns live from the sale of relics
a thread from St. John Bosco's cassock,
a pinch of dust from a tiny bone of St. Caralampius.
So too the Revolution has its relics and martyrs.
Felipe's peasant voice stored on a cassette
    is also sacred.
        The third of the three large islands is the Felipe Peña.
Donald, Elvis, and Felipe who died without a grave,
    you're saints now
like that saint who left the seminary
and said that we should all live like the saints.
Let no bigot, be he the Archbishop of Managua,
come and deny to us that you're alive (though he may not believe it)
        and that furthermore you are sacred.
Please God I might one day be sacred like you.
For all eternity everything about you has been recorded
down to the least shout as you played football.
    Lake Nicaragua reflecting the sky
        is all yours.
    The sky reflected in the waters
        is yours.
While the "Elvis Chavarría" comes and the "Donald Guevara" goes.

To continue the journey.
And that one fuck of a trip.
The phone-call out of the blue from Managua
to the farthest corner of the Antilles:
"Ernesto, Laureano's dead."
On the Trinidad-Barbados-Jamaica-Havana-Managua flight
gazing at the sea, and more sea, I could think of nothing else.
Since we've come into the world sentenced to death
best thing is to die a Hero and Martyr
as you died.
Of course it would've been better had you never died,
provided your wife and your children and your friends and the whole world
were never to die.
When I baptized him at the age of 20 in Solentiname
because he wanted to change from the alienated Protestantism of those parts
to our revolutionary Christianity
he wanted no godfather nor godmother
the whole peasant Youth Club were godparents to him.
Above all his obsession with the Revolution.
Fascinated by Marxism but unwilling to read up on it.
Highly intelligent, but unwilling to train his mind.
The most foul-mouthed person I've ever known.
But the one who uttered "swear words" with the greatest purity.
Once commenting on the Gospel in mass:
"Those wise men really screwed up calling on Herod."
Or, on the Most Holy Trinity (his summary):
"The three buggers are only one."
The night he confessed to me by the calm of the lake:
"I don't believe in God anymore nor in any of those shits.
I do believe in God but to me God's man."
Yet he always wanted to be my server in the mass.
Nobody could take that job from him.
His most frequent expression: I COULDN'T GIVE A FUCK.
My son and brother Laureano,
unruly and affectionate son
like any son with his father
and besides since I wasn't your real father

you were above all my brother
brother quite a lot younger in years
                        but above all compañero,
you prefer that word don't you?
      The one you loved most after the word Revolution.
Compañero Sub-Comandante Laureano,
            Chief of the Frontier Guards:
I say together with you, that we couldn't give a fuck about death.
              I didn't want to do this passage.
But you'd say to me in that poetic language of yours from those masses
later translated into so many languages, even Japanese
                                        (some job translating you)
"Son-of-a-bitch poet tell those fuckers my compañeros in Solentiname
that the counter-revolutionaries killed me the sons of fucking bitches
but I couldn't give a fuck."
      Like Leonel's "surrender your mother."
You were always telling me you wanted to join the guerrillas.
And me: "With your lack of discipline they'll shoot you."
Until your dream came true with the assault on San Carlos.
      "We're really going to fuck those fuckers."
The bullets the guardia sent your way. And your account after:
"paf! paf! paf! Holy fuck! I felt I was a dead one there."
Trouble-maker, reveller, womaniser,
bursting with life yet unafraid of death.
Shortly before you died you'd told me calmly in Managua:
"It's one fuck of a mess up there. Any day I could die in an ambush."
You haven't ceased to exist:
You've always existed
and will always exist
            (not just in this one,
      in all the universes).
But it's true,
once you were alive,
                        you thought,
                              you loved.
And now you're dead.
It's being like, let's say, the earth, or stone, which is the same,

"hard stone because it feels nothing at all."
But no, hard stone not a bit of it,
yes you *do* feel,
beyond the speed of light
at the end of space which is time,
absolutely conscious,
within the very much living
consciousness
of all that exists.
LAUREANO MAIRENA PRESENT!
The fucking plane running further behind at every stopover.
Night had already set right in over the sea. Couldn't get it out of my mind...
I'd like to die like you brother Laureano
and send a message down from what we call heaven
"My fucking old Solentiname brothers, I never gave a fuck about death."

Alejandro flying in a light-aircraft
over Laureano's grave in Solentiname
and having earlier seen the white flecks of foam
saw the circle of white stones on his grave
and thought (he says in a poem) that if he were to crash in that plane
"within minutes the circle of white foam would disappear."

"Midway between the unpredictability of matter
and the unpredictability of God" said Dyson.
Or might it not be the same unpredictability?
Or Martí again: "To die
is the same as to live and better
if you've already achieved what you had to." (XXX:22)

If I'm on this shore of the lake
the waves come in this way
if you're on the opposite shore
the waves go that way.
Have you seen this spot of the lake
—some hole in the center—
from which all the waves emerge

and go to their different shores?
Out in the lake the waves seem wild
as they come and go. They dance wildly.
But around the lake is the shore,
and it's a single shore all of it
the same there as here,
and the water doesn't move but merely the wave
which runs equally this way or that way
and thus every wave will find its shore
where alone, without any water, it will kiss it.

CANTIGA 36

The Grave of the Guerrilla

In the beginning...
To the question what was there before the beginning
it may be replied that nothing
but that nothingness is unstable.
"Creation from nothing seems to violate the laws
of the conservation of energy."
    Evening came and morning came: the first day.
In the beginning
the spirit of God hovered over the radiation.
God said: Let there be light!
and the sub-atomic particles began to light up
in the sea of radiation.
A second after the beginning
the creation of matter ceased.
Protons, electrons and neutrons danced in the light.
A million years later
electrons and nuclei embraced
and atoms were born.
The universe was very light, only hydrogen and helium.
Evening came and morning came: the second day.

He was not visible but spoke with them, the Pygmies.
Paradise was the forest.
All the animals were friends.
He ceased to live with them, he went down-river.
And this is the oldest tale in Africa according to Schebesta.
At the beginning he was with them the Pygmies.
In a hut. Arms with gleaming bracelets.
It so happened they were forbidden to eat the fruit of the *tahu* tree.
A pregnant woman ate it. One night he headed off down-river

and they never saw him again.

We scour the galaxy for technological civilizations.
But what if they self-destruct the moment they become technological?
Or astronomers like the Maya with no technology?
Set among the lugubrious structures of the black holes.
Only the soft whispers of radio static have been heard
or maybe it's a plane flying overhead.
Perhaps they are messages arriving at the speed of light
but from dead civilizations;
the ancient star now a black hole
where gravity entombed the light.
Possibly no other blue beaches, palm trees, loves
within a radius of a thousand light years.
A hundred million years ago flowers appeared.
The third of the planets around the sun
was the Garden of Eden.
Man was entrusted with its cultivation and ecological care,
and growth and natural selection.
In the beginning was chaos, instability, inflation and radiation.
20 thousand million years later
a herd recently descended from the trees,
on the wide-open plains, gazing at the stars
wonders...

According to the Urindi
in the beginning he dwelt amongst mankind in a village.
But they tried to kill him
and he withdrew.
The Yagua dwelt among tapirs and wild pigs in the heavens.
They didn't hide themselves in the jungle as now they do.
Likewise the Arhuacos: wild animals in the beginning
lived among the Indians in perfect harmony.
Or the story that animals used to converse with people
    (Caribbean linguistic family)
before they had fire.
        There was only fire in the hut of God.

Beyond particles of matter
particles of life,
and particles of thought
(or people).
And then what?
Life emerged from matter,
and from life thought (or people).
And then?
Perhaps one day there'll be no matter only life,
matter converted into life,
eternal life throughout the universe, in this
and in all possible universes.
Those who believe nothing's possible except for what has always been
(as though the astronomical immensities hadn't until recently
been discovered)
and given such discoveries, Chardin asks
could the universe come to an end in any other way
which was not in the immeasurable?

Or, so it goes in Nigeria, the heavens used to touch the earth,
and God used to replenish man's gourds.
He went off afar, as he is today.
Or there was a liana linking heaven and earth till it was severed.
The Djaga consider themselves punished
for eating the fruit of the mringa-mringa tree which was forbidden.
The Kuta tell that they ate the isuva fruit, forbidden.
The Maquiritare: a stolen fruit, which was the yacca.
But the Luba talk of some bananas.

At the beginning solely applied to thermal machines.
The second law of thermodynamics. Yet the fact is that all beings
are obliged to yield to the second law.
No technology will impede the inevitable destiny.
Unless it is something greater beyond technology.
Technology would always be economy: money or power.
Power thus against the restrictions of the physical laws?

When finally the sun begins to turn into a red sunflower...
How to move to another star system?
When many other stars are also burning out.
Unless in the final stages of cosmic evolution
gravity is no longer this gravity, gravity
is love.

The stillness of the nights... In our galaxy which travels
faster than a bullet.
    Silence of those worlds which terrified Pascal.
Firmament of immutable stars
moving at over 100 kilometres per second.
      Where is the Milky Way headed?
With a radius of 100,000 light years
and 100,000 million stars.
    Stars that are almost entirely hydrogen.
100,000 million suns almost entirely hydrogen.
Andromeda to the naked eye like a murky stain of light
        2 and a half-million light years away.
And the most powerful telescopes detecting galaxies
10,000 million
        light years away
            crammed together like protozoa.
"A business manager would reject
any natural process as inefficient and wasteful."
    In photos they appear like grains of sand on the beach.
Plus all the quantity of matter we're unable to see
dark, or transparent, or undetectable.
      A galaxy is a detail
      and a thousand million years a brief period.
      Being a part of something greater
      therein the entire history of the cosmos is condensed.
His concept of the universe is such, Einstein used to say:
that death to him seems insignificant.

We have reached the point now of being conscious matter. But
what other evolution lies way beyond consciousness?

What existence without matter and life no longer biological?
Even now a door of the universe remains closed
which one day will be opened to us.
        To have loved once upon the earth
        will be sufficient to exist forever.

We still preserve so much of bacterial movement.
The salinity of our blood the same as the sea's.
And how can we call ourselves separate individuals?
Is the oxygen molecule alive in the cell
but not in the air?
        Animate and inanimate matter
        the mystery is the same.
A plant's intelligence is it within it
or outside?

When a child eats corn flakes, Sagan says,
the child doesn't become corn flakes but corn flakes
become child. That, precisely, is life,
not a mathematical opposition, alas, to entropy.
Biology does not violate the second law,
the implacable second law of thermodynamics.
Order emerged from disorder,
and from order greater order emerges.
Yet the living being's order feeds upon disorder,
and shits a greater disorder, shit,
and only death is a greater disorder than his shit.
Which reminds me of Verlaine, drunk, saying to Rubén
in the cafe D'Harcourt: *La gloire!...La gloire!...Merde!...*
merde...encore! Pounding the marble table top.
We eat animals that eat plants, plants that eat sunlight,
in which we do not differ from non-living beings.
        But from birds birds are born
        and not sponges, nor sponges from rocks.
And now the direction of evolution
        Panida! Pan yourself, who led choruses
runs contrary to perishable matter.

It will need to transcend spacetime,
that's to say, an extra-planetary solution.
Anti-entropy!
The galaxies would be indefinitely dispersed...
this could be in some trillions of years
but nobody would like that.
Is nature so malevolent
that it has made us harbor false hopes?
He is subtle, but without malice, said Einstein.
If we have appeared asking questions, can it be
that the intention is that we shouldn't all end up in a black hole?
Our process has been from greater to greater improbability.

The winds and the waves come from the light of the sun.
Every movement on the planet caused by
imbalances in solar radiation,
snow melting, rivers which run down to the sea, heartbeats,
and even biological death.
But at the end of the day *what*:
A universe with no discernible finality,
an immense meaningless accident?
To know how the stable universe became unstable.
If equilibrium was a reality one day
how did it come to be divine disequilibrum?
Because total death is eternal equilibrium and nothing more.
The step from death to life
is this cosmic instability through the production of stellar light.

The universe is light.
Islands of light in cold space.
(Or energy.)
Jesus "the light of the world":
He who redeemed us from entropy.
A supernova above Bethlehem
(or Halley's comet in the 12th B.C.?)
And an empty grave.
Hope of the oppressed and the dead.

(Long before the Maya, stela C in Tres Zapotes, Veracruz,
there is a date close to that of the birth of Christ,
exactly year 31 B.C.
although the exact date of Christ's birth is unknown.)
Imprisoned, in a shit-awful state, the Baptist wondered
whether perhaps another would have to be awaited.

Every form is beautiful.
    Or everything is fire (Heraclitus).
Even a pond with lilies is fire.
        The universe burning continually.
And man burning.
            All light and heat.

There are many things about this new fire
        —outside his hut to the anthropologist—
that I could explain to you
if you could understand them.

        Silesia, Westphalia, Bohemia.
Bohemia: bonfires in the pastures and around them the dances,
garlands back and forth between girls and boys
through the flames. It's Walpurgis Night.
    Hungary:
The hills lit up with great bonfires.
Picardy, through the vegetable gardens and fields under crop with torches
exorcizing the darnel and blight.
        Prussia, the uplands aglare
            as far as the eye can see.
Castles of straw aflame
    on the hilltops above the highest beech woods.
Westphalia:
        new fire,
lighting up hilltop after hilltop.
Swabia, summer solstice,
    couples leaping across the flames
holding hands. Burning disks thrown

across fields of flax.
In Franconia, a straw figure, the Easter "Judas."
The whole of Auvergne lit up at nightfall,
first Sunday of Lent.
In Bavaria rolling lighted wheels downhill.
Dancing with garlands of sagebrush and verbana.
Firewood, from door to door, the young people
in Provence, for the great fire of the night.
Rustic dances in Lucerne around a fire tolling cowbells
and setting sparkling wheels a-spin.
Shepherds in Serbia with birch-bark torches
through the stables and sheep-folds.
Wales:
the new fire ushered out with two oak branches.
In Normandy
young men and women decked in flowers would light the huge bonfire
to the gentle ringing of bells in the summer solstice
and through the fields was borne the enormous communal loaf.
Malta, fires lit in every village.
The Tyrol, the mighty spruce aflame
and ringed with dance,
boys and girls with torches singing:
"The grain in the sieve and the plough in the land."
Silesia:
straw figures burnt on the outskirts of town.
Wheels of fire through the vineyards towards the Moselle river.
Rhineland: dancing around the flames,
leaping over the embers.
Scotland: the glare reverberating on mountain lakes.
Flocks passed through flames in Upper Bavaria.
Torches through the apple and pear orchards. Singing.
Lights on the move simulating will-o'-the-wisp fires,
through meadows, over hills, descending valleys.
Moravia, Saxony, Silesia, Rhineland.
Walpurgis Night.

At Frankfurt airport, the plane gingerly edges forward

on the runway, and picks up speed and lifts off.
            The clouds grey and pinkish
            (four in the afternoon in May)
      and a dense dark-green wood
      where the immense airport ends.
The airport buildings (there are several)
are square
            all their lines rectilinear
(unlike the clouds and the wood)
in cement, metal, glass,
some parts cement-colored, others painted,
the planes silvery-grey, I don't know which metal, which metals,
the runway asphalt, grey,
aloft on a building in giant letters: DORNIER
all this I see from my window aboard the Lufthansa flight
            taking off
                  travelling from Frankfurt to Vienna
and I wonder, from a formless nature
            like those clouds and the wood
how did man manage to extract all those materials,
cement, asphalt, metals, glass, paint,
the lights on these planes
switched on even though it's four in the afternoon,
the force that moves this plane,
the letters DORNIER the meaning of which escapes me,
how did he do all this,
these questions may seem foolish
but who answers them?
            Mathematicians should express it in symbols
            give us the answer.
They say that Faraday was less intelligible
because he used less mathematics.
A million years ago we were still pre-hominids
what does it matter if this is 20th or 19th century?
            "Planetary motion, of planetary majesty."
Or the question whether
a mammal is more advanced than a rose.

Certain scientists aren't sure.
            A girl and a rose?
Or is evolution aimless?
Humanity is the same gathering of particles
that we've already seen, but in this case the gathering
of conscious particles.
And would it be scientific for us to be the goal of evolution
and after us there'd be no more evolution?
      There is prehistory. Is our humanity static?
Our irrational demand (irrational?) that life
should be eternal. Or a survival of life.
            Or super-life.
Whatever you care to call it, comrade.
Something in the cosmos escapes entropy, wrote Chardin,
and it does so increasingly.
      Until all of us become
      "the equivalent of one person."
So many improbabilities the universe has thrown up...
            He is the light that illuminates the electrons
of any man who enters this world.
      All is fire (Heraclitus). And the new fire?
He has said that he came to bring fire upon the earth,
with this variant in the Gospel of Thomas:
"And behold: I watch over it until it is in flames."
And perhaps the sun already turning into the red sunflower?
There'll be no trumpet, said Sandino.
The Final Judgment will be the destruction of injustice on the earth.
"The trumpets that will be heard will be the clarions of war,
with the hymns of freedom of the oppressed peoples
against the injustice of the oppressors." And so the Gospel of Thomas
—after the fire passage—continues:
"The days you were devouring what was dead, you were making it alive;
when you enter into the light, what will you do?
The day you became One, you made yourselves two;
but having made yourselves two, what will you do?"
Pericles tells the Athenians (possibly
during the cold war with Sparta)

that we cannot see the gods yet believe them to be immortal
through the worship we give them and the favors we receive
and that the same goes for those who have died for their people.

At the grave of the guerrilla:
I think of your body which has been decomposing under the earth
becoming soft earth, humus once again
together with the humus of all the other human beings
that have existed and will exist on the tiny globe of the world
all of us together producing fertile earth on planet Earth.
And when cosmonauts gaze at this blue and pink globe
in the black night
what they are gazing at, from afar, is your luminous grave
(your grave and the grave of everyone)
and when extra-terrestrials from somewhere
gaze at this point of light of the Earth
they are gazing at your grave.
And one day it will be all grave, silent grave,
and then there'll be no more living beings on the planet, compañero,
And after?
After we decompose further, we will fly, atoms in the cosmos.
And perhaps matter is eternal brother
with no beginning nor end or has an end and recommences each time.
Your love indeed had a beginning but has no end.
And your atoms which were in the Nicaraguan soil,
your amorous atoms, which gave their life for love,
you'll see, will be light,
I imagine your particles in the cosmic vastness like posters
like living placards.
I don't know if I'm making myself clear.
What I do know is that your name will never be forgotten
and eternally they will cry: Present!

CANTIGA 37

Cosmos as Communion

In the beginning was chaos.
Chaos was only the first instant of the Great Explosion.
Thereafter everything became law in the universe.
Its creation was the momentary suspension of the physical laws.
A chaos in which something appeared from nothing.
            In the beginning was chaos
                        (Assyrio-Babylonian Genesis)
            when the heavens still had no name.
How did a chaotic universe transform itself into a structured one?
            Through telescopes and
            particle accelerators
                        we see the same reality.
The atom not only sings but sings in tune with the stars.
And the simplicity and informality of the universe:
            99% of it hydrogen and helium
            and the remainder impurities.
Hydrogen and helium, the two simplest atoms.
And like seeds in a freshly ploughed field
the basic molecules, it's said, are scattered
            throughout the blackness of space.

Made from the remains of stars that exploded
and later we will be part of other stars and planets.
            (In the garden of Tehran.) I think of the young people
            who died in the Iranian revolution
            and those who are dying in Nicaragua's.
                  They will live forever.
                        Their particles, will be eternal.
And their consciousnesses now in the Consciousness of the universe.
According to thermodynamics

no energy is lost in the universe,
so will the spirit be lost?
The evolution of love is irreversible.
In the garden of the palace of Baktiar,
the ex-Prime Minister.

Meteors impact on the moon
and pieces of moon cascade
to earth. So that the earth
is full of moon.
The first iron worked by man
was iron fallen from the sky as meteors.
They saw a colored arc in the clouds
and from there they invented the bow and arrow
and later the lyre.
Pythagoras discovered that all things are number.
If a string is twice the length of another
the tone is an octave lower.
Halley's comet perhaps now in Jupiter's orbit.
And you, dear girl, composed from all the elements of a comet.
On the other hand there also exists
the imperceptible psyche of particles.
We are witnessing in these days
the dematerialization of radiation.
The process of personalization of the universe.
What has united us all, Chardin discovered in the 20th century,
is that the earth is round.
And by the way
The Butterfly Effect
which physicists now speak of
(the air stirred by the wings of a butterfly in Peking
may turn into a storm in New York).
With Copernicus we were one planet among others.
With Newton the sun only one more star.
Hubble: the sky full of Milky Ways.
And now what else?
Applied sciences create reforms, the pure ones, revolutions

said the discoverer of the electron.
In the early days of the theory of relativity it was proposed
to call it not of relativity but of the absolute.
Light travels in grains but behaves like waves.
Which is metaphor.
But we cannot speak of light except in metaphors.
We see the sun rise and set, simply,
because the earth rotates on its axis,
but mornings are joyful
and twilights melancholy.
    (Reflection in a Tehran garden.)

The night is what permits us to peer into the infinite.
The night our shadow,
the earth's cone of shade in the sea of solar light.
And what do we see? Not a faint diffuse glow
but bright glints set amid vast lightless voids.
The universe then is not uniform. Due to the fluctuations
of the inconstant virtual particles it is not so.
Irregularities which had their beginning on a sub-sub-submicroscopic scale
attained in the expansion these cosmic proportions.
From the microcosmos the macrocosmos was born.
Our galaxy and the other sister galaxies.
We tend to have greater admiration for what is over our heads
said Descartes.
The majority of them having a planet with life,
it's supposed.
The moon was not a perfect sphere Galileo saw,
but irregular, imperfect like the earth,
with valleys and mountains.
    On Fraunhofer's grave is written:
        Approximavit sidera.
      He brought the stars closer to us.
And already from the XIV Meister Eckhart to his friars
in the refectory, during the collation (evening meal):
    "The earth cannot escape from the sky."

The extra-terrestrials, just how strange will they be?
Can they be anything other than like us?
Space and time we have in common.
Won't the extra-terrestrials be as terrestrial as us?
Certainly they'll have an economy.
They may also have their own Crucified Man.

I was sailing with Thiago de Melo in the Amazon,
the water beside the boat the color of smoked glass,
and beyond the jungle silhouette where the waters ended
the moon rose.
In contrast to the grey and desolate dusty moon
the earth is an enchanted garden of flower and song.
The Sea of Tranquillity, the Sea of Storms,
the Lake of Dreams, are nothing but deserts of dust.
All the infinite forms of beautiful life on earth
        spider, jaguar or Greta Garbo
are nothing but ordered forms of 20 amino-acids.
        Spider, bear no spite.
Manure on the grass, foul-smelling;
but the insect it attracts, mother-of-pearl,
iridescent, its melodious flight
        a gleaming thread.
                8 minutes it takes the photon
from the sun to the flushed rose-bud.
Salute the sun spider, bear no spite.
If from a single single-celled organism
                (dating thousands of million of years back)
we all come.
Today we swap words at the speed of light. Electromagnetic
waves of the beloved's voice on the phone!
And if the universe should manage to become a single universal being?
From the entropic explosion of the stars we've been born.
And it's a matter of triumphing over entropy.
An organic unity of souls.
Myriads of thought particles
which will be a single thought on a sidereal scale.

What colors will they see? Will they talk or sing?
What religion or religions will they profess,
or could it be something we'd not recognise as religion?

The heron casually descends on the lake (in a Solentiname islet)
quickly snatches a sardine, hastens
to place it crosswise—iridescent—into the beak of the heron chick.
And this is an analogy of the universe.
This is, I would say, like cosmology in miniature.
Biology which in reality is physics under the guise of chemistry.
To triumph over entropy.

Let the pupil observe that there are dark lines in the Sun's spectrum
which coincide with those of iron. This means
that in the Sun there's iron.
Or rather its gaseous exterior has iron vapours
which absorb light in lines which to us appear black.
The same that beats in our blood.
A lamp swaying in the penumbra of the cathedral in Pisa
with the same regularity as pulsating blood,
and Galileo gazing at that pendulum as a child, perhaps praying,
the lamp of the Most Blessed Sacrament, back and forth.
As the sea transferred to land with us, and salt
the common denominator of blood, sweat and tears.
And as the earth trapped sunlight and made of it trees,
green life charged with solar energy,
life which is light stored.
The green turtle of the Miskito keys
grazing on sun-drenched submarine pastures:
its succulent flesh, in the food chain, only
a link away from the sun.
As for what he knew of the immortality of the soul?
The entire earth is a single soul said the cacique.
From an inanimate planet all this life born.
Thanks solely to solar radiation not being erratic.
Light which comes from the heart of the sun makes the bird sing.

Guatemalan rites to awaken the moon,
so that the sun will step forth the first day of the year...
Or as the Omaha when a child is born invoke
sun, stars, hills, rivers, trees, insects.
And the Tarahumara, their dances learned, they say,
from animals. The dance of the turkey, of the deer, etc.
Dances which the animals perform for God.
They merely imitate those movements, they say;
praying with dance and the calabash.
And in San Ildefonso (U.S.A.):
        "We sing so that the maize will ripen."
In reality all children of the same primordial protoplasm.
        The unity we fail to see because of an optical illusion.
The same moon which rises on the horizon at dusk
sets for others in that instant on the same horizon.
Newton understood that the law of falling apples
applied equally to the moon not falling.
Now the atom is not a billiard ball but music and dance.
God commands all things to sing
says the Dakota song.
        "Say it. Say it outside."
        Drums are the cosmic rhythm,
        wind instruments the human spirit,
        intelligence the strings.
Church has been around since the creation of man according to Origen.
In this manner this was revealed to the Panamanian Cuna:
"God has left us here on the earth like a single person."

We still don't know what we are.
—The whole range of beings, from atoms to stars—
            We are incomplete.
We're not ourselves until we are celestially.
            What are we?
A compañero, in a city, in a country,
on a planet, in a star system, in a galaxy...
Fear of union. To lose ourselves individually.
But there's no human liberation without nature.

Which does not imply the liberation of all creatures.
The cosmos as though in Maternity screaming in labor.
Humanity is still multiple.
We save ourselves all or nobody.
The universe is One.
One in which we all are.
Friends, we save ourselves all or none.

The diamond-colored diatom
(microscopists attest to its beauty)
is eaten by the copepod,
and the copepod by the herring, and the herring by the squid,
and the squid by the perch, and the perch
dies and its detritus
fertilizes the diatom.
Berlin is built
upon a substratum of diatoms 23 metres thick.
The sea cradle of life.
And since then life is born from life,
and life lives, through death, on life.
Or all the cosmos as communion.
The humming-bird wouldn't exist without the flower
nor without the humming-bird the flower's nectar
"The Kingdom of Heaven is like a wedding banquet which a king..."
The flame-tree I planted in Solentiname
is this morning all scarlet, and the ground
beneath it, scarlet like a Persian carpet, and
the branches all thick with blossom as
if none had fallen to the ground. And
I heard a sound above me like a tiny
helicopter. The helicopter was a colibri
dew-colored with iridescent rays of sunlight,
the wings merely transparent shadow, the beak
a wire, longer than its body. (Doesn't it get in their way
when they sleep?) Drunk on nectar, changing flower
at each instant avidly, some it penetrates
and others not, from side to side like a jay-walker,

just as I in Paris would enter the boulevard bars and cafes.
It settled briefly on a branch, gorged on the blossom
and flew off.

Our other part of the I which is all matter.
"My kingdom is not of this world," in the Praetorium,
wasn't meant in a strictly astronomical sense.
        The union of the multiple and the one,
        in the orchestra for example,
                                    or in my body.
The union which differentiates.
A union we've been working on since the Neolithic.
        And how can all of me die
        if I am one united with the All?
If evolution has been towards more personalization,
could its end really be Total Impersonalization?
He preached nothing else but the Kingdom of Heaven
and not that it's coming but that it's close.
Or on the contrary the concentration of all personalization?
Because our work, what we achieved,
if something we did achieve, survives. But, and us what?
The general consciousness... And conscious beings?
Would we be forever conscious of no longer being?
It cannot be: That there should remain of us merely the shadow
or the shadow of a shadow in the memory of other shadows.
                Our dreams: memories
                of millions of years' existence.
And whoever you are, or however important you are,
you have millions of ancestors the majority of them
slaves or poor (they're always the majority)
and they're alive in your genes
and the genes of the rest of the people
that great majority.
Every species when it acquires its definitive form
tends to unite, to associate, to become socialized. But
if we're left with nothing but total annihilation
the human species would go on strike.

I read that electrons
do not travel indiscriminately to the right and left
but prefer the left.
And (I read)
"Yang and Lee were right: the universe would appear to be leftist."
Only now have we seen the depths of matter. And we never knew
matter would be so beautiful!
Why don't today's poets talk to us about it, said Feynman.
(About today's science.)
And I say: And about the heavens!
The entire universe is life!
Life divided qualitatively
and spread quantitatively.
The immensity of space and time which we call universe.
Accident or design?
"When physicists use the word 'fictitious' they don't mean
imaginary."
Chaos has now begun to unite all kinds of study.
In the purest diamond there are hundreds of billions of impurities.
A little drop of petrol which a car left
on a muddy puddle is lit up with the whole rainbow
the same as a colibri or a peacock or the dew
and the principle's the same.
But the colors of the rainbow are always in the same order.
Sister light.
Also the electron has psychic properties.
And like pearls reflecting pearls
each thing is itself and the other things.
"Science must rebuild itself again" Schrödinger has said.

Since the universe looks the same from any
galactic conglomerate...
Since the formation of planets seems
"as normal as childbirth"...
Could they be blue? (The atmosphere, the water, the distances:
blue like ours?)
How many inhabited celestial bodies are there in the cosmos?

We know only that we are or were one day on this celestial body.
        (In a universe for the most part hostile to life.)
                Surrounded by ashen stars
                        and black holes with their motionless time.
Reagan who's almost like a parrot
that repeats what's said to it. I say almost like a parrot
because he's not strictly a parrot, he has ideas,
but a few tiny, fixed ideas.
And who'd be surprised that the Central Intelligence Agency
should be keenly interested in studying
the new scientific revolution of this eighties decade,
the so-called science of chaos?
Naturally not for the order which emerges from the chaos
but to create more chaos in the chaos.
Space is an open field in all directions
and time is a train which speeds through it in a single direction.
But if time goes from past to future only
and it's from past to future that life elapses
and the direction of evolution is only towards the future:
mightn't it be that someone awaits us in the most remote future?
        He does not play dice said Einstein.
                Neither a pilot-less space ship
                wildly orbiting the sun.
In the most remote future or eternity.
The principle of all movements to Plato.
Moving the universe like a lover his beloved said Aristotle.
Towards where the telescopes are raised on the earth.
Until the last blade of grass enters Nirvana.

St. Clement of Alexandria had seen the interrelations
through the effect on molluscs of the phases of the moon.
        Annually the marriage of heaven and earth.
The feast of the first ears of wheat, with unleavened bread,
later came to be Passover, and later Body of Christ.
Also the Seminoles' dance of the fresh corn
and the ceremonies of the new yam on the banks of the Niger
are eucharists.

Solstices, harvests, grape gathering.
Catholic liturgy had the cosmic rhythm.
"The rains, the seasons..." (alluding
St. Paul to the ancient Cosmic Religion).
The semen of the sky scattered over the earth.
The joys of the solstices.
The ripe wheat, and the wine good now for drinking,
and the pruned vines.
Those in communion with Bacchus were called Bacchae.
And in autumn the Pyanopsias.
My lord has died. Tammuz has died.
The sad flute... (The remaining characters obliterated).
Offering maize, the Hopi offer their bodies
because maize is transformed in their bodies
and to the creator of maize their bodies give THANKS (Eucharist).
Later Catholic communion lost its nutritional value.
The Council of Laodicea, in 363, banned the agapes.
A transubstantiation without proteins.
While the question of transubstantiation of wine into blood
spilt so much blood.
A long time now since food was given in the churches.
With the platitude that
heaven is more important than the earth.

The preparations were at the full moon
and at the waning moon the celebration.
"I'm thirsty. I'm dying of thirst"
(whispered in the night).
In autumn at the sowing of the new wheat in Attica.
The *Lampadephoria*, dances in the night with torches.
The stars also formed part of the dance
and the waves on which the torches flickered.
The maidens suddenly without veils before the light
and the torches also reflected on them.
It was Demeter with her torch scouring the world for her daughter
and the cry was heard of the girl calling out to her mother.
"Goddess of the great loaves"

She who taught men agriculture.
After, the hierophant displayed the cut ear of wheat.
It was said that the first wheat was cultivated in Eleusis.
The golden wheatfields where Persephone returned to the light each year.
          Wheat returned from the grave.
In the dark, by the light of torches, on autumn nights.
"Unless the grain of wheat dies..." The ripe grain
was death, says Frazer, the final sheaf is called The Dead One
and children were warned not to venture into the wheatfields
because death is in the crop.
Christ became grain. (Analogy of grain and death, and also
grain and resurrection.)
In the darkness of the night, in temples or caves.
For those who contemplated the ear of wheat, a lesson
on how through death life is produced.
Recurrence of the cycle of seasons, of harvests, life.
The Eleusinian plain would be covered in wheatfields each year
through which Persephone passed like the wind gathering poppies.
Roots sunk deep into proto-history says Eliade.
The most perfect mystery of Eleusis says Hippolytus
was the silent exposition of the wheat ear,
the supreme revelation,
and then fearlessly you could face death.
The initiates' catch-phrase was
          NOT TO KNOW, BUT TO SUFFER
"to die is to be initiated," said Plato
and they'd cry out with their eyes raised to heaven, Proclus tells
     "Sky, rain! Earth, conceive!"
"Those who are initiated in the mysteries understand what I am saying"
(St. John Chrysostom in a homily on the Eucharist).
"The initiated already know what this means" (in another homily)
"The initiated know already what I mean" (idem)
          "...and what bread and what chalice are these."
They welcomed slaves and foreigners.
Cicero:—The most grandiose thing Athens has created.
          22 kilometres outside Athens.
The plain where the golden-tressed goddess gave wheatfields to the world

now chimneys, refineries, cement works, petro-chemicals;
the sea of initiations: shipyards, opposite Salamina darkened
by sulphur dioxide, nitrogen dioxide, carbon monoxide.

In the half light
(the meeting is clandestine)
laughing girls circulate between the small tables
bringing the olives, the sardines
Irene pours the wine
there are few of us
one glass for every mouth
one huge loaf
for all
one song on everyone's lips
the same song and the same glass,
we men kiss each other, the women kiss
a slave is among us, Erastus is there
the city treasurer, the ex-rabbi Crispus
Titius Justus the multimillionaire is there,
wheat scattered in the fields
brought together in a loaf,
dispersed in the barracks, the shop, the treadmill
we meet Saturday evening
separate grapes brought together in a wine,
Irene passes back and forth
we chat lying back
until midnight, beneath orange torches
what am I saying until daybreak Sunday.
There is one we don't see, the one who presides
the Executed Man, crowned with vine shoots
yes, we dine around a dead man
this is a funeral banquet. He
celebrated it thus before he died, so as
to unite us in his absence
("eat thus in memory of me") and he's alive in this wine.
Day breaks. The lights of the feast grow pale.
Farewell Irene

and in the misty streets we go our ways
but we go united.

How many faces together,
something like 2,000 young people,
thousands of blonds, undulating wheat,
sun through the church windows setting the wheatfield ashine,
undulating beneath the sway of the electronic music .
I give them communion, with
baskets of golden bread, and golden Rhine wine
in paper glasses. So many
grains of wheat together in one loaf
so many golden grapes in a single wine.
And also all united in the song.
So much song united,
so many throats together in the words of the song.
And all smiling, so many smiles together
like a single smiling face.
A face of 2,000 faces
lit up by the sun through the church windows,
something of the glory of resurrected bodies, I think.
The face makes us human. Animals
have no face.
(And they don't distinguish between our faces.
The dog can differentiate millions of smells, not faces,
but we distinguish infinite faces.)
Is this what's meant by
"in his image and likeness"?
This is the social being that God created in the beginning, I think,
social and one,
"male and female he created *him*"
All the faces together formed a single face of all
and a single face of one.
On the surface of the planet
Dusseldorf ever closer to Solentiname.
And the unity in the bidding prayers
One: "Lord

that in Nicaragua all their dreams may come true."
And another prayed:
"May there be many Nicaraguas in the world."

In radio contact with Solentiname,
in Managua writing about this mass in Dusseldorf,
I suddenly hear Nubia speak in Solentiname
and she signs off "Greetings to everyone there and good night"
"Good night, over and on the air"
and on the air the radio bore the Solentiname night
with the pocoyos cuasi-lechuzas that sing at night
no longer singing sadly as under Somoza
fuck-ed-up
but
we-fuck-ed-him
glow-worms a sky at ground-level
the lake color of moon under the moon
the repeated lapping of waves on the shore
over and over
frogs on the jetty singing of love
lovvvvvvvvvvve
and the thrum of the power generator.
The motor's about to be switched off.
Good night, over.

CANTIGA 38

Assaults on Heaven from the Earth

"In the beginning God created the heavens and the earth"
Genesis says (Although the earth
five billion years after the heavens).
        Quarks. Quasars.
In pre-scientific times they formulated:
    Smaller than the germ of a grain of millet
    bigger than all the worlds together.
The same as that:
            More subtle than subtlety.
And from the same recondite Sanskrit source:
        Dwelling place of all
        in all dwelling.
Unity and diversity:
    like a single moon in many ponds.

And the faith also of atheists. Or so-called.
"I will carry forth the faith you imbued in me"
        (letter from el Che to Fidel).
In rebellion in the heart of the mountains, but so as to bring it about
in the heart of man. It matters little
that certain terms are not understood, said Don Quixote,
"in time usage will work them in
so that they'll easily be understood
and that's what enriching the language is."
    Like KOINONIA. Communism and communion are the same.
"The ugly cocktail"
says Vargas Llosa "of politics and Christianity
which he has brought into vogue"
(me) (according to him).
Like the step from the inorganic to life.
It has to be understood.

In a non-static universe.
It has to be understood.
        20 Indians from Majipamba
working on the road to Cajabamba
each with his maize and his *máchica*: no one
eats his own: together in a poncho
the shared lunch.
The Indians of the Majipamba commune
            happy around the poncho.
80% huge estates (un-
like the common economy of the Majipamba Indians).
Its very basis
in man's biological make-up.
It has to be understood.
Right from the earliest ones, gathered in groups around the fire,
        and around them the millions of galaxies.
Faith in the invisible. Or the irreversible.
That's the thing, boy.
To adore God? Only in man.
Since he's his only image.
And that accounts for: he was always generous, said Inti
"el Che was always generous,
he'd treat enemy soldiers without ill-feeling
taking medicines away from his own people."
            The thrust of Evolution.
That's how it has to be understood.
Father Teilhard de Chardin excluded no one
from the Church who believed in Love.
            One, one single humanity, brothers.
                Each one in another another another.
Evolution didn't stop with the individual person,
it has yet to reach its limits.
The discovery of the roundness is
that the earth is in the heavens.
Faith in the future. The invisible and the irreversible.
            "I will carry forth the faith you imbued in me."

Forces which reach us from the depths of the universe.
    This vast solidarity of all that exists
    in the totality of space and time.
The lunar rhythm
is the rhythm of the sea
and the reproductive rhythm of the sea creatures.
Flowering occurs through light.
Through seasonal variations in light
the plant breaks out in flowers instead of bundles of leaves.
You will discover that your body was the whole universe,
and the universe a single body,
body with infinity of souls
united.
And in thousands of spiral nebulae, like us they are longing.

Members of a group of 17 galaxies.
    All of them revolving like musical spinning tops.
We don't know what the universe is. Nebulae
and suns, the parabolas
of comets, the intergalactic spaces,
dead stars like worlds of coal.
To Sandino the struggle was not only of this earth:
    Other planets were also involved.

Planets perhaps where the atmosphere is methane
and the sky is green.
Perhaps other types of biology with different chemical bases.
    The galaxy Virgo A
        comprises maybe 10 trillion stars.
Only explicable by a love beyond measure.
    And all the astronomers in all those galaxies
    and poets too with cosmic canticles.
        Universe dwellers.
Standing before my hut in Solentiname I urinate
gazing at the stars.
The earth from Mars must be luminous like Mars.
And how beautiful we would see our galaxy from outside of it.

From that flickering point of light, I sing to you:
Love, creator of the stars.

What the Chinese call—or used to call—the Heavens.
"He works without speaking.
Without words he governs the sequence of the seasons."
    Absolutely no beggars,
an extraordinary thing in an Asiatic country.
And Western doctors have found no trace of
venereal diseases—completely gone.
    The revolution begun in the heart
    and which is conscious evolution.
        Science utopia.
      The Great Harmony Mao called it.
The kingdom of heaven on the blue earth.
An earth to make us hungry,
a sky to sustain desires, without satiating them.
For centuries with their wooden ploughs
and suddenly with their hands they made steel,
five centuries in five years, in two years,
with spades and wheelbarrows the drainage
or irrigation canals,
for dams, fish farms, electricity,
socialism without machines, with hands,
6 million peasants giving talks
on the nature of soils, fertilizers,
previously unable to read.
        A change in the heavens' mandate.

    The biological need for association.
Cells could get no bigger though they might have wished to.
They would have tried for three thousand million years
in vain.
Accumulation of a million independent cells
didn't help much.
This did little to improve the sponge and it remained a sponge.
Accumulation of many cells *in community*

that was the revolution.
With division of labor and so on...
                    Until the Body of Christ.
"We have unleashed the assault on all heavens"
my friend Roque wrote shortly before his death.
            The fact is we die so that others may be born.
Why others? That's Evolution.
            Others better than us,
                    and others better than those others...
                                        To what end?
The fact is that that's the meaning of death.
Evolution was our past
is our present
will be our future.
            All of it united in evolution.
Evolved out of universal matter; with
evolution not yet over.
"One day we will see in the dark"
                    (Roque Dalton. In unfinished poem).

Heirs to the purest of chromosomes.
            The difference from animals:
                    changing reality.
The reporter from the capitalist magazine
couldn't help but observe that
no team in the professional world
could produce such impeccable positioning
on a baseball diamond
("the truly remarkable harmony of the Cuban team")
Animal society is incapable of progress because
the young always learn the same things,
their young,
                forever the same things.
'Incredible harmony, that cohesion
of coordinated movement
from the Cuban team.
Not mere individuals but baseballers...'

(Sports editor in Somoza's Nicaragua)
"Proclaim..."
The revolution is compassion
(in old Hebrew).
And zas! new housing,
dairies, schools, hospitals.
Revolution making itself singing.
Posters like Cuban light itself.
In 1959 Fidel spoke out like Deuteronomy
says Matthews
(against usury)
And all the banknotes in Cuba signed: che
no capitals
"I will carry forth the faith you imbued in me."
Already on the threshold
of liberation from the law of natural selection.
It has to be understood in that light.
The dawn still murky. The non-light scarcely dissolves.
What we will see later!
Harmonious structures without government.
The evolution of love an entire geological period.
Republic of Heaven.
He ordered the proclamation: "it is at hand"
(although it wasn't quite so).
Which is why he was considered more subversive than Barrabas.
It wasn't quite so.
But: "I will carry forth the faith..."
Farewell letter from el Che to Fidel.

The old dream of a world without poor.
With harmonious rains upon the meadows
creative work for the good of all.
No one said that things were his only
(*only*)
all things for all
(quoting whom?)
The primordial of basic necessities, love.

And there was even rice in the airport
almost up to the runway.
The beautiful conic hats are for the women only.
Children with books under their arms out in the paddy-fields
having returned from school.
Hole after hole after hole
full of water
bomb craters
turned into peaceful ponds.
Fish and ducks in the ponds.
Paddy-field after paddy-field with their network of canals.
Huge bridges destroyed now rebuilt.
Land of much water and a smiling people.
Streets jammed with cycles.
Green bamboos and palm trees. And the peaceful ponds
like this Vietnamese people.
Lines, lines of people, on
the road, on the bridges.
Balancing their two baskets.
Baskets of rice. Or even of earth.
During the war they carried messages
in the tubes of cycles.
Green billiard baize: young rice reaching to the horizon.
People with baskets fetching water
from one strip to another
very quickly so as not to let it escape.
It was March. Paddy fields, with rice seedlings.
This is what we saw. Millions of human beings
with hoes, with baskets, with bare hands, changing
nature for the future society.

Pithecanthropus: the first work-tools,
rudimentary work, and society.
First forms of work and society.
Through work: from the Australopithecus to the Pithecanthropus.
Evolution of the hands, brain, vocal cords
through work.

Through work, language.
The song of the Pithecanthropus.
Production made man,
that is, social process, history, song.
Until Las Casas said (Las Casas I believe)
"All the nations of the world are men"
Like saying that the entire earth is the Body of Christ.
Or will be if it isn't.
In the heaven of the future, as someone said.
"The grammar of those peoples
makes no distinction between past and future."
And in this whole affair food is a mystery.
The great mystery.
Inside a 30 inch sea bass which Bosco brought from his island
a 6 inch sardine swallowed whole.
Was this allegorical?
The entire universe is allegorical.
Functions, and the body is only one (CORINTHIANS)
Functions, and not classes.
A biological union is what will occur.
Or is there another planet to emigrate to?
We are not at the mercy of large numbers
I tell you. Since living organisms organized themselves
we have cooperation, society.
We will get There through evolution.
Some form of final unity.
There's no rational irrefutable proof.
But that it's union, it's union.
Where the factory stands was once swamp. Now
there is an artificial lake
and next to it an auditorium
and dances.
Boating pavilion. Theatre groups.
Is this the one who is to come or shall we await another?
Without fangs, nor claws, nor defensive shell.
He owes his progress to
Muller says

astuteness and camaraderie.
Astuteness and love. (The serpent and the dove.) His weapons are
intelligence and attraction towards his own kind.
Nothing can stop him from reaching the culmination
of his evolution.
The exploiter will become man.
"...a handshake or a Hail Mary, Country or Death!"
said el Che.

Brother, day has broken. Look.
Already we can see the Masaya volcano
and its smoke
rising out of the crater, and the green lagoon of Masaya,
further off the deep blue Apoyo lagoon,
the Sierras, and the mountain ranges sky-colored,
as far as the eye, the truth is,
that our earth is the color of sky,
farther off, do you see, the Pacific,
almost pure blue under the sky,
the truth is we're in the sky and don't know it,
look, on the other side Lake Managua, and Momotombo
close to the water like
a triangle of lake raised up or
a pyramid of sky.
All this was there before
but a dark night enveloped it,
and it couldn't be seen. The night of temptations.
Each one had his temptation.
The temptation of the false dawn that can't yet have come.
Lying in bed in the middle of the night it's daybreak.
Daybreak has come now, Pancho Nicaragua,
all is lit up
around this hut.
Earth and water. You can see it.
And in that little house I hear singing:
"How happy and fresh
the break of day."

CANTIGA 39

"The Desired of Nations"
(Of Peoples)

According to Plutarch, the Oracle of Delphi was the depository
of an ancient and secret prophecy:
a birth.
Son of Apollo
would bring the kingdom of justice on earth.
Also Tacitus: that in his time the belief was common
that a saviour of the world would come out of the East.
Prophecies hung in the air. Prophecies
that something was coming.—And, whatever it was,
it would be from the East it came.
Reason why the Eastern religions became fashionable.
Down to the bread and water banquets of the Mithraic mysteries.
For St. Augustine there were Christians from the beginning of the world.
And Newman: It is not a paganism in Christianity but
Christianity in paganism.
The sowing of grain as a solemn funeral rite says Frazer.
In Boeotia, in November, the Pleiades departing, says Plutarch.
"If the grain of wheat does not fall into the earth and die..."
words which had a very ancient background.
Then came sacrifices in the threshing floors to Demeter. The first bread
with wheat recently threshed.
Oh Osiris, first born among the dead!
(Isis screaming).
Longings for Christ, says Guardini!
Osiris, Apollo, Dionysius, etc.
Tammuz was a shepherd.
He a shepherd too.
(Perhaps of those other sheep that were not in His fold.)
With the blue lapus-lazuli flute

the song in order for him to rise (Tammuz).
"Let the dead arise from their graves."
The same as with the flute, the silent song on a Sumerian tablet:
"Once again I open my eyes
once again I open my mouth"
And the folk song sung by shepherds:
"Flower with roots pulled from the earth."
Also the shepherds' Pan.
First only the shepherds in Arcadia venerated him.
The caves of Arcadia consecrated to him.
(And an official cave at the foot of the Acropolis in Athens.)
The caves where the shepherds took shelter.
Later through his name *Pan*, "Everything",
became the God of the Universe.
Later a birth in a cave... And incidentally
Rubén's: "Bethelehem bound, the caravan passes"
St. Jerome, lodger in that cave, speaks of the ancient cults.
Around the year 4000 copper. Then bronze.
In the Holocene, following the last ice age
the Mediterranean civilization,
cereals, and sheep with their milk and wool.
Which brings us to Luke (3:1) where: "In the fifteenth year
of the reign of Tiberius Caesar, Pontius Pilate being..."
and what Plutarch relates, that in the time of the Emperor Tiberius
some Greek sailors were sailing through the Ionian Sea
and as they skirted the tiny island of Paxos,
famed for its mysterious caves and olive groves,
they heard a thunderous shout which proclaimed THE GREAT PAN
HAS DIED!
—The shepherd was playing his syrinx (common reed
which was Pan's Flute)
and sometimes *panic* descended upon the flock
the sheep suddenly scattering, mysteriously
seized with terror—
Idolatry as a belief in *mediation* (A. Nicolson).
Around that time the oracles fell silent. All the oracles
everywhere. There having been so many.

Which is why Plutarch wrote his book
ABOUT THE ORACLES THAT HAVE CEASED AND WHY
Plutarch pin-pointed the decadence of Delphi.
Despite the millionaire budgetary assignations of Hadrian.
The conservative, colonialist oracle, who spoke the ambiguous
language of Bishops' Conferences. Which explains Heraclitus:
"The god of Delphi neither reveals nor conceals."
And what was it he said; the last thing said by Delphi?
The message to Julian: "The waters of the language have run dry."
(Worse. Now Athens will extract aluminium silicate
according to the paper of a few days ago, 1987 A.D.
for the rich beds of bauxite, you know; and acid rain
will fall on the nearby Parnassus; sulphur dioxide turned to sulfuric acid
on the temple of Apollo, what's left of it,
caustic soda flowing to the Castalia fountain.)

Eusebio of Cesarea tells that also around the time of Hadrian
human sacrifices of expiation came to a halt everywhere.
Already in clay in the Library of Asurbanipal it was prophesied
the stain of slavery cleansed
the chain broken
(some Assyrian liberation theologian)
and Eleusis is the same; *Eleusis*: "the coming,"
Eleusis was that, the coming,
the coming of God (Schelling).
Until the final fulfillment of the myths.
The throwing away in Greece of old garments
and reception of the new year with dances:
Old man—New man
St. Paul's "dress oneself in the new man"
was not like now for old parrots in their pulpits.
Greece's lamps all with the same light.
"Ah Attis, the sacred green spring!"
The myths, the grainfields, were signs
of the plenitude of the times.
Proof was the cyclical birth of the sun and the seasons
according to Theophilus of Alexandria. Is there not resurrection in the
harvests?

24 March, *dies sanguinis* for the Romans:
lugubrious liturgy for the death of Attis.
And that pagan Holy Week mentioned in Plutarch,
the women in mourning for the death of Adonis,
Alcibiades' fleet setting forth thus with bad omens.
They used to flog a criminal annually in Athens
so as to expiate the sins of the people.
A possible act of alliance with the invisible.
Criminal, quite likely revolutionary.
Would explain Tacitus calling Jesus *ignoble.*
In the scant reference he made to him.
All the ignobles there've been since then
and had been before him it would appear.
But the body of Attis in the earth did not decompose.
His hairs like plants continued to grow.
Following the newborn solstice
sun in the misty winter
nights growing shorter
and days longer.
To Lucilius, Seneca writes:
"A man adorned with divine perfections
that one day will be given to us to contemplate
to whom we could say in the words of our Virgil..."
The Sibyls had announced a Universal Monarch says Cicero.
And later the Sibyls fell silent.
Then it is that Virgil sings:
"Now the final age of the Sibyl of Cumas is at hand,
the great series of new centuries now begins,
the Virgin is returning, the kingdom of Saturn is returning,
from the high heavens a new progeny is descending.
Take care, Lucina, of this child, who will end the Iron Age
and will bring forth the Golden Age throughout the world."
The Sibyl... The Church likened her to the prophets.
(*Teste David cum Sibylla*). St. Augustine speaks of one in Eritrea
who wrote very clearly of Christ ("He will cut down the hills
and raise up the valleys... The mountains will be levelled with the fields")

and Heraclitus, who apparently did not believe in oracles, Heraclitus
who said (fragment quoted by Plutarch)
"I consulted with myself"
speaks of the Sibyl with delirious lips making herself heard for thousands
of years
"thanks to the God that is in her."
And the Golden Age of Saturn... Without wars, or money-grubbing or
discord.
Slavery and private property were unknown.
Neither slavery nor private property. All possessions in common.
God of the grape harvest and the peasants.
He was expelled from heaven. In honor of Saturn
slaves were set free for the *Saturnalias*
and the masters among friends cooked for each other
"Blissful age and blissful centuries those
to which the ancients applied the name of golden."
Another fragment of Heraclitus was
that we live from the death of the gods.
Barbarian wisdom and Greek wisdom, to Clement of Alexandria
saw the truth in certain rendings or crucifixions.
Like Merejkovsky: "Christianity is the truth of paganism."
"Christ in part known to Socrates" (St. Justin).
And Plato prophesied the crucifixion in *The Republic.*
The Just man, as Plato saw him,
"held by the worst of men, without ever having committed
the least injustice... will be scourged, tortured... Later
they will crucify him" (Republic, II, book 2)
which Seneca translated: *Extenda per patibulum manus.*
Or the archaic stone with Orpheus crucified.
That stone on which Orpheus is crucified.
Faked? Perhaps not. In any case with this truth:
Orpheus torn to shreds by the Maenads, figure of Christ.
Whom they called "bacchic Orpheus" in the catacombs.
(The legitimate Orpheus for Clement of Alexandria.)
And on a chalice in Damascus: surrounded by vines like Dionysius.
The fresh orphic fountain.
From the beyond. On the orphic tablets.

The Babylonian text where Tammuz is
"in the underground corral"
The other sheep *not* in His fold?
"the seasons produce all things" is in Heraclitus.
What did he mean by that?
Anniversary of the creation
was spring
for Philo of Alexandria.
They had prophets according to St. Augustine.
They were Christians considered atheists, to St. Justin.
Paganism which was then the true religion.
Their revelation: the rain, the seasons...

It would be out of the East he would come
and Suetonius as well: he of
"The ancient and persistent conviction throughout the Orient
that Judea would provide leaders for the Universe."
And when king Astyages dreamed of that tree
whose branches covered the whole of Asia.
"All these things, Lucullus, are hidden
from us in dense fogs..."
Parmenides spoke of a road to salvation.
Empedocles felt claustrophobia in the universe.
He felt himself to be in a dark cavern.
Cave. Cave. The Orphics always with their cave.
Before the Gospels he was in the Gnosis.
Under various guises.
His parables archetypical symbols:
king, father, water, fire, weddings, grain, wine,
the light and the shadows.
OSIRIS KNOWS THE DAY IN WHICH HE WILL CEASE TO BE
(Book of the Dead)
To Frazer, Osiris was the cereal that is born and dies.
But isn't it rather the reverse: the cereal, Osiris?
"oh beautiful adolescent, come."
Chesterton is amused that Jupiter should symbolize the thunderbolt
and not the thunderbolt Jupiter.

Everything was one huge myth to Sallust
worthless in itself except for what it symbolized,
the meaning. Which conceals and reveals.
        Osiris dead and resurrected among the dead.
In the time of the XVIII dynasty
those clay Osiris-figures with seeds. Theban tomb (1,500 B.C.)
with one, life-size, of barley and earth,
the barley germinated in the earth 8 centimeters 35 centuries ago.
Frequently represented raised up from his coffin.
                All mummies identified with him.
                His name on each mummy.
In the great temple of Isis at Philae that chamber
with the corpse of Osiris germinating wheat and the inscription
"Osiris he of the Mysteries, who springs from the waters that return"
        —The most pious of men—said Herodotus.
The whole mystery of Egypt, for Merejkovsky,
the whole mystery of Egypt is being the shadow of the body of Christ.
St. Peter speaks of torchlight in a dark place.
Darkness of the caverns of prehistoric man...
                And already in Neanderthal graves
                the dead facing eastwards.
Like the mummies in the Andes turned towards the East.
        All those ragged Chibcha mummies towards the East.
"His name is East"   (the prophet Zechariah 6:12)
He had exchanged the West for a new East
says Clement of Alexandria.
        In the West are the dead. There where western
and Christian civilization resides. But in Matthew it says:
"As a flash of lightning comes from the East and shows itself in the West..."
                Western west Christendom.
And for 20 centuries now in the Canticle of Lauds,
almost 20 centuries, the monks, at the Hour of Lauds,
"save us from our enemies and from all who hate us...
...bring light to those who lie in the darkness and the shadows of death"
with the theme of the path of peace, etc.
                What the Orphics already asked for
liberation from the sad and tired wheel

or the broken tablet in the Asurbanipal library in Nineveh
asking for the coming of liberation, the theology of liberation.
Isaiah's, awaited by the islands.
Which islands? The islands are all of us.
Solentiname also.
Hye, Kye
In the Eleusinian mysteries they called out
Hye, Kye, "Let the rains come, may you conceive"
with eyes raised up to the sky according to Proclus,
which signifies the marriage of the heavens and the earth according to
Proclus.
And the Church still says it in Advent.
To him were directed all tears for Tammuz.
Who was like Osiris, a *god that dies.*
Tammuz-Adonis, the husband of the fields.
..."with pious myths" said Xenophanes.
And for him was the wait for the Saoshyant (Future Liberator)
with the nectar of immortality, from the times of Zarathustra.
The door-locks were covered in dust
says a cuneiform text, in the mansion of the dead.
Myths are for the time being, said Plato
—conjectures, hopes...—
until a safer boat was available for the other shore.
The Feast of the Flowers. This was in Greece
in spring. When the vines were pruned
and the wine ready to be drunk,
the wheat ripe,
the fields full of flowers.
And what they were drinking, like gleaming blood in goblets,
primitively they called it Dionysius.
Demeter, *Mater Dolorosa*
Tertulian saw the analogies.
The women of Elis called out across the waves, Dionysius!
so that he would arrive at his white temple by the sea.
In the rites of Attis it was recited for centuries
muttering it *kymbanon...kernos...*nuptial bed
as Clement of Alexandria relates.

I slipped into the nuptial bed.
Christians: from the beginning of the world to Augustine
Although only later did they call themselves Christians.
Was not Orpheus the first founder of monasteries? (*orfanoi*)
Heraclitus, Christian to Justin,
or for Philo of Alexandria he took from the Bible
the doctrine of contraries.
Which makes relevant the business of "the cycle of seasons"
of Paul in the Areopagus.
Cycles. Seasons. "So that albeit gropingly they might find him."
Feeling their way, in the darkness, stumbling...
In the darkness.
That constant terror of mankind.
(See Theophrastus.)
Fear, says Plutarch, fear of the sea, the earth, the sky,
of darkness, of the light, of voices, of silence.
The pain "explained in the mysteries to the initiates
as expiation for a very atrocious crime". (Cicero)
Anaximander's painful world
all things atoning for the injustice of each against the other.

They said into the ear of the initiates in Eleusis:
"I am thirsty, I'm dying of thirst"
They prophesied water. They asked for water.
But the mysteries were not sufficient.
Socrates had scorned Eleusis.
Diogenes the hippy did not believe in the mysteries:
it wasn't possible that a gangster initiate could be saved
and compañeros Epaminondas and Agesilaus should be condemned.
The way to Hades, the Orphics were searching for.
How not to lose oneself in the lands of the dead,
is very complicated, said Plato.
Since I know very little of the other world... said Socrates.
That they should not listen to him but to the Logos, is another of
Heraclitus's fragments.
The mysterious Eclogue IV
announces that he already arrived.

"Erased the traces of our ancient crime
the earth liberated from its perpetual fear.
The child will receive divine life.
Will see the gods mingled with heroes
and he himself they will see in their midst
and he will rule the entire earth at last brought to peace"
What Zeno the Stoic longed for: human beings compatriots.
A human species without nations.
The flock with the common law of a common pasture.
Or as Diogenes exhibited his world citizenship: *cosmo-polita.*
("Tyre, the Ethiopians, all born in Sion" for the psalmist)
The earth like a common city, which the Stoics wanted,
says Cicero; common to the gods and to man. As
Cicero also qualified mankind:
"by nature suited to cities"
Marcus Aurelius: "Born for cooperation."
He said like one being the feet, another the eyelids:
"members"; of the organism of rational beings.
Members of Christ is the same. Or communism is the same.
Seneca saw that clearly: to be members of a huge body.
With no greater limits than God himself, said Seneca.
"...eyes obscured by your vision..." (Hermetic text)
The division not between Greeks and Barbarians for Eratosthenes
but between the good and the evil. Orpheus already sang says Apollonius Rhodius
that the sky, earth and sea were a single mass
and from that mixture of discords they were differentiated.
Orpheus whom Proclus called "theologian". As Cleanthes sang:
"This universe which rotates in circles around the earth
obeys You." Our souls, to Pliny
"particles of the heavens". Plants rooted in the heavens
to Plato. Thales likewise, pioneer of cosmology according to Heraclitus,
"the first to scrutinize the stars"
Thales likewise, saw that everything was full of God.
Gazing at the stars, says Aristotle, men believed in God.
Such movement and order!
Like watching from Mount Ida the advance of the Greek army.

Kingdom of Saturn. Kingdom of Heaven.
"Everything is full of God." The only phrase to come down to us from Thales.
And it is the most sublime in philosophy to Plato.
He said God or gods depending on the translation: better to say Godgods.
Everything: he meant the familiar reality which surrounds, and also *Everything.*
The Kingdom of Heaven is like a woman with a jar of flour...
In the middle of the present post-glacial period he was born.
The Desired of the Myths, also in an Advent antiphon.
The Apollo whom the shepherds in the woods implored
for protection against the wolf.
"The flocks will have no fear" (Eclogue IV)
And referring to merchants:
"There will be no ships to exchange merchandise" (Eclogue IV)
O muses of Sicily!
The return to those times Empedocles pined for
in which there were no wars nor gods,
with only Love as king,
before this Age of Hatred.
Men of wisdom monotheists in ancient times according to Democritus.
Eros: pre-dating all the gods, Orphic doctrine in Aristophanes.
"Behold I come to fulfill all the myths."
They never existed, but always are, according to Sallust.
O muses of Sicily!

CANTIGA 40

Flight and Love

"In the beginning was the Tao.
And the Tao was in God.
And the Tao was God...
And the Tao became flesh and dwelt amongst us"
        (Translation of the Gospel into Chinese by Dr. Wu)

According to dialectical materialism
matter never emerged,
it has always existed.
Not in the most minute particle can it be increased.
No being disappears or emerges from nothing.
            There is no nothing.
Nothing comes from nothing
            and nothing returns to nothing.
Matter is immortal and eternal.
But
if the universe is eternal, life is eternal,
        and consciousness, eternal.

A wedding of all male and female.
All male and female
            with the All.
        For we are more than living organisms:
Consciousness that doesn't die with the cells.
        (Perhaps girt with bodies of hydrogen?)
                Of consciousness dying
                we have no consciousness.
The question what will come after communism.
As St. Paul says (1 Cor: 15:19)
if Christ didn't rise again

we're a bunch of pricks.
Man's a process, an entity in gestation.
Towards being each one two,
and all one.
It's in our genes.
It's in the interest of our genes.
Love is for survival.
Without which a true revolutionary
does not exist, said Che.
Life is irreversible?
Is love irreversible?
The first cause of the universe,
of matter expanding ever more
and more, that's for the reader to determine.
The equations don't spell it out.
Our existence dependent upon so many coincidences
that one might think of an Author of the coincidences.
The resurrection of energy and of life:
if there is no other life
we're fucked.
The girl's alone at this party.
I'm waiting for you, compañero.
Come.

At a tremendous distance from its island,
the Caribbean green turtle (from the Mesozoic)
finds its way back to copulate there guided by the island's smell.
From Brazil perhaps
to its tiny island in the Lesser Antilles.
Salmon by the smell of their native stream,
and up-river, against the current, leaping onwards
to where they were born, and where love calls them.
And whales and dolphins, whole oceans...
The fact we won't settle for the finite.
Born to wed with the heavens.
Ah, Leibniz, the reason why something exists
instead of not existing.

And that not everything can be pure chance.
My former love, still loved.
Lovers' love imperiously demands
the immortality of lovers.
This plan, whose?
Or his existence as though practically necessary.
Or if the totality of it all were all by chance?
And the finite the only absolute?

Most unbearable
for being the most incomprehensible!
While the universe descends into entropy.
And we like insects towards the light.
But as to whether he's personal, he's personal.
And not someone who's been created out of anxiety.
Ad Deum qui laetificat juventutem meam
old Fr. Cassini would say at the altar step
"God who is the joy of my youth"
that's how the elderly psalmist recorded it
and the old priest would recite it at the altar step
in the pre-conciliar mass, I a child, acolyte, on my knees
or better translated
who is my joy and my youth
who is still my youth
not was,
is my youth
and the youth of old Fr. Cassini at the altar step
and a child kneeling at his feet in a small red cassock
or that archaeological cry, perhaps from neolithic times
"from my father's semen you knew me"
in the hymn dug up at Qumran.
And where do hydrogen atoms come from?
and:
Creator and Matter as male and female?
Like Bride and Groom?
The Maker of stars...
The cause of being of all that is

is his beauty
says the sculptor quoting St. Thomas who quotes
Dionysius the Areopagite.
The eternally young.
"He whose teeth are always perfectly intact"
says Fernando González.
He escapes entropy.

The desire for a kiss more real, embraces more real.
Not those fleeting kisses, unreal like in the cinema.
That though 1000 years may pass or a 1000 million years
the kiss might not pass, the embrace not pass.
Love untimed
unmeasured out in minutes on the minute hand.
Beyond the death of solar systems.
Now broken all our molecules.
That thing
for which the Revolution has no answer.
Or has it an answer?
Sacrifice, immolation, are
Darwin's law.
Martyrdom:
is evolutionary.
Not just heroes and martyrs,
every living being dies for others.
Being alive is for giving life
and ceasing to be,
to die
for the new life.
If lasting longer were the important thing
granite has beaten us all.
"It is path and not terminus," said Martí.
Also, if I'm not mistaken: those were the laws of light.
And: harmony is arrived at through agony.
Pain is *useful.*
Thus he reached his sacred island.
The sacred island of liberty.

"Cuba and the night..."
And why is there a universe?
And an expansion of the universe
in which we cannot be the center of the expansion.
Oh Wakan-tanka of the Sioux, who bestows the buffalo
and for which reason the buffalo is holy,
and you give the things and the knowledge to use them,
how to find the holy plants, encircle the buffalo...
Help us to be attentive!
THE UNIVERSE IS A THOUSAND TIMES LARGER
HARVARD ASTRONOMER DISCOVERED
(Boston Sunday)
Shortly before I was born.
The dear old man dreamed of a universe a thousand times larger.
But it was merely
a small fraction of the universe.
Individuals don't count in science said M. Curie.
Madame Curie who discovered radiation
which killed her and transformed her forever into radiation.
It's not having life but being life. And
even without biological life we are life.
Elvis Chavarría, I dreamed you were alive on your Fernando island
in Solentiname, your mother's island,
as though you hadn't fallen
after your assault on the San Carlos barracks,
and you were going to take me to meet a new child of yours,
like the girl you'd had earlier
the dark little mite
whom they said was yours and was the image of you
and I envied you this new child,
because you could do what was denied to me, because I denied it to myself,
and then I awoke and remembered you were dead
and that your Fernando island's now known as Elvis Chavarría island,
and you could no longer have that new child who looked like you
as neither could I,
you were dead like me
although we are both of us alive.

Ay, man cries out the moment he leaves the womb
wanting to return there.
And spends his whole life longing
to return there.
The myth of Mother Earth
where we're buried
and the dogma of Mary's Assumption into heaven
(its complement).
Yes, because why only the earth.
Each planet comes from a star.
And there we shall return.
All together.
To heaven's womb.

To go is to return.
"Returning is the motion of the Tao"
(Lao-tzu).
Cycles.
Expansion and contraction.
"The yang having reached its climax yields to the yin
and the yin having reached its climax yields to the yang."
The shady and sunny sides of a mountain.
One and the same mountain.
"That which lets now the dark, now the light appear is *Tao*."
Day and night, male and female, above and below.
Yang Heaven (masculine) and *Yin* the Earth (feminine).
She on her back, gazing at the heavens, and he face-down, at the earth.
He is movement, and she rest.
Understanding and intuition.
All is rotation. *Yang* revolves around *Yin* and *Yin* around *Yang*.
Each one the seed of the opposite.
Copulation of contraries is the cosmos.
Going far means returning and returning means going far.
Man is the sun and woman the shade.
I renounced those girls for the cosmic sexual act.
All that was born of hydrogen:

flowers, women, music, the Mona Lisa...
The unity of all things is patent in the atom
and still more within the atom
and more: below the atom.
Heat is the love of molecules.
Love is movement.
In the cosmic immensities
as in bed
love is movement.
That one who is Love is Movement.
History governed by the "law of LOVE"
(A.C. Sandino).
The laws of light. The reason the sky's black at night.
But light which travels at 300,000 kms. per second,
where is it going?
What's the probability of the Beyond?
If beyond that there's another reality,
more reality?
Is it merely a question of bigger telescopes?
Eckhart longed for a God bigger than God. Which is why
according to Dr. Rosenberg Nazism comes from the XIV century:
God bigger than God was the god of National-Socialism.
But the business of a God bigger than God was correct.
As he also said that everything said of him is false.
Not that Eckhart was a Nazi.
And I one day understood
that to be in love with God
was to be in love with nothing.
And passionately in love.
Or I thought I understood.

The 12 year old girl feels independent.
In that tiny hotel in Santiago de Chile.
Fr. Cortés came in, a religious in the MIR; armed
and semi-clandestine although it was in Allende's day.
The 12 year old girl believes she can live on her own,
he tells me, in that modest little hotel,

expounding atheism to me.
She's forsaken dolls now but she's still not a woman.
One day her body will mature and she'll feel incomplete.
That's when the Bridegroom will come.
Now she must not be upset.
It's wise to mention to her some time about her future union
so she won't grow up selfish, or turn lesbian
or, feeling herself alone, commit suicide.
Contemplatives are sexual cells of the girl's body
which have now matured.
In the little hotel in Santiago de Chile.

Some ephemeral molecular structures
in a minor planet, revolving around
a medium star,
in a marginal region of a galaxy.
But love is infinite.
And the heart empty:
like empty space which is not nothingness but which has
infinite energy.

The male represents creation,
as woman also represents creation,
and their union
represents the union of creation.
From the union of pistil and stamen
comes the new seed
which is the seed of new seeds
of new unions.
Subject and object.
Give and take.
Centripetal and centrifugal force.
And the object in its orbit around the subject.
The universe is dual
and all beings are two.
But
while the others are not you are not.

The stars are rubbing, sexual act, orgasm.
That's why they're so hot.
Orgasm of Antares in Scorpio,
Betelgeuse in Orion, Aldebaran...
The atmosphere swells unrestrainedly and turns a red hue.
All is movement, sexual movement. Rubbing, coitus.
The Trinity is movement. Pure Act.
Or pure sexual act.

Once she played with dolls, listened to fairy tales,
relied on mummy and daddy. That was religion.
Now she feels she can go it alone,
wants to be independent.
The priority: that the girl should develop.
The priority is the Revolution. Still
there are only human beings, not Humanity.
            Fr. Cortés's point in the Chilean hotel.
Some sexual cells mature earlier,
feel the need for union earlier.
The hermit is also revolutionary.
            That was in 1971. He died in battle after the coup.

      And whales and dolphins entire oceans.
            'I knew a love like the pitahaya flower
            which is flower of a single night'
Where did I hear that song? Don't even remember if it was a song.
The pleasure was so intense and was so fleeting, and was gone.
We poor little things, chasing fleeting intensities.
The smooth part of woman beneath the tight fitting blue pants.
From the birth of first life to the invention of sex
may have taken two billion years. Why so long?
Until the first plants' invention of sex.
The pitahaya flower is of a single night. Don't know
whether it was a song or something I took from a science book.
Way before, the self-sacrificing, sexless green alga cell:
which strangles herself and separates into two daughters

and ceases to be her. Why?
So many things one wanted
but the will has not wanted anything other
than the totality.

After the Era of Radiation came Matter's
and with it the galaxies, stars and life.
There'll be another, that of life beyond matter.
And like an evolution of the same evolution.
"About to try it out now
the slow separation of life and matter."
        A new cosmic development so to speak.
                Non-biological man of the future.

At dusk tenuous grey clouds hang over the lake
which are not clouds
        they're clouds of chayules
so tiny that they get through the screen
and keep us from reading
        on many pages of our books they're stuck
        transparent and greenish the size of a letter
and sometimes we have to put out the light. Next day
on the terrace there are heaps of dead chayules
which need to be swept up. They live for only 24 hours
and never once eat
        they don't even have a digestive apparatus.
They say they come from murky corners of the San Juan river
where the larvae lie 2 meters down. Sometimes,
by Las Balsillas, dawn breaks over the calm lake, covered
with a layer of dead chayules, about 1" thick
huge fish all around leap up to eat them
and in its wake the boat leaves a sort of channel...
        They're very similar to mosquitoes, but don't bite
                —what if they bit—
You'll want to know how they live without eating, how they grow.
        They don't grow: they're born as they are.
Yet before they had a different existence

in which they were tiny black worms swimming in the water
    and then they just ate.
Now their entire lives are a wedding, nothing but wedding.
Do you know what the chayules are? They're winged sex.
    We think their only purpose is to bug us
but those minute air-fleshed creatures
are like an allegory of something, there in the air:
Of a different existence mankind may have
    in another element and with other functions
a little like transparent chayules, in a certain way
    —only flight and love.

CANTIGA 41

The Canticle of Canticles

In the beginning...
Big Bang.
Let's go back to the first origin, the spark
from which everything comes:
Neither matter nor motion nor space nor time existed.
And the Great Explosion
A beginning defined in time
and a defined beginning of time
and space was born curved like an egg.
First a very small universe. Let's imagine
a thousand million tons in the space of an olive.
Then the first nuclear reactions:
some neutrons and protons in pairs
procreating nuclei of deuterium.
When the universe was about a million years old
atoms appeared. (Nucleus with electron.)
An electron spinning around a nucleus.
When the universe filled up with atoms
it became transparent and light was able to pass
from one extreme to the other of the universe.
Neither galaxies nor stars nor planets yet existed.
The beginning
was that love was converted into energy.

In the beginning
the cosmos was shapeless and empty
and the Spirit of God brooded over the radiation.
The universe was still radiation and not matter.
And time began.
Matter and anti-matter

burst forth from pure radiation,
from pure energy.
Perhaps for millions of years
everything remained in deep darkness.
First only what was simple existed. (Without light.)
Then corpuscles appeared:
protons, electrons, neutrons, photons.
A proton joins with an electron
and the first atom has been born:
hydrogen.
There was a time when there was nothing but hydrogen,
none of the other elements of the stars and life.

There was nothing but hydrogen atoms in empty space.
"Before Eros united all things in pairs" said Aristophanes.
And how did all things physical stem from hydrogen?
Hydrogen engendered helium
helium engendered carbon
carbon engendered oxygen
etc.

The first copulation, it appears, was between single-celled algae.
Not sexual union exactly but certainly a union.
First from one two were made, and each of these
from one two were made, until one day
two became one.
Perhaps two that were incomplete.
And they became a single cell.
Perhaps they simply collided by accident
and liked each other and then coupled for evermore.
It wasn't exactly copulation because the two were the same.
They'd been the same life once, separated
by successive divisions, and now together again.
It wasn't out of fear of death, since there was no death
rather an unending multiplication of identical cells.
This was before the invention of sex and with it that of death,
and all were immortal.

The case of the single-celled blue-green ocean alga
which dividing itself for two thousand million years
has yet to die.
Occasionally accidental mutations occurred in those cells.
And one day, two slightly different cells came together...
Not so different as to be incapable of coming together
but different enough certainly not to be completely mistaken one for the
other
and now they were together in their difference, and that was sex.
Which has not ended, in the planet's life will not end,
not even later, no matter how much evolution occurs:
    that great novelty that appeared,
        invention and mischief.

Fauces half-agape as though to eat each other.
Or belly against belly, he ravishes her. Or
they explore each other's thorax, elytrons, with their antennae.
    Kissing with their jaws.
The delicate nibbling at her silky neck feathers.
Mysterious chemical changes make them court each other.
    Antennae facing antennae,
    wings embracing wings.
They sing
when the light has swollen their germinative glands.
    Chemical calls from hormones to other hormones.
        Melodious whistles, iridescent plumage
for the other sex.
When the days are longer in the northern hemisphere
because the pole is inclined more towards the sun
there's more time to find a mate and more time to make love.
    Belly upon belly, the numerous legs entangled.
Hormones give the message that spring has arrived.
        The rubbing of one skin against another skin.
  in the mating season
  fantastic dances with veils and fans
  strutting back and forth,
and they spread their feathers like a flower,

they open their beaks.
The embrace of wings and the kiss of beaks.
Each song for a female and a thousand songs in the grass.
Quivering tentacles in sea abysses
to locate and caress each other.
Like flowers, glands exhale sexual smells.
After a long, colorless life, as a larva, perhaps for years,
short days of an adult life
merely to love and copulate among the flowers.
One towards the other
running, flying, swimming or slithering.
Each in search of the other half of itself.
Of its lost unity.
Unity of the earliest days of the primitive ocean
when there was a single life.

All sexual life is for the union of two cells.
Two cells that copulate,
and become a single cell.
Anxious extension of protoplasm,
from one to the other
and they become one.
Once concerned merely with finding food,
and now vehemently drawn one towards the other
and they become one.
Mysterious attraction, more than chemical in nature,
with which they become one.

—Beloved:
We shall embrace beneath the pandanus branches.
We shall eat again of the apple-rose.
We two beneath the pandanus.
There the oyien flower flowers unseen
and you can hear the calls of the kagl and the waugle bird
which always sing in pairs.
On the little island where the pandanus trees grow
where a hut stands abandoned.

—My love: your smooth dark body of turned mahogany,
your tongue like the flame-tree flower.
Your teeth a row of herons on the banks of the Ululali.
Your breasts are the color of medlar
and their taste of milky medlar.
How beautiful the string of pink begonias around your neck.
 Among the yellow elderberries I will love you.

Sex came out of the water like life.
Translucent *Ectocarpus* cells
or transparent, I don't know
 (the brown algae of the sea coasts)
swim around devoid of any sexual attraction,
until a female attaches herself to a solid surface
and secretes into the water an irresistible chemical substance;
hordes of males besiege her with their flagellae
but only one male cell penetrates her
(and her alluring secretions cease
and the other suitors disperse.)

At night under the moon tuneful wolves call to each other.
The grasshopper makes music with its legs for its loved one.
The male cricket gingerly steps forward,
then strikes the first strophe with its musical wings.
Spiders pluck music from the threads of their web
and at other times it's lovesick telegraphy.
 Deep-water fish and cephalapoda
 exchange sexual signals
 with their numerous photofores.

 Penises and vaginas of the flowers.
 Which is why Linnæus was considered to be obscene.
Even a very simple flower (buttercup let's say)
is not just genitals: there is the green calyx,
the colored petals, the corolla:
but nearer the center the stamens with their filaments (phalluses)
and in the center, the pistil with its style (female organs)

in the inner recesses, the penetralia of the flower.
The Bishop of Carlisle was scandalized
by the idea of genital plant life.
Linnæus spoke of plant betrothals, nuptial beds;
Goethe was also among those scandalized by
the business of *labia maiora* or prepuce, *labia minora*;
and, in the *Sponsalia Plantarum*, words like *Clitoria*
("which perhaps the virtuous student...")

The first couple, the hydrogen atom.
"The fact is the universe is constructed in such a way
that it can never create an electron on its own or proton or any other thing,
rather it is always in pairs: particle and its antiparticle."
Just as to the Pawnee all things are two:
The two eagle's eggs (Tirawa's bird).
Man and woman. The sun and the moon.
The sun and the moon make one two (with its shadow).
"Or look at a feather, each eagle's feather
is also two."

—My love:
The orange *elequemes* are now aflame with flower,
the breadfruit are ripe,
golden orioles are cawing in the pawpaws.
The island *icaco* plums are now blushed.
Monkeys are howling in the mahogany trees
and the toucan sings among the avocados.
Come to the village.
—In my bed of palm leaves
my beloved is like the black ura-fish
tattooed like the black fish of Ifaluk.
Like the dark ura-fish
he has come from a distant island.

Pairs of pelicans on their ancestral cliffs,
first squabble together,
their beaks clash like swords.

Then gentler now,
with their beaks they kiss,
and gentler still, lovingly preen each other's feathers.
Snakes coil one around the other,
two snakes in one.
The male seal snatches the female: seizes her with his teeth
and drags her off to the coast, and fucks her.
Two amoebas press together until their nuclei entwine.
The lovemaking of polyps
with tentacles all the color of fireworks.
Whales, like drifting ships, belly against belly.

Flowers are sexual organs,
and a cherry tree ten thousand open sexes at once.
Orchids with a single phallus
and the baobab tree blossom with two thousand phalluses.
No diversity of sexual organs and of sexual
practices greater than in plants.
The colors and scents of flowers
which are loves.
First there were only ferns.
Silent, colorless, without flowers, without insects and birds.
The ferns of the luxuriant rainforests
so sexless; they don't pair up or copulate;
ferns release their spores
which germinate, not like ferns but sexual organs
which copulate, and from which new ferns emerge
to cast their spores once more into the moist solitude.

Also the sexuality of the atom.
We could say that the universe *is* sex.
The whole of matter a vast sex.
Also infusoria that embrace
rupture their membranes,
blending their nuclei and protoplasms
becoming a single one, and they separate
each one transformed into half of the other.

This is in fresh water.

—Perfumed with balm of ginger
sweet is our encounter beneath the palm trees.
I chose you above all others in the tribe.
Your skirt is like the plumage of the pa-i bird,
like the plumage of the golden oriole,
with paint on your cheeks
and paint around your eyes.
Your oiled and smooth-combed hair.
Coconut milk you gave me that night
coconut milk.
My skin on your skin
on your dark skin bearing amulets.
Your fingers perfumed like tamarinds.
—My beloved comes at night
to my straw-mat
he holds me tight against his tattooed chest
and squeezes me with his tattooed arm.

Ah, the rain of ripe pollen through the whole planet
even in the cities. 30,000 grains per square centimeter
in Sweden, for example. All this pollen searching
for a female surface only.
To be imprisoned by the fleshy, downy,
viscous female filaments.

Off the Bermudas the sea turns phosphorescent
as though an aurora borealis were reflected in its waters,
due to luminous worms that at every instant light up
flooding the water with eggs and sperm
and then the lights of males and females slowly fade
and drift down to the sea bed and to their death.

When two hydrogen atoms meet they hug each other like lovers,
in the magnetic clinch of positive and negative.
"Stone that loves" the Chinese called the lodestone

and Thales thought it had a soul because it attracts iron
(the Magnesia lodestone, or that of *magnetism*).
Electrons and positrons are born in pairs.
Similarly mesons are born in pairs.
    Are born and die in pairs.
The same sex for which flowers are scented,
for which birds sing at daybreak
and butterflies are a flurry of color.

The chromosomes of spermatozoids and ova are incomplete.
United they complete each other.
Tiny infusorian couples seek out and find each other,
their nuclei coalesce (a kind of copulation).
        There is a sexual impulse in infusoria,
            a longing for happiness,
                recognition of the other.
If you separate sponge cells
they fuse together again.
    A chemical phenomenon which fuses them.

—My love with her perfumed skin
and glint of sun in her beautiful necklaces
in her golden earrings and nosepiece.
Her embroidered beads like the scales of the ka-hob fish.
Her braceleted embraces in the undergrowth.
Her anklets jingle among the flowers.
Far away our village drums resound.
Her anklets like sea serpents
    and so beautiful her amulets.
Far away the drums resound.
—My beloved
like a deer leaping in search of water.
        Beneath the great bo tree
        my beloved kissed me.
Could they be his
those gentle steps on the leaves?
Could they be his?

The colors of butterflies (like the flowers' too)
were painted by love; they are for love alone.
        Love which hastens the turtle's pace.
The smitten male camel calls to the female with his tail.
        Stag in rut, day and night bellowing at the sky.
Birds of passage which cross half the hemisphere to make love.
            We too inhale the cloying love-scent
            of the skunk's urine at night.
Toads make love again in last year's pond.
The roar of fur-seals more violent that the reef:
a kilometer of male fur-seals braying for their females.
And the butterfly that dances back and forth before its own shadow.
Fish from the depths, in eternal darkness,
locate each other with their love lanterns.

The fusion of cellular nuclei is fecundation.
            Ephemeral cells which one day wed
            are now fossils in age-old rocks
            when man and woman had yet to appear.
The first living creatures bumped into each other.
It depended solely on chance encounters.
Lovemaking emerged 3,000 million years ago.

—Her body all painted in signs
like a lagoon eel.
She comes sheathed in her wrap of beautiful drawings
her wrap painted with *curcuma* dye.

All things are two in the universe.
            A photon
may break down into a pair of electrons
of opposite charge
                like saying divide into two sexes
and then they can reproduce
        and the rest follows from there.
                A gas which gives origin to the stars and life.

And light years?
Stars shine in the distance of time.

The poor plants' need for mobility in order to make love:
insects, birds, quadrupeds, the wind.
The ferrying of a flower's male dust
to the deep female organs of another flower.
Pollen by water
towards the lobes of female flower stigmas
to adhere.
Pollen which falls on the moist stigma
and thanks to that dampness swells
penetrating deep, deep within the stigma,
heading towards the ovary, to an ovule.

—Where did my beloved's canoe go?
His decorations like the diadems of the bird of paradise.
—Let us go to the reefs to watch the colored fish
let us bathe in the clear waters of Vau-Aka
to watch the colored fish among the corals.
In reed fykes we will catch crayfish and lobster
and in the coconut grove we shall eat coconuts.
—On the island of Nusa
he stowed his canoe.

The *Heliomaster longirostris* humming-bird,
helicopter of sapphire, emerald and ruby,
culls the fragile ephemeral *ephemiridae*
which hover above the water and drunkenly sucks
among the tubular flowers down to the depths of the corollas,
passing pollen from flower to flower, its beak gushing nectar,
so as to dance later before the female
with circles and arcs and vertical ascents and sheer dives,
winged jewel, its wings unseen at imperceptible speed,
(two hundred movements per second)
and then it hangs in mid-air excitedly motionless;
it turns one eye and then the other

upon the female in heat, and the two disappear at once
        imitating the sky and scintillations of light.

Morse light: two flashes and a pause...
                two flashes...
The males' lights flutter above the vegetation,
and sky-wards the female hoists her illuminated sex.
The male approaches that light in a gentle glide
and falls directly into the coitus of two lights.

        Sex-appeal was already in the stars.
The implacable attraction of matter to other matter,
        or GRAVITY which sustains the unity of the universe.
Gravity was a natural inclination, Copernicus discovered.
In our bodies and in the sun and the planets.
        Gravity which acts solely to bring together.
        A gravity which separates is unknown.

The female flower lubricates like a woman.
The shiny surface of the stigma is sticky and moist
in preparation for sexual relations with pollen.
Sticky secretion which tends to be sweet to the taste,
with much sugar.
But pollen must lust after the female flower
and the female the pollen. In other words the pollen's irregularities
should match those of the stigma. To slot one into the other,
so as to make very intimate contact
and then union occurs.

—I shall bring you more colored beads
        by the river mouth.

In the calm blue inlet of Cabo de Palos
spring has also descended into the sea.
Down below the light lasts longer now,
and the phytoplankton is reproducing explosively,
the zooplankton finds more food and reproduces,

the opisthobranchiates intertwine their merry tentacles.

Pliny had already realized that palm trees hug each other.
That the branches of male and female clung together with a sigh.
It seems that earlier Theophrastus had hinted
in a few lines at the love among palm trees. Cautiously.
        (Socrates was not long dead.)

—Above us the whisper of palms
and she is like a necklace of pretty stones
of pearls and colored stones.
        She is like the lush-feathered wena bird.
—And I smile with my love.
                Her smell of apple-rose.
We have loved each other beneath the mangoes.
Oh, my love, beautiful are your adornments.

The attraction of each galaxy to any another galaxy.

Fireflies' love lanterns.
Forest fireflies do not randomly light up
rather on and off and they flash in unison.
        It's sexual light.
                The two sexes' dialogue in light.
The two sexes burning like lover stars.
The female displays to the male her blazing belly
encased in an aura of greenish light.
        The females' sexes glow in the grass.
Like when you gaze from the street, at the beloved window
shining in the night.
Dragonflies dart over sheets of water
left by the rains, making love-talk with their wings,
wings color of water, color of air, quivering with love;
        immaterial as two ideas,
they are a perfect circle of fragile transparency and light
iridescent,
        and gentle arabesque will be the copulation of dragonflies,

that fuck in flight. Transparent
skyfuck.

"The sexual urge of oxygen"
(to unite with other elements
to the point of cremation).
Sodium and potassium with a solitary extra electron
longing to meet someone lacking one electron
to unite with him, and they never rest until they find him.
The sexual phenomenon is right there in chemistry.

Stamens longing in the breeze for the ovaries.
The creamy fleshy flower redolent of ripe fruit
a-tremor and enticing there in the air
so as to scatter its sperm.
The stamens are the men, the pistils women.
The virile pollen blindly flies in the wind
searching for a pistil to stick onto and penetrate
first the ovary and then the ovule.
Colors, shapes, smells (poppies for example)
to please the pollinators.

Sexed termites grow wings
(the rest of the community is sexless)
in their underground nests, wings for the nuptial flight,
and they see the light, only then do they see the light,
with wings in the light only for lovemaking.
They fly far, and shed their wings
and copulate on the ground.
From their union a new community is born.

Peach ovaries overflowing with nectar.
Butterflies joyfully sup from those calyxes
fertilizing the likewise overjoyed flowers.
The butterflies go for the nectar,
sweetness of the love-flight from flower to flower.
The honey bee favors flowers with a slim silhouette.

The Bee Orchid, *Ophrys apifera*, opens its flowers
before female bees appear
so that the male flies in vainly attempting
to copulate with them. It squeezes them, and rhythmically and frenetically
humps and humps
never reaching orgasm. Frustrated
it bears down upon another Bee Orchid
and in this way cross-fertilizes it, but still without orgasm.
There are no sexual taboos in nature
neither are "natural" and "unnatural" known.

But the proton is attracted by a certain particle alone.
Why?

And the nereis. The nereis hear
the love-call in the sea depths.
The males at high tide with the new moon
begin to dance and release their sperm
which travels to the females at high tide.

And perhaps life was born from the wedding
of the planet with a comet,
the comet spurting life throughout the planet.

The magic number is 2.
Attraction is the basic reality of the universe.
"Every dynamic in the cosmos stems from the reproductive instinct."
The same as saying that
union and reproduction are intrinsic to matter.

With the apple in blossom,
zigzag flight, up and down,
the male *Aglia tau* searching for a wife,
butterfly wife.
The inviolate doe trembles in the woods for fear of the buck.
Mallards raise their wings
as though fighting

male confronting female.
In woods where evening darkness has fallen
the dark woodpecker flies hesitantly
and with opaque song, towards a female
in an even darker corner.
A duck drops into the water, out of the sky, next to an unknown female.

From the light come the hormonal signals
which produce flower cells
instead of leaf cells.
Plants day and night attentive
to the shifting of the planet,
the length of the days,
and one day of a precise length
their flowers burst forth.
At sunset the pollen descends
and settles
on the recently opened female flower.

—Your necklaces of animal teeth
tear my skin.
Fragrant coconut oil in your hair.
The sand in the estuary gleaming under the moon
and crickets singing to the stars.
He is honey in my mouth.
—Coconut milk and honey
I have on my tongue.

In the high tides of new moon and full moon
silver-plated sea-elves leap over the waves,
leap onto the sand, for their night of love,
gleaming like the moon, and all the sand with them.
Sand full of gleaming love like the moon.

Corollas bent down like bells
protecting their pollen from the rain,
or the petals enfolded across the pollen.

Peonies open by day with the dry air
and close at night or when rain threatens,
hermetically they seal away their pollen.
        Hidden nectars,
                well-guarded sweetness
so that only whoever carries off the pollen
may savour it,
                at the cost alone
of a thorough dusting of pollen as he goes.

—The flowers on the hill of Ha'ao
are like the foam of my beloved's canoe.
When will we be together again,
and hear the agula bird that sings so prettily?
Like heron feathers the foam of his canoe.
        If your reef were not so far away
        your coral reef by the sea!

Association is nature's process.
Each particle is attracted by the others
as it also attracts all the others.
Attraction which makes the stars. Gravitation
generates the spherical form.
        Association is the process.
Molecules seducing other molecules.
                The curvature!
        The universe is curved,
            curved upon itself,
                and the curvature is gravity.
        Force affecting the whole of matter.
Gravity is love.

The problem was
how to unite sexually
two separate creatures rooted in the earth.
Whether they wed through the wind or butterflies,
there are flowers meant for birds,

or, smaller ones, for ants.
    Color signals in flowers
guide the pollinator to the nectar's source
as the lights and yellow stripes of airports
    do to planes
        (hence the yellow and violet of wild pansies).

The lone aria in the sea depths
heard for miles and miles,
    of one whale calling to another.
Each song lasts half an hour
and time and again is repeated, note for note as though following a score.
Songs which have been heard, they say, like laments and groans,
and roars, and barks, and a woman's screams,
whistles and buzzes and howls, the sound of an outboard motor
at low speed, the tolling of bells, chirrup of birds
and gentle strokes like an orchestra tuning up.

Flowers which muster many colors, or
crowd many together in bunches
to be clearly seen by the fertilizers
and wither only when all are fertilized.
Others with scents, or with nectar, or, like roses,
pollen protein for their fertilizers.

The fern violently ejaculates its spores into the wind
towards unknown but somehow beloved dampnesses.
The pine expels its thirsty pollen into the wind
towards distant drops of sticky female liquid.

—Girl dressed like the forest parrot
I will loosen your wrap so lavishly dyed
with many drawings
and so beautifully dyed.
More beautiful than all the other women
who dance with garlands of flowers
among the palm trees.

—I know that you will wait for me
under the orovol tree and the otsonol tree
with its many branches.

Love drives the orchid to the jungle heights.
And the orchid has a million ovules.
The hairy bumble-bee weighs the forget-me-not down to the ground.
Magnolias flood the night with perfume, they long
for the hornet that unites one magnolia with another.
The taciturn ivy attracts pollinators
opening its flowers in autumn, when by then in autumn
all other flowers have died.
Blue and yellow petals attract bees,
but red ones birds and butterflies;
and opaque and faded flowers
insects, with ultraviolet.
Ophrys orchids indiscriminately seduce wasps and bees
and Huxley called them whores.

The female moth scatters its perfume in the night
for the distant antenna of the male who doesn't see it.
And so as to detect molecules of female perfume in the night
its giant antennae.
Emerged from the chrysalis with a single aim, to copulate.
That is the minuscule secret of their flight,
tumultuous flight,
their brief night of life, perfumed and warm,
through which they live without eating.

All those scintillations are for love.
Thousands of examples amid the flowering palms.
Each one of them lights up twice a second.
Ghostly will-o'-the-wisps in the palm trees.
(In Jamaica, like:
"a lamp-lit feast of newly-weds")

—Let us go to the inlet

to hear the sea sing on the shore.
We will catch lobster, we will catch crayfish.
—My love bedded down on the shore like the new moon.
The perfume of cardamom flowers
            close by us.

How flowers compete, like luxurious shops
announcing their wares.
Blue cells overlaid on scarlet produce
the black tulip. Purple in the bracts of Bougainvillaea
from nitrogen in molecules.
Sepals and petals of the bird-of-paradise flower.
And orange sepals and blue petals delight
the eyes of the white-eyed bird. White flower to us
is blue-green to the bee who sees the ultraviolet.
Attracting through color, scent, shape or size.
    Rafflesias with its flowers a meter in diameter.
        High calorie pollen and nectar.
      Others attract insects with non-floral smells,
      such as smells of feces, or urine, or decaying meat.
Orchids with perfumes with complex chemical structures,
for the male insects and disguised as their females,
all their colors copied even down to the genitals.

Attraction between their atoms lit up the stars,
that fascination of some atoms for others.
A pair of passionate hydrogen nuclei
draw close and join together forming a helium nucleus.

The kingfisher carries a small fish to his companion
asking for copulations. The starling
a flower.
The penguin a pebble, or perhaps snow.
The bird-of-paradise: its fantastic palaces
made from shells, twigs, gravel, flowers,
cigarette papers.

The male royal heron leaps in the air above the female,
flutters its wings, gently glides, neck tucked back on the shoulder
and then stretched forward, the feet brought up,
it flies in wide turns, beats its wings against the wind,
its snowy breast tense, it descends finally to the beach,
marches solemnly into the water, on high stilts,
its wings still, it curls and uncurls its neck,
now in an S shape, it reaches out with it, grasps in its yellow beak
a dry twig on the shore, it's for her: the nest's first.

Arum conocephaloides, with traps to imprison insects;
others warm within so as to attract them at night
and they will release them only when they are smothered in pollen;
or those that hurl a cloud of pollen at the insect.
Orchids spring-loaded to reach the bee.

Pine, juniper and cypress pollen borne on the wind.
        The pop music of wind laden with pollen.

The asexual cell only produces twins
and more twins of twins.
        There's no evolution.
But from the simplest cells to the most complex cells
and with cells with nuclei, the union of two cells,
and sexual reproduction.
                The "supreme function."
Although with the formation of the first organism there also appears
the function of death.
Springtime: flowers open, sexes open. There are songs,
        games, courtships, couples,
salmon race back up the rivers
leaping across every dyke,
                                to love and to die.

The wind blows where it will
and the pollen never knows where it is going.

Fish make love upon the eggs. They scatter
their semen over them, driven wild
by absent females
whom they never saw nor touched.

The sexuality of oxygen, it is said,
because it joins to other substances so readily.

The butterfly perched on a branch emits love perfumes
and the male will fly towards the perfume and copulate with her.
From the ocelli which embellish its wings, and are not eyes,
emanates the love-perfume which calls to copulation.

—The loved one opens up
and her beloved enters.
All about, thick underbrush
and far off the roar of tigers.
The kundombo tree is scattering flowers
        and in its branches
        kinde and wendo birds sing.
Roar of tigers in rut.

The palolos' nuptials governed by the moon
or the ebb and flow of the sea?
Ephemerons eat nothing, they spend all their hours
dancing and mating.
Cicadas: their entire brief life is love and song,
singing to the sun, drunk on love.
Eels make love only once and perish. In mysterious
depths whence they come, they disappear.
The ardent male bumble-bee copulates day and night until its death.
Then the female lays the eggs and dies too.

Orchids with aphrodisiac perfumes for insects
which are those used by man to attract woman.
The rustle and purr within the fragrant female organs.
        The lascivious and foul smelling mushroom

erect like a dog's scarlet penis
attracts insects with its putrid smell.

The male goose sits upright, dips its neck in the water
and cries out.
It was desire that heaped colors upon the peacock.
The crab with its large claw beckons its beloved
to the hidden sandy chamber.
The deer rushes through the woods looking for a doe.
The female viper has a fragrant hormone (pheromone)
which only the bifid tongue of the male detects on the wind.
Albatross couples rub their powerful beaks together,
beaks of aggression now merely beaks of tenderness
Towards the end of summer throughout the woodlands of Europe
male butterflies squabble over patches of sunlight
where virgin butterflies will come to settle.
The male sperm whale on the trail of female perfume
in the desolate ocean.

The day has to be sunny.
The sumptuous eyes which cover their head
like radiant crowns, do not recognize her
until she soars in the blue.
Beneath the sun's splendor they flock after the princess,
the royal bride, on her first and final nuptial flight.
Twenty, thirty swarms join them from elsewhere.
Thousand of suitors and only one will be the chosen
for the unique nuptial union of death in joy.
The rest will flutter in vain around the intertwined couple
and soon they too will die never glimpsing again the shining
sinister love
they never knew.
She stepped out onto the lintel
when the sun shone brightly,
surveying for the first time her vast floral domain
and flew like an arrow, unseen to the opaline summit,
the luminous zone other females will never know.

The males pick up her scent which flows into flowers and apiaries.
Only one will reach her in the solitude of the ether.
Intoxicated with blue air he sings the song from his tracheal sacs.
Higher, higher, higher he rises.
Only one among them all can attain such heights,
he penetrates her, the upward gyre of intertwined flight
is momentarily more vertiginous in the mortal spasm of love.
The giver of life must die in the moment of his surrender.
Memory that persists in human kisses says Maeterlinck.
The penis comes away from the male along with the entrails,
it remains inside trailing the male's entrails,
the wings sag, and the empty body tumbles in a spin.

In spring when the sun warms them
plants feel themselves prisoners of love.
The flower petals are the nuptial bed
hung with beautiful drapes and perfumed
for the wedding of plant bride and groom
and there the groom embraces the bride
and then the *testiculi* open
and genital dust shoots out
and falls into the vagina
and fertilizes the ovary.

The coats of tremulous shrews merge.
Crabs intertwine as if killing each other.
Mongoose mounted upon mongoose.
Two robins squeeze their red-breasts together for an instant
and a shudder runs through their ingravid bodies,
they separate, arrange their ruffled feathers
and fly off.
Male frogs with their love-croak call to the females
who arrive leaping or swimming.
Frogs now paired, go hopping, hopping,
one upon the other,
back pressed tightly against belly.
Sponges all release sperm and eggs

in the same phase of the moon so that the moon will unite them.
Multicolored chaffinches of pastel hue
(bluish, greenish, leaden, brownish, pinkish)
with their tails erect, cloaca against cloaca, copulate singing.
        Two lumbering rhinoceri shadows
                mounted one atop the other
        against a red, burning background of sunset.
In coitus the rhinoceri become tender,
only then.
The female crocodile picks up the rhythm
of his amorous dance in the water.
She draws closer. Nestles her scaly jaw
beneath his. Closes her eyes...
Green grasshoppers: Fabre never got to see their union
which takes place at night, but he witnessed long preludes,
the slow caresses of soft antennae.
And Fabre watched the female devour the male after lovemaking
—ferocious Marguerite de Bourgogne—.
Female and male buzzard, in a commotion of ruffled feathers,
trample over the carrion with love-cooings
amid the cracking of putrefied bones.
The gentle elephant's trunk furled in the other's trunk.
Turtles poke out their heads and withdraw them,
they perform their aquatic dance before copulation,
then for two weeks stuck together they drift at the mercy of the waves.
Mucous hermaphrodite sea snails
entwined in viscous embrace
exchange painful lances and delicious semen.
The male praying-mantis mounts the female
and for half an hour rocks back and forth on her
as she devours his head; his rocking later grows frenzied,
all inhibitions now lost
and his head lost.

"...a wedding banquet which a king prepared for his son".
The festive wedding of the spermatozoid with the ovule.
From among all the spermatozoid suitors

the ovule chose only one.

—My love, your belly smells of fresh-ploughed earth
and of earth recently wet.
—Of furrow recently wet by my beloved.

All matter is constructed with two particles:
protons and electrons;
positive protons and negative electrons,
male and female.
A birth is not by accident
but through a union.
And protons and electrons in the stellar gas
were sexed.
Whence the evolution of the universe.
An irresistible attraction
between positive and negative subatomic particle.
From this the atoms, the stars, us.
This is the cohesion of the universe.
Essential love
who art at the heart of the universe!
Attraction which has created all things.
And reason for the centrifugal rotation of the galaxies.
Antelopes dance in hidden depths of the forest
and whales intone their songs beneath the sea.
And the reason for every being:
a being is born only from two that make one.
The entire universe is a wedding.

—Our kisses among the butterflies
in a bed of ferns.
Your thighs redolent as the ham-zah flower.
Your body with colored beads
oozing coconut milk.
I sucked your breasts.
—My beloved
the scent of your semen like that of the milky kassamano flower.

Engendered by that law
which also governs kisses.
Fragment of stellar matter,
an atom of yours is like a solar system, and your body
like a system of galaxies with millions of suns.
Attraction. Attraction.
Electrons orbit within atoms,
satellites orbit their planets,
planets their stars
and the stars of a galaxy circle
a common center of gravity.
Gravity which moves the sun and the other stars.

CANTIGA 42

A Certain Something That They Still

Hidden and ambivalent.
Neither personal nor not personal.
Not personal and personal.
Yet could he be anything other than anthropomorphic?
Each one of the two
already both.
One already both, and
two each of them both.
It's not a vague black hole full of nothing.
Cosmic copulation.
How else other than anthropomorphic?
As in quantum mechanics experiments
the question of God:
That's to say depending on the question
(wave or particle?)
Is he infinite? He's infinite but not merely that.
And were we to prove his existence, were we to prove,
he'd be beyond that proof.
From the marriage of the large and the small, Eddington said;
and to me that reveals more than he intended.
In what other form then?
That he should come,
should come to me and take me,
that he should come.
I had something going with him and it's not a concept.
His face on my face
and each one not two
but a single face.
When I called out that time
you are God.

Gaze gazed upon.
Gaze gazing on gaze.
In Baghdad, or perhaps in Damascus
that: Oh you, who am I!
And also what al-Hallay exclaims:
If you see Him, you see us both.
But at the same time that other voice:
Between You and I there is an I am that torments me.
—That opening of the arms
and I embrace air—.

Beloved in the beloved great nothing transformed!
Until I sink, I merge, I am confused.
To be possessed and to possess you my GREAT NOTHING
beloved GREAT NOTHING.
Hurled with all my force towards you and I feel nothing.
I embrace nothing more than my two arms.
Like the dark region beyond which the universe peters out.

The animus can know everything except itself
(this is Meister Eckhart)
since it knows nothing except via the senses
and thus it does not know itself, it is without idea of itself,
it is ignorant of nothing more than of itself,
and thus it is free, innocent of itself
and thus it may be united to God who is also pure and without idea.
(Meister Eckhart of the Rhine mystical movement.)
Oh two nothings entirely denuded
the all with the nothing
a nothing transformed into its all
I tarried and forgot myself
leaving my past
among the quasars forgotten.

It is felt
and is not felt
is felt

but it is as though not felt
or in reality it is that it's not felt.
Something within me, not in my body but deeper within
is embraced, embraces and is embraced,
united having in some manner two in one, two one,
gentleness with gentleness, in a single gentleness,
pleasure of the other pleasure, the two pleasures one
without anything being felt sensually, let it be said:
it is as though I have embraced the night
black and void
and I am void of all
and want nothing
it is as though I had been penetrated by
the Nothing.

The sunny and shady slopes of the same mountain.
Yin/Yang identity of opposites.
For which reason the invention of sex.
In the antennae the presence, in perfume,
even at a kilometer away.
Love is the pain of being one alone
and not two (two in a union).
A hand in my hand which is not my hand...
...the mouth that is not your mouth.
I am scouring the universe for a lover.

I feel that he's kind of lonely in the universe.
God searching for love like me.
For whom I renounced that day
a girl or two.
Although they'll no longer be so, to me
they remain beautiful.
Just as they were that last time.
Renunciation of what is
the least spiritual of the soul, or
the most spiritual of the body.
For that instinct of being one united with the One

in whom all divided things are united.
I surrendered my little bag of illusions, my handful of dreams.

To Pseudo-Dionysios he is the universe and is not it.
All that is
and nothing of what is.
The same as that:
'I know and do not know him' (a Babylonian)
or that
'generation succeeds generation
and always hidden' from a hieroglyph.
By the sea, Numenius, saw that it was like looking out at the blue waters
and there away in the distance a tiny fishing boat,
a dot, nothing more,
you can't see it, but if you look right,
you catch a glimpse
for an instant...
Worse Erigena's observation, that:
"he may be called without impropriety Nothing"
The problem is that being in all things he is beyond all things.
I am scouring the universe for my lover.
In the perfumed Baghdad night.
For want of His face Ibn-L-Farid
contents himself with the full moon.
Or in the green-black forest that Amazulu:
"Unkulunkulu:
in reality we know nothing of him save his name."

The question of
whether he has existed for all time
"for all time" what does that mean?
Older than the oldest antiquity
he is neither old nor has an age according to Chuang Chou.
Like trying to imagine what the outside of the universe is like.
Is it true that somehow the universe began by chance?
But whether it be dice or cards or roulette
or two kids playing hopscotch on a corner

or plucking daisies, he loves me he loves me not:
Who on earth knows anything about chance?
And that nature has no need of God
is an attribute of God.

Strolling through the old back streets at dusk
before the bridge, in the shadow of the castle, Rilke understood
"only in him is there community."
And because we all come from he who is everywhere,
said Pursued-By-Bears,
there are men who understand the songs of birds,
the calls of animals.
But he is everywhere like our dead,
whose voices we cannot hear,
Pursued-By-Bears clarified.
A hidden force in things (the best that Meister Eckhart
managed to come up with) which wants them not just to be alike
but that they be joined together. Made one with the One.
The Universe that Juliana of Norwich saw,
bounded in a hazelnut, and felt
that it exists and will always exist through the one that loves it.
I open my opaque hotel window and gaze at the stars,
twenty floors up in the Caribbean Hilton.
I am alone in your universe.
Fish that scatter their semen in the sea:
those who are alone in your creation.
The aim of my Canticle is to console.
For me too that same consolation.
Maybe more.

If he loves you more than you yourself
your you is superficial and he is your deep you.
In the center of our being we are not us but Another.
If the iron in my blood is the same as that in rails,
my calcium that of cliffs,
where my God is this I of mine that loves you?
Part of your tenderness, I feel,

are these particles of mine.
Pleasure of knowing that you made me.
God of the absurd numbers
of the dementedly large and the dementedly small.
If he is infinite
he must also be infinite madness
infinite spontaneity.
That one day you and I might caress each other
as lovers do, with their eyes closed and gasping,
in an infinite place and on a date eternal
but as real as saying meet me tonight at eight.

Day once again in Solentiname
and it sings in the Silk Cotton-tree gazing at the sky
its song virtually unchanging
company company company
you and me you and me you and me
union union union
and sings also
compassion compassion compassion
the same song every day
the bird clamoring for its mate.

Looking out over the lake
where the Managua Intercontinental hotel now stands:
the lake raised above the roofs
and the boats seemingly drifting in mid-air
and above the lake the blue mountains
and above the mountains the blue sky.
Water and earth the color of sky.
And it was then I said:
But when will I see you face to face?

Patiently
like the hunter
and the fisherman
you waited for me

and I never gave you a thought.
You waited many years for me.
Years of my wild life and even before my life
and before the mountains.
    Once I was off my guard
and when the moment came
        like the hunter
        and the fisherman
                you were very quick.

We're so close to him that we don't see him.
It's not He or She; greater than God, says Eckhart
and Meister Eckhart begged not to understand him.
    That day I betrothed myself to my people.
I close my eyes
and you draw closer
in the night of nothing
how well I know your taste
and you mine,
lover and beloved, sighs
tremulous like those on the shore
silent caress
in the dark night of nothing.
    In order to be full empty yourself
                (this is from the TAO)
He's not up above, but there before you,
    present in all things
yet so absent from all things
that it is perfectly rational
to be an atheist.
I read the theologian Schillebeeckx
    "God coincides with nothing."
Well, so be it.
    And I have abandoned myself entirely to him.

WHEREIN IS DESCRIBED AN INSTANT OF THE DARK NIGHT:
In the darkness, half-asleep,

my naked body on this hot Managua night
brushes against the wall, smooth
and cool as a skin
and, awaking, in the darkness
the wall brings me back
to my endless solitude.

A solitude that will end only with death.
        Alone but with the people.

I've no complaints. Meister Eckhart used to say:
They prostrate themselves and genuflect not knowing to whom:
why genuflect when he is within you?
Hounded by the Inquisition, the Gestapo of his day.

We are like those two St. Nicholas doves
that when one runs away
                the other tags behind
and when this one takes flight
                the other follows on
but they never stray far from each other
        always travelling in pairs.
When you draw away from me
                I tag behind you
and when I'm the one that moves off
you follow on.
We are like those two St. Nicholas
                                doves.

In every dimension we see rotation, from the proton
to the galaxy. One wonders
with good reason, whether the entire cosmos isn't also
rotating.
            And then: around what or whom?
Something that maybe lies at the heart
of all the solutions to Einstein's equations.
And well might I say:

a planned creation.
Matter which is no accident.
The creation of a Materialist God.
Or is the universe mere chance?
And the deepest part of our being
mere chance?
Or Chance merely another name for him?
the infinite Chance?

Solitary cell lost in the primeval sea
without a cell with whom to fuse.
One who wanders alone through the cosmos,
but some day we'll be united You and I,
cosmic event as
when the first two cells united
in one the two.
Or are you an unnecessary hypothesis?
The cosmological coincidences.
Through whom the universe is not merely of red dwarf stars
or giant blue stars.
Birds of passage that carry in their DNA molecules
a detailed map of the stars.
The tremendous imaginative capacity of orchids.
I see your smile in the rainbow
or the iris of a girl's eye
or the iridescent scales of a *machaca*
—machaca or sabalete in Solentiname—.
Since the creation of my lakes and volcanoes you desired me
and even before.
Water cries out to the thirsty man who drinks it.
Each thing tremulously reflects a blurred perfection.
I'd say: he exists in all beings
not as essence but as cause of their existence
if these sounds make any sense. Better
to say simply:
the hard rain falls upon the asphalt
and the drops leap like filigree.

You see through him and do not see him
as though he doesn't exist.
Or does he merely intervene
in the uncertainty laws of quantum mechanics?
Beyond all light years, unreachable
and closer to me than my moan:
Our love is sad.
Oh, a union greater than electromagnetic interaction!
Oh, a union greater than that of proton with neutron!
Perhaps better avoid the word God.
"False things are acceptable to God"
(bilingual text in the Asurbanipal Library).

Upon which the ancient poets are united
says Aristotle.
And: Sing to him through action, Cleanthes sang.
Since: His Word harmonizes the discords,
draws order out of chaos
Cleanthes sang.
It appears that all things are born from the One
and in Him they are dissolved,
sang Museus (or in the songs attributed to him).
The world was "vision of the invisible" for Anaxagoras,
and although no thing is entirely separate from the other things
the Spirit is the only thing different from any other thing
and is always the same in the large and the small
although no thing is the same as any other thing
and each thing is individual. Anaxagoras who to Aristotle
was like a sober man among drunkards.
The gathering of all things, separated by discord,
was how the Orphics saw it.
They called him *One*, says Proclus [the Pythagoreans]
and Pherecydes says that Proclus says that Zeus became Eros
in order to make the world with opposites.
Infusing in all things their individuality
and at the same time a unity that penetrates the all.
Standing with a smile on the carriage of the Essence

says Numenius.
            And for Empedocles:
                without downy genitals
                and only swift thought.
Aphrodite was the principle of union for all beings,
for every pairing up in the universe. He, Empedocles, saw
Eros as a quicksilver passing through all things.
To Empedocles Eros was
cause of all union of cosmic forces.
Love is what unites the cosmos and hate divides it.
    Eros the cornerstone of philosophy to Plato.
Within the material world like honey in the comb for Zeno,
the I in You and You in me in the liturgy of Hermes,
he is all you see and all you cannot see according to Seneca,
driving the chariot of the soul said Philo of Alexandria.
Aristides who knew the ecstasies...crying with pleasure...
    ("who is initiated knows and understands it").
The animals with their idea of him, according to Xenocrates.
"A portion of Zeus in each of us" (Marcus Aurelius).
Anaximander's Unlimited embracing the all.
    He'd never write on that theme,
Plato wrote.
Light of light, said Plotinus, whatever it was
he meant to say.
It was thought that in Tierra del Fuego they had no God
but the Yamanes said (before their extinction)
that they'd never spoken of Watauinewa
because they hadn't been asked.
They told Gusinde.
                        The ethnological proof of God.
    "I long to see Watauinewa face to face
    but where to meet him?"
                        (Gusinde's expedition).
For whom the Bushmen's nocturnal dances,
the Hottentots' prayer asking for honey and roots,
Pygmy liturgy, that Schebesta describes, under the stars
by the light of wax torches offering up sweet potato to God.

Who also through the rainbow reveals to the Pygmies
his great desire to bond with them.
    "The Atman is silent."
We are born of the invisible like the fig tree
from the fig tree invisible in the seed.
It's like a piece of rope on the road at night that looks like a snake.
By day the rope can be seen and the snake vanishes.
"Not to be able to contemplate his beauty, I the painter Neb-Râ."
    From whom the Nile comes to us.
    Through whom the gods exist.
    And the pleasures of the light.
Unkulunkulu, Unkulunkulu
of the Amazulu, about whom the Amazulu say: no one, not even the chiefs
can speak about him in a true way.
"What we were and what Unkulunkulu created
we do not know in this life we lead
since he ceased to exist. The way of Unkulunkulu,
so to speak, was not given to us on our pilgrimages.
He is beyond we know not what.
In reality we know nothing but his name."
The intrinsic principle of created things
that Chuang-tse discovered in the silent universe,
dark and formless, he seems not to exist
and he exists. The *yin* and the *yang* follow upon each other
and the four seasons... But he remains.
He encompasses the greatest immensities of space
but even the smallest bird shit in autumn
awaits his power to give it form.
    Like the tender tiger cub in its mother's jaws;
    like the waters of the Ganges to the sea...
The Kaffir said to Monsieur Arbousset:
"Your teachings I awaited.
Twelve years ago I was on the move with my flocks. There was mist.
I sat down on a rock and I asked myself sad questions.
Sad because I could not answer them.
Who made the stars?
The waters flow day and night. Who makes them flow?

I cannot see the wind. But what is the wind?
Sitting on that rock I hid my face in my hands."
Mystical Red-Skins in the XVIII century, or simply Red-Skins
heard the cocks
and saw the smoke in the huts of heaven.
    "So much evidence of the invisible things"
    (...things told by my grandfather Confucius).

CANTIGA 43

Omega

The "Sole Innumerable" of Polynesia.
Hunab Ku, 8,000 times God (and to them simultaneously,
the Maya) "He of a single Age".
Nyongmo (Gold Coast) with the stars
ornaments hanging from his face.
Mawu, of the Ewhe: the blue is his veil
and the light the oil with which he glosses his skin.
Bayame of the Waradjuri-Kamolaroi-Euahlayi, cannot be seen,
        on a transparent throne of rock crystal,
            only heard and felt.
Ta'aroa of the South Seas,
        from eternity to eternity changing shell,
            permanently young.
Meim num'-vater (Daddy of the Skies) of the Samoyed,
        the rainbow the trimming of his mantle.
The Urün Ajytojon of the Yakut, 6 heavens above.
Makonaima, "He who works by night" (in Venezuela).
            "The Great Wanderer" of the Sinkyone.
Bhgwan, of the Nhil, in the beginning utterly alone,
to whom they pray: "Do not keep us far from cereals!"
Bahkkoore-Mahishtsedah ("He who created")
                    was composed of the vapors
that existed before the world was made by him.
        Murungu of the Kikuyu of Kenya
                invisible presence everywhere.
The "most luminous *Khan*" of the Beltires
        and the Vogul's "good golden light of on high."
Juok to whom the Anuak pray: "I have no other."
Kiho of the Polynesians:
                First cause of the constant unfolding.

First cause of the changing growth.
Constant hand that there is in the trees.
That dwells for ever in the mysterious abysses of the Night.
Leza of the Ba-ila in Zimbabwe
That one-from-whom-all-things-come
(not so good now as before the whites).
Mu-lungu of the Bantu, word which has no plural,
the one who sets the taboos so that men will be in control of themselves.
"Ancient Secret" in the Popol Vuh.
"The Great Chief of the Mysteries" of the Salishan.
"The Chief of the Air" of the Trimshi.
Ngewo reveals himself in the lightning and the waterfall
and in certain men. They call him in Siberia
"Universe," also "Existence."
To the Tlingit: "In the origin of all things,
in the world of deep darkness".
Atnatu of the Kaitish (Australia): "prior to death."
To the Tunusians he gives the good and the bad,
they don't know on what criteria.
"The Great Darkness" invoked by the Iroquois in their songs.
Io-te-pukenga of the Maoris: from whom memories come.
Too big say the Tumbukasi to think of us.
In Melanesia a diffuse force in all things
totally different from any material force.
"The Lone One" of the Ashanti
to whom all men have access.
No path of man crosses with that of another.
A little piece of him there is in the body of each person.
African names of:
"The Lighter of Fire," "The Unexplainable,"
"The Contemporaneous Pool of All Things"
"He who Was Found."
The rainbow is his hunting bow, to the Pygmies.
With which he hunts storms.
The moon a sandal he left behind (Bushmen).
The Pawnees' *Tirawa* to whom they sing in Arkansas
"Listen, up above, in the blue silence!"

("But we don't conceive of *Tirawa* as a person.
We imagine him in all things.
Nobody knows what appearance he has.")
The Koryak call him the One on high.
The one that exists.
He dwells in the village in the sky.
A'wonawil'ina (He-She) with nobody in the universal void.
Who produced Sky-Father and Earth-Mother
and from that union all creatures come.
When the air takes the shape of a bird
He-She is part of that bird.
"The Something which moves" of the Santee Indians
and *Pon* ("Something") of the Yukaguiros.
And the Alaska thing, to that ethnologist:
"Something above watches over us all the time."
Jumê of the Cheremisses, which means "Heaven"
and *Nhandeyara* in a branch of Guaraní (Apapocuva-Guaraní),
beneath his hammock the blue tiger of the sky.
Wakan-tanka of the Oglala: only the blue sky can be seen of him
but he is everywhere.
The Macu call him *Uake* ("Superior to God").
Among the Yukis: "he who goes alone."
Daramulun
this name is known only by the initiated
and they listen to him by night seized with terror amid the jungle noises.
"*Dzimbé*, who rains, refreshes the drought!"
"He is still alive" the Wiyot-Wishok said
"and will exist for as long as the world lasts,"
Californian tribe now extinct.
And the Maoris again:
"That one-in-whose-presence-all-things-are-united."
Death is something which does not come from *Io*.
The Bantu: "*Nzambi* has abandoned us. Why
bother ourselves about him?"
For other tribes: *Anyambie* ("Idle God").
For others he went away to work in other places.
And the Diola in swamps, their swamps of the Pagny: "God is dead."

And Olson to the Motilones:—Why without figures of him?
—We haven't seen him, how can we make figures of him?
(But this Olson says that since they do not know him and do not see him
they believe him to be everywhere.)

We the smallest ones, pray the Pygmies.
The Lele are very grateful to him for giving them the forest.
To the Nicaraguas, dark-skinned: "the same color as us Indians."
Kari of the Semang, close even to the most distant things.

Veiled in the darkness according to the text of the *Che king*.
Imana knows everything to the Batwa of Rwanda.
Puluga of the Adamaneses is always in midday.

The stars, his eyes, to the Alacaluf.
Mareigua sometimes descends to la Guajira. Then there are downpours,
and greenery springs forth from the sandy ground.
Unkulunkulu? "Of *Unkulunkulu* (the old-old man)
we no longer know anything.
He was the first being; he burst forth in the beginning.
The old people say that *Unkulunkulu* is [exists].
He made the first men, the ancients of long ago."
In Tierra del Fuego where Darwin found no religion:
one like the wind, that cannot be contained,
without body, nor wife nor children, and there are no images of him.
"The white people think these songs are lies"
(the Yamana woman).
To the Maidu, Sacramento, Calif., U.S.A.
(on their reservation) *Wonomi* ("Immortal"?) says to them:
"Within your hearts you must know us.
It is pointless for you to see us and touch us.
The light of the camp-fires is not needed because there is the interior light."
Frequent in California the reference to interior light, says the author.
As also the Great Spirit strolls by the light of the moon
on an island of his in Lake Superior.
They translate "the Great Spirit" but it is "the Great Mystery."
Ta'aroa, already mentioned above, the ancestor of the gods,
before creating the universe
was squeezed in his conch in the dark depths,

his conch tumbling in the limitless space.

In ancient China they spoke to him with bonfires in the mountains.
Zulu prayers are of one word: "Cow!"
"Rain!"
or "Children!"
In Bonny, God, sky and cloud, are the same word.
For the Swazi his name is Great Premier.
(Shepherd of the cloud-sheep...)
(He knows the trail that a bird leaves in the air...)
Khopry is reborn from himself.
To Hartland, impossible, that men without clothes,
incapable of counting to seven, impossible!
with sublime philosophical concepts.
What makes us see a stone is the reflection of divinity in it,
it is its *aria*, say the Maori.
The Dakota say: we never see the real sky,
but merely an aspect of it, the blue sky.
Nor the real earth either, nor the real rocks,
merely its image of God.
The manner in which the Winnebago boy dreamed of *Maona*.
He fasted and fasted in order to dream of *Maona*.
And he dreamed of all things but not of *Maona*.
A stone revealed to him that that was to dream of *Maona*.
And he ceased to want to dream of *Maona*.
The Sky is a person to the Zulu.
Ever since creation they have not seen him again
say the Bantu.
Cradle of all children to the Ainu.
Man-not-known-on-the-earth created all the things
but the water and the earth were not separated,
there was deep darkness all around
(as from a chaos of notes about the God of the primitives,
jottings, tiny slips of paper
this canto can emerge)
and he created the first couple
and that couple dreamed that all the things were being created
and when they awoke there were all the things that they had dreamed of.
The Wiyot of California mentioned above

have said: He does not work with his hands.
What he thinks exists.
Sila of the Eskimos which also means "Universe".
Nobody has seen him, say the Eskimos,
because he is close to you but infinitely far away.
To them it is impossible to explain him with ordinary words.
He is not heard by men in ordinary words,
but through storms, snowfalls, the flux of the tides.
And another manner of revealing himself: the days of sun, the calm sea,
small children playing who understand nothing.
The children hear his mysterious soft voice, almost like a woman's.
The word he says to them:
Sila ersinarsinivdlugo
("Do not be afraid of the universe").
Kiethan, in Massachusetts,
against whom Hobomock (the devil) himself can do nothing.
For the Maidu of California he shines like the light of the sun
but no one has seen him, except the Evil One,
who once set eyes on him.
The *Yuok* of the Chilluk of the Upper Nile, according to Lienhardt
is not the supreme being above all beings
but a supremely contingent being.
Is he body or spirit? They answer: he is "spiritual like the wind."
Also: that on one side he is spirit and on the other side he is spirit,
and in front and behind he is body.
And Dr. Heasty: "He appears to be one and nevertheless plurality."
(He is the presence in everything, the material and the spiritual
without being spirit nor matter.)
"He remains there always
although the sun falls in the evening"
(Gold Coast).
There is no atheistic people on the earth, according to the evidence of
Artemidorus of Rhodes.
"Have you not gone off to hunt and have you not heard his voice
when the antelopes run because he calls them?"
(To Mr. Orpen, the Bushmen).
Immutable center of the shifting infinite.

You saw me bring a pumpkin, said the Ewhe,
and you are watching me make from it a vessel to drink from.
The seed within is very tiny.
I place it in the earth and it becomes a vessel to drink from.
This thing I cannot do. Nobody knows him.
    Tamakuel, before all the ancestors,
he made the first firmament and the first earth,
        but he has never come to the earth.
    He is far behind the stars.
            From that time he exists.
Whom the gods adore (*Amón-Râ*). Child of love.
Akongo of the Ngombe in the Congo.
All peoples give him a different name say the Ngombe.
To them: "Beginning," "Without End," "Unexplainable."
    You can deal with him very easily.
He has never been man—although he has the features of a man.
    "All names are yours"
                (St. Gregory of Nazianzus).
"Our Father" is the *Mungan ngaua* of the Kurnai.
Imana created the world from nothing, because there was nothing,
but he does not interfere.
    The banana gives fruit.
(The scholastic distinction of first and second cause
says Maquet.)
He has emotions. He has very long arms. He is not material.
Imana gives, he does not sell.
            He is so good he requires no worship.
Above the palisade of this world is the sky,
where the stars fly like fireflies.
    And above, the other palisade.
            "He is beyond the beyond" (Hindi).
Bodiless to the Baria. He dwells
in those deep African jungles.
He has not grown angry with man. He is good
but he sleeps.
The Batak see his dew drop on a plant
    (for food of man).

I don't know according to what mystery the Quiche called him Beautiful
Gourd.
(Also Clear and Hidden, and Hurricane of the Sky.)
Tao, in existence before the void and the silence,
before the primeval nothing,
who set the motionless universe in rotation at the beginning
and started the chain of the emergence of beings from non-being
and the return to non-being.
No one has seen him,
said a Yuki to the German Ivar Lissner.
But I believe someone must have seen him,
because if not we would have no knowledge of him.
Wan-Aisa ("Our Father") of the Miskitos.
Ma-Papak ("Our Father") of the Sumu.
"Father" is the most primitive form of addressing him according to
Schmidt,
the formidable German with 20 volumes on the subject;
the oldest tribe of the oldest tribes of Australia
knows no other name for him.
His name in Tierra del Fuego is never uttered,
they use other terms.
In Africa the Banen call him "Death."
The God of the Samoyedos, called *A*.
In Australia his name revealed to the neophytes in secret,
which we do not know.
"Zeus", whoever he may be if that name pleases him said Aeschylus.
And the Apollo of the Oracle of Claros said:
"Zeus, Hades, Helios, Dionysius, are the same."
In hermetics he is: *anonymous* and *polynomous*,
nameless and having many names.
Just as for the Purana of India there are 330 million gods,
but above them there is a single God.
And a people from North Africa calls him *Yus*
word for which there's no known etymology or meaning.

"Being existent before all and different from all
without limit where he ends and without part or form

and the being that he is is act by himself
of himself giving existence to himself and through himself,
neither quality nor quantity, neither moving nor motionless,
neither in place nor in time but uniform in himself
and before truly formless, prior to all form,
and prior to movement and to repose, without being essence
only being able to say that he is transcendence to being
which is not to say what he is but merely what he is not,
without being able to assign any name to him other than the name of One
and without being even able to say of him that he *is*,
nor that he is good, but simply the Good without the *is*,
being able to say what he is not but not what he is,
and not possessing in himself either the not good nor the good
he possesses nothing and finds himself alone and separated from all,
splendor that makes a statue beautiful
and a living person more beautiful than a beautiful statue,
and where is the creator of so much beauty?
he can be none of the beautiful things
since he has no form rather from him all forms are born,
and his beauty is a beauty transcendent to beauty
but from him all beauty is born and all things aspire to him
divining almost that they cannot exist without him,
being he the Good that is present in everyone
and also those who are sleeping are in him,
and it is not him who desires us to be around us
but we desire him to be around him
and the harmony of the dance around him is of a divine dance
and the soul loves him in harmony with nature
wanting to unite with him with the beautiful love of a beautiful virgin
and that joy we can conjecture from earthly loves
seeing how much joy it is to possess what one loves,
but the beloved objects in this world are mortal
and the loves are simulacrums of loves like in the theater
since the beloved is not our good nor the one we are searching for,
he is not decked in a separating flesh, the true beloved,
and the soul has then another life and has no need of another,
stripped of all other things so as to be alone in him and to be him alone

in a flight of the entire spirit towards Him alone
there on high where color is beauty in flower
or rather all is color and deep beauty,
there one and what one sees are no longer one exterior to the other,
rather that he who sees penetrates in himself the one he sees,
and the soul seeing the beauties of this world suspects
that none of those beauties are the one he is searching for,
and when he sees them in a continual flow he knows full well
that what shines forth in them comes from somewhere else,
but where is the creator of so much beauty?
He must be above all forms,
infinite beginning, without form, from which all forms proceed
and thus one has to reject the vision of things
and look merely towards that one through whom one sees
like when one sees a thing without wanting to see other things
and lowers the curtain of the eyelids producing thus the light
or like when one screws up one's eyes and sees the light there is within him,
not seeing sees in the darkness and sees more than ever since one sees the light,
the other things were luminous but were not the light,
and in order to have him one does not have to have anything but solely him alone
(this initiation is in some manner known to the initiates)
and thus he appears in oneself and no longer are there two but two One alone
being an imitation of this lovers and their beloved
who prefer intoxication to drinking the drink with moderation
and it is difficult to describe the vision in which they are not two
but he who sees is transformed into one with the seen,
not occupied with beautiful things but beyond the beautiful
like someone who has entered the inner-most place in the temple
after the statues: upon leaving he will again see the statues."

The light that travels at 300,000 kilometers per second
takes 8 minutes from the sun to here.
A being that travels at twice the speed
would take half the time.

A being moving at infinite speed would be everywhere at once
and therefore in the interior of everything
        and therefore would know everything
                and knowing everything would be all-powerful.
Since time is merely
our inability to see everything at the same time
this being would be without spacetime,
                infinitely present.
And since what we see as present
and as future cannot yet see
nor as past, everything is present,
he would be in an eternal present.
Also an infinitely mobile being
would be motionless.
And a motionless being in the interior of everything,
would have to be the motor of everything,
in other words the creator of everything, and therefore
        infinite love.
And then you ought to be able with this love
                        to make love.

The Catio had a ladder.
It was also closer then.
They could hear the songs from here.
In the Orinoco, dances and eternal intoxication.
For the Guajiro, in their sandy and arid land:
crossed by wide blue rivers
                (something unseen in La Guajira).
In Patagonia: a larger and more beautiful region than the Pampa.
In Greenland a warm sky beneath the earth,
a sheltered and blissful place (hell is above in the sky,
a cold and desert place where great winds blow).
In the Amazon, an immense River of Life, called *Meshiarene*,
which flowed over the earth but later withdrew from mankind,
it is in the sky and can only be seen on starry nights
        (it's the Milky Way).
Men were rejuvenated in this Amazon of Life.

The Yagua's heaven is not in the sky but much higher up.
A most beautiful forest, without villages because they are not needed.
For the Macu there are two extra-terrestrial worlds:
    one is above, where there are only good people;
    another beneath the earth where there are also good people.
    Only here on earth are there good and bad people.
The Mataco of the Gran Chaco tell of the times
when the heavens and the earth were united by a tree
and the Indians could ascend the tree to hunt in the heavens.
The Yekuana build their round huts in the style of the sky
    (place where eternally and untouched maracas play).
The Yaruro asked the anthropologist for a photo of heaven.
They wanted to become extinct quickly in order to reach heaven.
The Iroquois "Soul country," where bad people never enter.
    "The tents on the other side" of the Crows.
The Village of the West, of perpetual dance, of the Ottawa.
They have reached there in their canoes through the lakes, the Algonquins.
To the Tarascans its gate was Lake Pátzcuaro.
An Agrarian Reform like that of the Incas, for the Chibcha.
The roof of the hut of the world for the Talamancans of Costa Rica,
in the middle of the hut there is a tree which is the center of the world
and it is in Chiriquí (Panama).
"Invisible forest" of the Paraguayan Guayaki
where the strange trees are, the eternal trees.
To the Arapaho, now almost completely vanished,
all the vanished buffalo graze there in prairies.
The Cuna will have very busy streets there, they say,
buildings with many stories but of gold.
There is a lift to get up to that city of golden skyscrapers.
There God has a telephone and he sits in a revolving chair.
The whites sell bananas in the streets,
as now the Cuna do in Panama.
        There are few whites in heaven.

And it's that we are on this earth, said Seneca,
just as the maternal womb keeps us for ten months.
The gravitational collapse of the universe.

And so what?
The One scattering himself created all things
which will once again be the One.
The One, the Ly, of Confucius
silent and secret, in hidden action.
    That one from whom all evolution stems
    and in whom all evolution ends.
"We'll come out of this all right God willing"
    (THE LIVING THOUGHTS OF SANDINO, Ed. 1961. p.139)

I gaze at the polished-glass waves from the prow of the *Solentiname*
observing that there are never two waves the same.
Created by someone who has made no two of us the same
but so that we are all made one.
    All one.
The different islands of the Galapagos
made the animals of those islands different
Darwin discovered in the Galapagos.
Plutarch attributes to Anaximander the theory that we come from fish.
And Empedocles said: "I have been a bird
and a silent fish in the sea."

        ALFA is OMEGA.
In Egypt it was written:
All that is came after him.
    Atum, who created himself and became himself.
Tao, of whom it is said that he comes to meet us
as the origin of everything that is.
All things tend ardently towards a common center .
        Omega point!
"That supreme will has brought us together here
to obtain the freedom of Nicaragua."
    "God will speak through the Indian of the Segovias."
"We will win, with God's help"
        (to the North American journalist Carleton Beals).
"God will crown our efforts."
"Do not be afraid, my dear brothers:

very soon we'll have our once-and-for-all triumph in Nicaragua."
"...against the imperialisms of the earth".
Not only here:
Cuzco means "navel."
In Bali the volcano Gunung Agung (the highest)
is the navel of the world. Babylon was the navel of the world
and its temple the center of the cosmos.
Egypt considered itself the navel of the world.
And China, the Middle Empire, center of the world.
Delphi was the center of the earth, and it had in its temple an *omphalos*,
an umbilical stone.
Similarly the temple of Quezaltepeque in Guatemala.
Easter Island was called *Te Pito Te Henua*
"The Navel of the World." Jerusalem
also was an *omphalos*.
But the Samaritan woman asked Jesus if it was Jerusalem or Samaria
and he said it would be the whole earth.
The entire planet the navel which unites us with the heavens.

Love is the synthesis of the universe
(like the chemical synthesis of substances in a compound body).
It recapitulates the universe, gathers it together in a single point.
But synthesis which has to transcend the universe
or entropy will triumph.
Romeo's voice ringing out in the night:
"Hang up philosophy! Unless philosophy can make a Juliet?"
And since the galaxies will fall upon themselves.
Once again the Second Law of Thermodynamics:
Heat does not travel from the cold body to the warm.
Carlos Martínez tells me that M.Z. died of a heart attack.
And I think of the Second Law of Thermodynamics.
"...after which it collapses upon itself and returns to nothing."
But the incompatibility that there is between total death
and the intention that lies behind evolution.
Death, victory, said Martí. (Identical to Darío's
"victory of human progeny.")
Also the same Martí:

"Death is the hardest to understand."
Alfonso talking to me about Chocano in the asylum
as though he were alive in Lima. I said to him. "He's dead."
And he: "Well who knows... I think he's not dead."
Another time I told him his friend Fr. Pallais had just died.
"I don't believe it. I think it's a political conspiracy
or something like that."

Alfa and Omega.
The prophecy of the Gâthâs
that someone would come to "re-cloth the bodies."
On whose account in Western Africa the skulls
are painted red.
Killing a god dates from the most remote times according to Frazer.
Those Redskins
seeing the whole world full of blood,
as though painted with blood, they say,
and that's why there are red rocks,
and that's why the world is beautiful.
The hieroglyphics on the tombs of Tell-el Amarna:
addressed to him.
in the XVI century Ricci encountered
most ancient Jewish communities in China
waiting for the *Moscia* (some time within 10,000 years).
And Confucius said:
You do not leave except by the door.
You do not walk except along the path.
He came to unite all our totems and all our clans.
To set us free from all the taboos.
The saviour of the tribe.
A Mediating Saviour in the Upper Nile,
who is not dead according to them in the Upper Nile.
Mictlan Tecuhli Nahuatl, the Lord of the Mansion of the Dead.
The sun. The one that feeds us
and by night lights up our dead.
The primitives in their myths, according to Frobenius,
never mention the technical process of that discovery

(fire) but that it is always from a god, an outsider.
Fire was *stolen* also in Polynesia
(Island of Mangala). Thanks to a hero, people have light
    and can cook their food.
A humanity in deep darkness, the Zuni recall,
crowded together, climbing one on top of the other like reptiles,
until the great wise man brought them out of there
to the surface of the earth, to the Sun-Father.
That *agraphon* of Christ's:
    "Raise up the stone and there you will find me."
(He's been around since the Palaeolithic.)
The stone that God worked (Chilam Balam de Chumayel)
there where formerly there was no sky.
In the Strait of Torres
Mutuk was inside a shark.
Yetl (sun god) inside a whale.
Jonah, deeply rooted in the mind of primitive peoples
says Frobenius.
Once again Frobenius. Dear Pound.
The hero defeats the monster in the Pygmy myth
delivering from it the men that it had devoured.
"Difficult to know what he will be like" Confucius said,
"the saint awaited for a hundred generations."
A generation (*chi*) is 30 years;
that is, awaited for 3,000 years.
Also: That the two first dynasties have not
been able to satisfy the heavens.
"You have said it. I am king." He said in the praetorium.
Which you have to interpret in the orthodox manner:
I am the People. And the People are king.
    I am the proletariat.
        And the proletariat is king of history.
"Many times you have heard me speak of a Final Judgment of the world."
(Sandino to his troops.) "By Final Judgment of the world you should
understand
the destruction of injustice on earth
and the reign of the Spirit of Light and Truth, that's to say Love."

Jesus also specifies:
the Judgment will be undertaken by someone who was hungry, was
imprisoned...
According to the ancient Persians
we owe the order of the cosmos to the just.
And it says in the Gospel of Thomas
that the kingdom of heaven is spread across the earth
but mankind does not see it.

Jesus free of Oedipus complex called him *Abba* ("Daddy").
For more than a million years we have seen him
(confusedly) in thunder, the woods, animals,
the sea, the wind, fire, rain, the stars.
Ptolemy used to say that gazing at the stars he was touching him.
Epicurus was pious.
His doctrine was not to fear the gods.
He said they were comrades of ours.
The Redskins affirm that his power is beautiful
and that he delights in this.
"You who also made the animals that
eat rotting and decaying things:
buzzards, flies, cockroaches
and with them feed their young
and their young suffer no diarrhea..."
"Watauinewa!" (the barefoot woman kicking the sharp-edged ice).
"That you might have made us a present of a whale."
The Pygmy woman who wants to eat snake meat prays:
"Mugu, allow me to kill a snake!"
His passage through the forest is announced by strange nocturnal sounds
but above all is manifested to them in dreams.
And the tribe for whom praying is crazy.
And an insult to Bayame who knows everything.
"Each atom is his throne" said that Sufi,
although now thrones and atoms are different.
To Empedocles he was a sphere, in all parts equal to itself.
Just as Origen theorized that resurrected bodies were spheres
(why? because they'd have no entrails nor rectum

since God creates nothing in vain).
Not so ludicrous, since
the curvature of the universe
which folds in upon itself
is reflected in the earth's curvature
which spins upon itself
and in the consciousness of the earth
which reflects upon itself.
The Sioux say that he placed them on the great island (U.S.A.)
with knowledge so that they would be acquainted with all things.
Two curvatures, says Chardin,
the roundness of the earth and the convergence of minds
on this earth. Within the great curvature, the universe.
The Canticle never ends.
        That's to say, the poem's theme is endless.
A planet of persons first,
and after of super-personalization.
                Now the tendency of the species
                is the convergence of all its tendencies.
        All to the same convergence.
The dream of all mystics, says Chardin.
Chardin once again. Dear Fr. Ángel
(because of cancer of the pancreas now all light).
                "Sonorous light"
                        said Alfonso.
And elsewhere:
That God dreamed Aphrodite in words.
If the poem has little congruence
its theme the cosmos is less congruent.
The convergent force of the universe towards its center
is love.
        The idea that each part tends towards the Whole
    this is a *cliché* in my poem
    but it comes from Plato.
It must have been like an ecstasy, in his madness, when Alfonso said:
"Here everything, even time, becomes space."
This may be hermetic, but not hermetic à la Octavio Paz.

Center of convergence of the universe,
do not exclude me from your kisses and your embraces!
Mystery of being more the other while more the same.
Center of centers, irradiating from the center of a system of centers
like a single point. Omega point.
Where nothing more will fit together.
In our most intimate being, closer to everyone.
There is our end,
because where we are going is where we came from,
the beginning.
Having had a common origin, says Wells we will be united
in a common destiny in a tiny planet among the stars.
Thy kingdom come.
May the revolution come to the entire earth.
Until revolution and earth become extra-terrestrials.
A perfect humanity nothing less—which is no small thing–
or which transcends even that?
A society of planetary units?
Simone Weil's conclusion was that everything that is less than the universe
is subject to suffering.
The clay eggs found in Russia and Sweden
were metaphors for immortality.
Or the dead buried close to the waters in the Megalithic.
Zulus associate the snake with resurrection
because it changes its skin.
The whole is entire in each of its parts
as the mystics have seen
and not just the elite of mystics.
The whole sings in each one and each one in the whole.
Union which will be the fruit of the tree of life.
Collectivity of consciousness or collective consciousness
or super-consciousness.
An extra-planetary destiny.
Spiritual atoms?
Hominization even of death itself
in the words of the mystical palaeontologist.
Now all confused with the All, and persons with the Person

in an All that is Person
and Person that is Love.
Matter was merely the tenuous veil over your face.

Transcendence of the visible universe.
A change as when life began on earth:
a completely ethereal humanity
(and the entire universe has been change since the beginning)
mere atoms in space communicating with each other through radiation,
and becoming finally, perhaps, completely light,
which could just as well be either the end or the beginning...
This is Desmond Bernal in 1929.

And what do we see when we gaze at the night sky?
In the night we see simply the expansion of the universe.
Galaxies and galaxies and beyond galaxies and beyond quasars.
And further back in space we'd see neither galaxies nor quasars
rather a universe in which nothing would have yet condensed,
a dark wall, before the instant the universe
became transparent. And earlier
what would we finally see?
When there was nothing.
In the beginning...

Other Books by Ernesto Cardenal

Ansias lengua de la poesía nueva nicaragüense. (Nicaragua), 1948.
Hora O. Revista Méxicano de Literatura, 1960.
Epigramas: Poemas. Universidad Nacional Autónoma de México, 1961.
Antología de la poesía norteamericana. Translator and editor at large with Jorge Montoya Toro. Aguilar (Madrid), 1963, Alianza (Madrid), 1979.
Literatura indígena américana: Antología. Translator and editor at large with Jorge Montoya Toro. Editorial Universidad de Antioquía (Medellín), 1964.
Gethsemani, Ky. Ecuador 0°0'0', 1960. 2nd edition, with foreword by Thomas Merton, Ediciones La Tertulia (Medellín, Colombia), 1965.
Oración por Marilyn Monroe, y otros poemas. Ediciones La Tertulia, 1965. Reprinted, Editorial Nueva Nicaragua Ediciones Monimbó, 1985.
El estrecho dudoso. Ediciones Cultura Hispánica (Madrid), 1966. Editorial Nueva Nicaragua-Ediciones Monimbó, 1985.
Poemas de Ernesto Cardenal. Casa de las Américas (Havana), 1967.
Antología de Ernesto Cardenal. Editora Santiago (Santiago, Chile), 1967.
Mayapan. Editorial Alemania (Managua, Nicaragua), 1968.
Salmos. Institución Gran Duque de Alba (Avila, Spain), 1967. Ediciones El Pez y la Serpiente (Managua, Nicaragua), 1975.
Homenaje a los indios americanos. Universidad Nacional Autónoma de Nicaragua, 1969. Laia (Madrid), 1983.
La Vida en el amor (meditation, with foreword by Thomas Merton). Lohlé (Buenos Aires), 1970.
The Psalms of Struggle and Liberation. Translation by Emile G. McAnany. Herder & Herder, 1971.
Hora cero y otros poemas. Ediciones Saturno, 1971.
Antología: Ernesto Cardenal. Edited by Pablo Antonio Cuadra. Lohlé, 1971. 2nd edition, Universidad Centroamericana, 1975.
Poemas. Editorial Leibres de Sinera, 1971.

Poemas reunidos 1949-1969. Dirección de Cultura, Universidad de Carabobo, 1972.

Epigramas. (with translations from Catullus and Martial). Lohlé (Buenos Aires), 1972.

En Cuba. Lohlé (Buenos Aires), 1972.

To Live is to Love. Translation by Kurt Reinhardt. Herder & Herder, 1972.

Canto nacional. Siglo Veintiuno (México), 1973.

Oráculo sobre Managua. Lohlé (Buenos Aires), 1973.

Poesía nicaragüense. Compiler and author of introduction. Casa de las Américas, 1973. 4th edition, Editorial Nueva Nicaragua, 1981.

In Cuba. Translation by Donald D. Walsh. New Directions, 1974.

Homage to the American Indians. Translation by Carlos Altschul and Monique Altschul. Johns Hopkins University Press, 1974.

Love. Search Press, 1974.

Cardenal en Valencia. Ediciones de la Dirección de Cultura, Universidad de Carabobo (Venezuela), 1974.

Marilyn Monroe and Other Poems. Translation by Robert Pring-Mill. Search Press, 1975.

El Evangelio en Solentiname. Ediciones Sigueme, 1975. Editorial Nueva Nicaragua-Ediciones Monimbó, 1983. Reprinted in four volumes, Orbis Books, 1982.

Poesía escogida. Barral Editores, 1975.

The Gospel in Solentiname. Translation by Donald D. Walsh. Orbis Books, 1976.

La santidad de la revolución. Ediciones Sigueme, 1976.

Poesía cubana de la revolución. Extemporáneos, 1976.

Apocalypse and Other Poems. Translation by Thomas Merton, Kenneth Rexroth, Mireya Jaimes-Freyre, and others. New Directions, 1977.

Love in Practice: The Gospel in Solentiname. Search Press, 1977.

Antología. Laia (Barcelona), 1978.

Epigramas. Tusquets (Barcelona), 1978.

Catulo-Marcial en versión de Ernesto Cardenal. Laia, 1978.

Canto a un país que nace. Universidad Autónoma de Puebla, 1978.

Antología de poesía primitiva. Alianza, 1979.

Nueva antología poética. Siglo Veintiuno, 1979.

Zero Hour and Other Documentary Poems, Translation by Paul W. Borgeson and Jonathan Cohen. Edited by Donald D. Walsh. New Directions, 1980.

La paz mundial y la Revolución de Nicaragua. Ministerio de Cultura de Nicaragua, 1981.

Love. Translation by Dinah Livingstone. Crossroad Publishing, 1981.

Psalms. Translation by Thomas Blackburn and others. Crossroad Publishing, 1981.

Tocar el cielo. Lóguez, 1981.

Nicaragua: La Guerra de liberación der Befreiungskrieg. With Richard Cross. Ministerio de Cultura de Nicaragua, c. 1982.

Los campesinos de Solentiname pinton el Evangelio. Monimbó, c. 1982.

La democratización de la cultura. Ministerio de Cultura de Nicaragua, 1982.

Nostalgia del futuro: Pintura y buena noticia en Solentiname. Editorial Nueva Nicaragua, 1982.

Evangelia pueólo y arte. (selections from *El Evangelio en Solentiname).* Lóguez, 1983.

Waslala: Poems. Translation by Fidel López-Criado and R. A. Kerr. Chase Avenue Press, 1983.

Antología: Ernesto Cardenal. Editorial Nueva Nicaragua Ediciones Monimbó, 1983.

Poesía de la nueva Nicaragua. Siglo Veintiuno, 1983.

The Gospel in Art by the Peasants of Solentiname. Translated from *Bauern von Solentiname malen des Evangelium,* selections from *El Evangelio en Solentiname,* edited by Philip and Sally Sharper. Orbis Books, 1984.

Vuelos de Victoria. Visor (Madrid), 1984. Editorial Universitaria, (León, Nicaragua), 1987.

With Walker in Nicaragua and Other Early Poems, 1949-1954. Translation by Jonathan Cohen. University Press of New England, 1984.

Nuevo cielo y tierra nueva. Editorial Nueva Nicaragua-Ediciones Monimbó, 1985.

Antología Azarias H. Pallais. Editor. Nueva Nicaragua, 1986.

Quetzalcoatal. Editorial Nueva Nicaragua-Ediciones Monimbó, 1985.

Flights of Victory. Translated by Marc Zimmerman. Orbis Books 1985. Reprinted by Curbstone Press, 1988.

From Nicaragua with Love: Poems 1979-1986. Translation by Jonathan Cohen. City Lights Press, 1986.

Golden UFO's: The Indian Poems: Los Ovnis de Oro: Poemas Indios. Translation by Monique and Carlos Altschul. Indiana University Press, 1992.

Cosmic Canticle. Translation by John Lyons. Curbstone Press, 1993.